Avant-propos

AVEC Password Tle ENTREZ DANS LA LANGUE ET DANS LA CULTURE DES PAYS ANGLOPHONES

À l'horizon de cette année de Terminale, il y a le Bac mais aussi l'entrée dans le monde des études supérieures ou dans la vie active : autant de situations où vous serez amené(e) à tirer parti de tout ce que vous savez dire et faire en anglais.

- **Password Tle** vous aide à développer vos compétences de communication en anglais : lire des textes de nature différente, comprendre des messages oraux variés, pouvoir en retour s'exprimer personnellement, découvrir et comprendre la culture de l'autre.
- Chacun des neuf chapitres privilégie ainsi, au travers de tâches variées, un apprentissage en situation et en contexte où interagissent oral et écrit, compréhension et expression.
- La découverte des notions du programme constitue le fil rouge de vos apprentissages cette année. Tous nos choix (thèmes, documents, tâches et activités) ont visé à rendre cette exploration aussi vivante et attrayante que possible.
- Nous vous souhaitons une belle réussite et un grand plaisir à pratiquer et faire vivre la langue anglaise dans toutes ses dimensions.

Les auteurs

Password T^le et le Bac

Au fil de ses neuf chapitres, **Password T^le** vous accompagne dans votre préparation aux épreuves du baccalauréat afin de les aborder avec confiance et méthode.

Explorer les notions du programme

- ***Le thème du chapitre*** est lié à l'une des quatre ***notions du programme.***
- Il est abordé sous forme de ***problématique*** pour assurer une construction rigoureuse et dynamique des savoirs.
- ***La préparation au Bac*** est systématiquement intégrée au parcours.

Consolider compétences et connaissances

- ***Un parcours par étapes***, à partir de documents à écouter, visionner, regarder ou lire, enrichit vos connaissances culturelles et consolide vos compétences de communication.
- ***La pause récapitulative*** est l'occasion de faire le point sur un aspect de la notion étudiée.

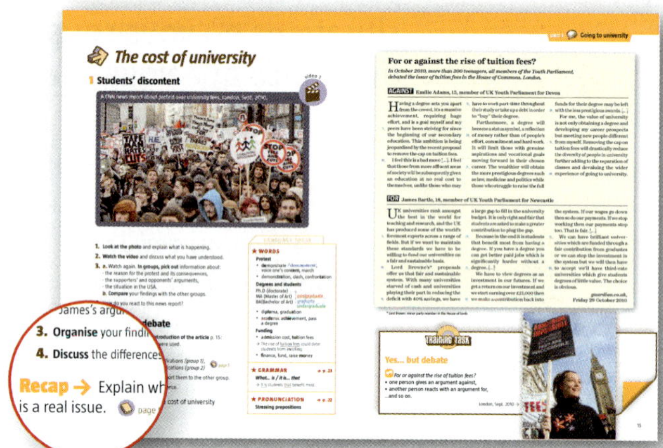

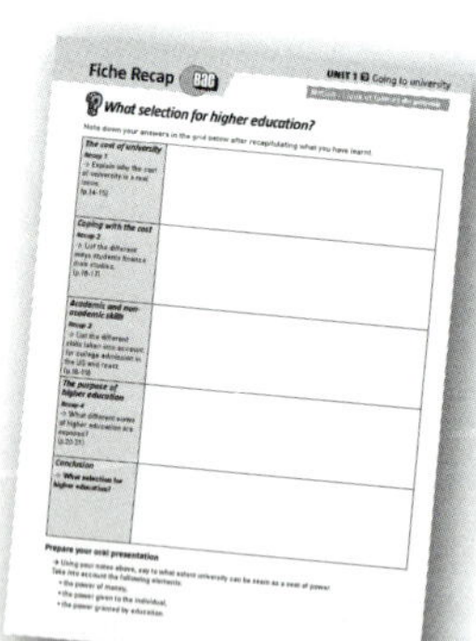

- ***La fiche* Recap Bac** :
  - pour noter ce que vous avez appris,
  - progresser dans la découverte de la problématique,
  - établir les liens avec la notion du programme,
  - établir des liens entre différents chapitres traitant une même notion.

dans le workbook
ou sur **www.didierpassword.fr**

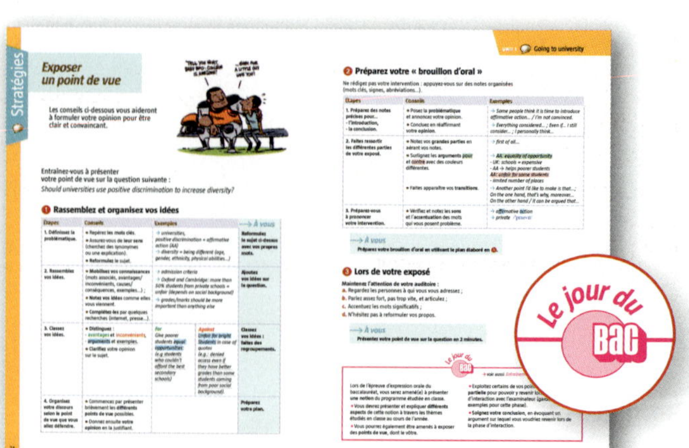

- ***Les pages Stratégies*** développent conseils et aides méthodologiques dans l'activité langagière dominante du chapitre.
- ***Le jour du bac*** replace ces conseils dans la perspective de l'examen pour vous aider à les mobiliser efficacement le jour J.

- ***Language Tools :*** des exercices de langue en contexte (grammaire, lexique, prononciation) vous aident à vous exprimer avec aisance sur la notion.

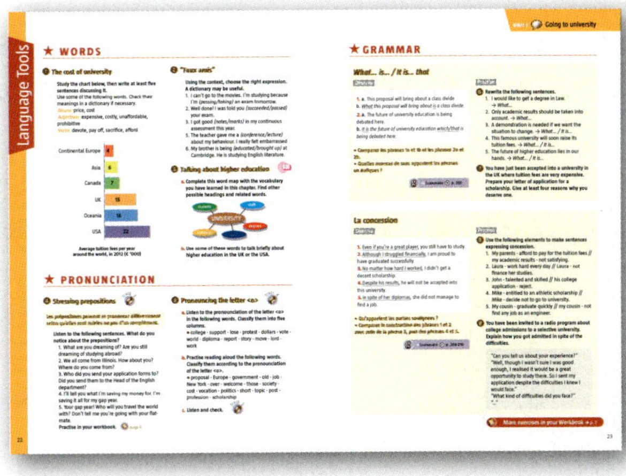

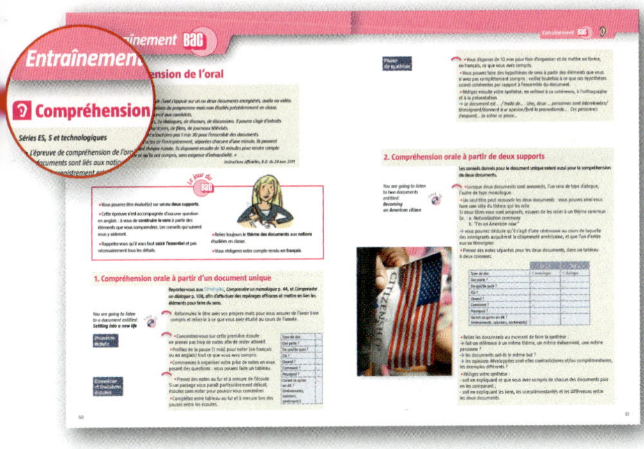

▸ S'entraîner aux épreuves du Bac

- ***Cinq entraînements*** **Bac** proposent un dispositif complet pour vous familiariser avec les nouvelles épreuves, à l'écrit comme à l'oral :

- les textes officiels pour toutes les séries,
- des documents supports calibrés et des protocoles d'évaluation,
- une aide méthodologique favorisant l'entraînement en autonomie.

- ***Évaluations*** **Bac** : un protocole d'évaluation complet, en lien avec la notion explorée dans le chapitre, est systématiquement proposé en fin de parcours.

→ appareil d'évaluation, critères et barème dans le guide pédagogique

Bien repérer

track 7 — Écouter la piste correspondante du **CD audio** de l'élève

page 7 — Aller à la page correspondante dans le **Workbook**

video 7 — Visionner la séquence correspondante du **DVD** classe

Aller sur le **site Internet** www.didierpassword.fr sur lequel vous trouverez les supports utiles à la réalisation de certaines activités et les fiches **Recap Bac**

Sommaire

Chapitres | Culture Documents | Communication

1 Going to university

Faire une intervention orale argumentée pour défendre une opinion

• Comprendre des faits et des opinions dans une motion ou un témoignage
• Comprendre l'explicite et saisir l'implicite dans un texte de fiction

Comprendre une information spécifique ou une explication dans un reportage ou une interview

2 The new Americans

• Comprendre les points principaux d'une expérience personnelle
• Comprendre les points clés dans un reportage télévisé

Poser/répondre à des questions sur une expérience personnelle

• Comprendre des informations et des opinions dans un article de presse
• Comprendre les faits principaux, l'identité des personnages, leurs actes et leurs motivations dans des témoignages personnels ou des textes littéraires

3 Tech-less world

• Décrire et expliquer par écrit les conséquences de la disparition de la technologie sur la vie quotidienne
• Imaginer et rédiger un texte narratif décrivant la vie, les sentiments et les réactions des personnages dans un monde sans technologie

Comprendre les faits principaux et les sentiments des personnages dans des témoignages personnels et des textes narratifs

Présenter par oral une expérience personnelle

Activité langagière dominante du chapitre : couleur foncée *(exemple pour unit 1)*

Activité langagière associée : couleur claire *(exemple pour unit 1)*

Langue	Tâches d'entraînement	Stratégies	Évaluations finales
Lexique • *Protest* • *Students and degrees* • *Financing and difficulties* • *Non-academic skills* • *Transformation and accomplishment* **Prononciation** • Accentuation des prépositions • La lettre <o> **Grammaire** • *What... is.../ It is... that* • La concession	Réagir à un point de vue sur l'accès à l'université en présentant des contre-arguments → p. 15 Expliquer de manière argumentée les solutions envisagées pour financer ses études → p. 17 Après quelques recherches, présenter une activité extra-scolaire proposée par une université américaine → p. 19 Exprimer de manière argumentée son opinion sur le rôle de l'université → p. 21	Exposer un point de vue → p. 24 **Entraînement** Expression orale → p. 30	**Tâche** Défendre une motion concernant les critères d'admission à l'université **Tâche** Identifier les opinions de différentes personnes et leur associer la motion correspondante → p. 26 BAC **Évaluation** 4 situations d'évaluation → p. 27
Lexique • *Immigration* • *Obstacles and success* • *Work* • *Feelings* • *Integration* • *Achievements / Can-do spirit* • *Prosperity / Want* **Prononciation** • Rythme et formes faibles • Accentuation des noms composés • Les mots se terminant en *-ion* **Grammaire** • *Want/would like/expect sb to...* • *When/If...*	Après quelques recherches, rédiger une entrée pour un livret de présentation du musée de l'immigration à Ellis Island → p. 35 Faire un bref exposé pour présenter et commenter une photo → p. 37 Rechercher et échanger des informations sur des personnalités américaines d'origine étrangère → p. 39 Discuter la définition de l'expression « le rêve américain » dans le but de rédiger un tweet → p. 41	Comprendre un monologue → p. 44 **Entraînement** Compréhension de l'oral → p. 50	**Tâche** Prendre part à un débat radiophonique sur les nouveaux Américains **Tâche** Choisir un invité pour une émission télévisée → p. 46 BAC **Évaluation** 4 situations d'évaluation → p. 47
Lexique • *Electricity cuts* • *Discontent / Satisfaction* • *Obstacle / Failure* • *Dependence / Independence* • *Deprivation* • *Dislike* • *Benevolence / Malevolence* • *Success* • *Abundance* **Prononciation** • Intonation dans les questions • Intonation dans les listes **Grammaire** • *Present perfect + since/for* • *a/the/Ø*	Faire la voix-off d'un extrait vidéo → p. 55 Rédiger et présenter à l'oral le compte rendu d'un « week-end sans numérique » → p. 57 • Rédiger la suite d'un texte narratif décrivant un monde « post-apocalyptique » → p. 59 • Rédiger une carte postale → p. 61	Écrire un texte narratif → p. 64 **Entraînement** Compréhension de l'écrit → p. 70 Expression écrite → p. 72	**Tâche** Imaginer et présenter par écrit un monde « post-apocalyptique » **Tâche** Associer des textes de quatrième de couverture aux couvertures correspondantes → p. 66 BAC **Évaluation** 4 situations d'évaluation → p. 67

Chapitres | Culture Documents | Activités langagières

Activité langagière dominante du chapitre : couleur foncée *(exemple pour unit 1)*

Activité langagière associée : couleur claire *(exemple pour unit 1)*

Langue	Tâches d'entraînement	Stratégies	Évaluations finales
Lexique • *Symbols of the monarchy* • *Political systems* • *Myths* • *Speech tags* • *Authority and ambition* • *Feelings* • *Duty and leisure* **Prononciation** • Groupes de sens dans les phrases longues • Accentuation des informations essentielles • Terminaisons en *-ed* **Grammaire** • Le discours indirect • *Wish*	Enregistrer un audio-guide sur un sujet relatif au règne de l'une des trois reines d'Angleterre → p. 77 • Réécrire un épisode de la vie de la reine Elizabeth I en changeant de point de vue → p. 79 • Écrire une lettre pour rendre compte de sentiments personnels → p. 81 • Imaginer et rédiger un dialogue entre la reine Elizabeth et l'un de ses conseillers → p. 83	Comprendre un texte narratif → p. 86 **Entraînement** Compréhension de l'écrit → p. 92	**Tâche** Rédiger un court épisode de la vie de la reine Elizabeth II à partir d'un fait divers réel **Tâche** Comprendre et reconstituer un texte dont les paragraphes ont été mélangés → p. 88 Bac **Évaluation** 4 situations d'évaluation → p. 89
Lexique • *Talking about films* • *Soldiers* • *On screen portrayal* • *Trauma* • *Cruelty* • *Disillusionment* **Prononciation** • Accentuation des adjectifs dérivés • Intonation et contraste **Grammaire** • Formes passives • Utilisation des noms comme adjectifs	• Après quelques recherches, présenter à l'oral un film de guerre américain → p. 99 • En tant qu'assistant de Steven Spielberg, expliquer et commenter les choix du réalisateur pour une scène particulière → p. 101 Réagir à un commentaire sur un site de critiques de films ; rédiger sa propre contribution → p. 103 Écouter une interview et prendre des notes dans le but d'écrire une critique de film, puis justifier ses choix → p. 105	Comprendre un dialogue ou une discussion → p. 108	**Tâche** Rédiger la critique d'un film de guerre américain **Tâche** Associer critiques et affiches de films → p. 110 Bac **Évaluation** 4 situations d'évaluation → p. 111
Lexique • *At work* • *Statistics* • *Business* • *Work efficiency* • *Relationships* • *Feelings/personal reactions* • *Decision making* **Prononciation** • Accentuation des arguments personnels • Accentuation des quantités **Grammaire** • *Modals* • *Make/have/let someone do sth*	Discuter de l'évolution des modalités de travail en s'appuyant sur des titres de journaux → p. 117 En tant qu'employé, convaincre son employeur des avantages du travail à domicile → p. 119 Participer à une enquête en ligne en rédigeant une réponse à la question : « E-learning : aimeriez-vous étudier en ligne ? » → p. 121 Donner son opinion à tour de rôle sur la motion : « Le télétravail devrait être un droit pour tous les salariés » → p. 123	Comprendre un texte argumentatif → p. 126	**Tâche** Prendre part à une campagne radiophonique ayant pour but de promouvoir le télétravail **Tâche** Associer des textes promotionnels aux cibles auxquelles ils s'adressent → p. 128 Bac **Évaluation** 4 situations d'évaluation → p. 129

THE TIMES
The cursed crown
Cloud of ash empties skies
TIMES ONLINE

Activité langagière dominante du chapitre : couleur foncée *(exemple pour unit 1)*

Activité langagière associée : couleur claire *(exemple pour unit 1)*

Langue	Tâches d'entraînement	Stratégies	Évaluations finales
Lexique • *Restitution* • *Museums* • *Pillage* • *Agreement / Disagreement* • *Heritage* • *Virtual repatriation* • *Identity* **Prononciation** • Intonation des questions rhétoriques • Les liaisons **Grammaire** • *Questions rhétoriques* • *Talk sb into doing sth*	Après quelques recherches, présenter brièvement à l'oral une œuvre patrimoniale → p. 135 Comprendre et classifier les arguments utilisés au cours d'un débat → p. 137 Prendre part à une conversation en donnant son opinion et en s'appuyant sur des exemples → p. 139 Rédiger un court article pour présenter une exposition d'« arts premiers » → p. 141	Défendre un point de vue, justifier, convaincre → p. 144 **Entraînement** Expression orale p. 150	**Tâche** Prendre part à un débat télévisé **Tâche** Choisir les meilleurs partenaires pour constituer son équipe dans le but de participer à un débat → p. 146 BAC **Évaluation** 4 situations d'évaluation → p. 147
Lexique • *Symbol* • *Heroes and characters* • *Tolerance* • *Sailors and adventurers* • *Personal traits* • *Companionship* • *Admiration* • *Eccentricity and humour* **Prononciation** • Le "*-s*" dans les pluriels • Accentuation des formes négatives **Grammaire** • Verbe + *-ing: Being British...* • *Have-en / had-en*	Après quelques recherches, présenter à l'oral un héros de série télévisée britannique → p. 155 Rechercher et échanger des informations sur de grands explorateurs anglais → p. 157 • Écrire le compte rendu d'une conversation dans un journal intime → p. 159 • Imaginer et créer un *flyer* pour promouvoir un événement caritatif → p. 161	Écrire un texte explicatif → p. 164	**Tâche** Rédiger le portrait d'un personnage emblématique de la culture britannique **Tâche** Identifier les personnages de fiction britannique susceptibles de plaire à différents profils d'internautes → p. 166 BAC **Évaluation** 4 situations d'évaluation → p. 167
Lexique • *The press* • *Gullibility* • *Reliability* • *Editing and exposure* • *Censorship/Freedom* • *Contributing* • *Audience* • *Worth* **Prononciation** • Accentuation pour marquer la différence entre le passé et le présent • Terminaisons en "*-ate*" **Grammaire** • *Used to / would* • *The more..., the more...*	Mener et présenter une enquête sur les habitudes en matière d'information → p. 173 • Rédiger un commentaire à poster sur un forum → p. 175 • Rédiger un tweet pour réagir à un article de presse → p. 177 • Écrire une lettre de candidature pour un poste dans le journalisme → p. 179	Écrire un texte argumentatif → p. 182	**Tâche** Participer à une discussion sur un forum en ligne à propos du métier de journaliste **Tâche** Comprendre un article de presse et identifier le tweet qui en rend compte le plus fidèlement → p. 184 BAC **Évaluation** 4 situations d'évaluation → p. 185

UNIT 1 Going to university

↑ An American university campus

What selection for higher education?

Look at the title of the chapter and the photo.
Explain why high-school students choose to pursue their education.
Discuss what you know about higher education in the UK and the USA.

FINAL TASKS

P. 26

Motions

Speaking
Defend a motion about admission to university

Reading
Match motions with people's opinions

CULTURE

- Learning about higher education in the UK and in the USA:
  - the admission to university
  - the tuition fees debate.
- Exploring the purpose of higher education.
- Literary works:
  - Tom Wolfe, *I am Charlotte Simmons*
  - Jeffrey Eugenides, *Middlesex*
  - Philip Roth, *Indignation*

COMMUNICATION

Voicing an opinion about higher education issues, giving arguments and examples.

- Understanding key facts and arguments in articles and personal testimonies.
- Understanding explicit and implicit meaning in a narrative passage.

Understanding news reports and personal testimonies.

TOOLS

Words
- Protest
- Degrees and students
- Funding and financing
- Facing difficulties
- Non academic skills
- Transformation
- Accomplishment

Pronunciation
- Stressing prepositions
- Pronouncing the letter <o>

Grammar
- *What... is... / It is... that*
- La concession

Bac

The cost of university

1 Students' discontent

video 7

A CNN news report about protest over university fees, London, Sept. 2010.

1. **Look at the photo** and explain what is happening.
2. **Watch the video** and discuss what you have understood.
3. **a.** Watch again. **In groups, pick out** information about:
   - the reason for the protest and its consequences,
   - the supporters' and opponents' arguments,
   - the situation in the USA.

   b. Compare your findings with the other groups.
4. How do you react to this news report?

2 Teenagers' debate

1. **Study the title and the introduction of the article** p. 15: imagine what arguments were used.
2. **Read the article**. Highlight:
   - Emilie's arguments and justifications *(group 1)*,
   - James's arguments and justifications *(group 2)*

   page 5
3. **Organise** your findings and report them to the other group.
4. **Discuss** the differences with France.

Recap → Explain why the cost of university is a real issue. page 9

LANGUAGE TOOLS

★ WORDS

Protest

- **de**monstrate /ˈdemənstreɪt/, voice one's con**cern**, march
- demon**stra**tion, clash, confron**ta**tion

Degrees and students

Ph.D (doctorate)
MA (Master of Art) — postgraduate
BA(Bachelor of Art) — graduate
undergraduate

- di**plo**ma, gradu**a**tion
- aca**de**mic a**chie**vement, pass a degree

Funding

- ad**mi**ssion cost, **tui**tion fees

→ The rise of tuition fees could deter students from enrolling.

- **fi**nance, fund, raise **mo**ney

★ GRAMMAR → p. 23

What... is / it is... that

→ It is students that benefit most...

★ PRONUNCIATION → p. 22

Stressing prepositions

For or against the rise of tuition fees?

In October 2010, more than 300 teenagers, all members of the Youth Parliament, debated the issue of tuition fees in the House of Commons, London.

AGAINST Emilie Adams, 15, member of UK Youth Parliament for Devon

Having a degree sets you apart from the crowd, it's a massive achievement, requiring huge effort, and is a goal myself and my peers have been striving for since the beginning of our secondary education. This ambition is being jeopardised by the recent proposal to remove the cap on tuition fees.

I feel this is a bad move [...]. I feel that those from more affluent areas of society will be subsequently given an education at no real cost to themselves, unlike those who may have to work part-time throughout their study or take up a debt in order to "buy" their degree.

Furthermore, a degree will become a status symbol, a reflection of money rather than of people's effort, commitment and hard work. It will limit those with genuine aspirations and vocational goals moving forward in their chosen career. The wealthier will obtain the more prestigious degrees such as law, medicine and politics while those who struggle to raise the full funds for their degree may be left with the less prestigious awards. [...]

For me, the value of university is not only obtaining a degree and developing my career prospects but meeting new people different from myself. Removing the cap on tuition fees will drastically reduce the diversity of people in university further adding to the separation of classes and devaluing the wider experience of going to university.

FOR James Bartle, 18, member of UK Youth Parliament for Newcastle

UK universities rank amongst the best in the world for teaching and research, and the UK has produced some of the world's foremost experts across a range of fields. But if we want to maintain these standards we have to be willing to fund our universities on a fair and sustainable basis.

Lord Browne's* proposals offer us that fair and sustainable system. With many universities starved of cash and universities playing their part in reducing the deficit with 40% savings, we have a large gap to fill in the university budget. It is only right and fair that students are asked to make a greater contribution to plug the gap.

Because in the end it is students that benefit most from having a degree. If you have a degree you can get better paid jobs which is significantly harder without a degree. [...]

We have to view degrees as an investment in our futures. If we get a return on our investment and we start earning over £21,000 then we make a contribution back into the system. If our wages go down then so do our payments. If we stop working then our payments stop too. That is fair. [...]

We can have brilliant universities which are funded through a fair contribution from graduates or we can stop the investment in the system but we will then have to accept we'll have third-rate universities which give students degrees of little value. The choice is obvious.

guardian.co.uk, **Friday 29 October 2010**

* Lord Browne: a member of the House of Lords, wrote a 2010 report on the university funding system

TRAINING TASK

Yes... but debate

For or against the rise of tuition fees?

- one person gives an argument against,
- another person reacts with an argument for,

...and so on.

London, Sept. 2010 →

Coping with the cost

1 A personal story

How I avoided student loans

by Crystal (March 2011)

When people learn that I managed to avoid college loans, I'm often asked how that happened. It was a mixture of work, luck, and help.

Planning for college

For as long as I can remember, I knew I'd go to college. It was a given. I can't remember my family overtly pushing me that way, but my grandparents and parents went to college, so I was going to go too. My family is also open about money, so I always just seemed to know that college would be expensive. So, I started babysitting and pet-sitting when I was twelve years old so that I could save for those magical four years of college education. I also planned to get a "real" job as soon as I turned sixteen. My plans changed, though, when we moved overseas. [...]

We moved back *nine months* before I was scheduled to start college, and I still had long-distance courses that I needed to finish before I could graduate from high school. [...] That is also when I applied for my first "real" job — as a help-desk attendant for the 24-hour assistance desk in my future dorm.

Putting the "Work" in Work-Study

Luckily, I received a few scholarships, including a very large Academic Achievement Award that covered a big part of my actual class expenses. But my parents covered my dorm room and food for that first year. I also worked at least 20 hours a week at the help desk and applied for other on-campus positions.

By my second year of college, I was engaged. [...] I was still trying to pay my own way through college, but I kept falling short about $1200 every semester. I was living as cheaply as possible, splitting a room for $288 to save money, and even staying under $3 a day for food. But making $5.25 an hour just couldn't cover everything my scholarships left behind.

I worked part-time in the Games Room on campus throughout my last three years in school. During my last year, I was a blackjack dealer for office parties (the legal kind of gambling in Texas, where the players could win raffle tickets for prizes). I also found a third job as a tax-office receptionist during my last semester. I took loans from my parents for whatever my scholarships and my paychecks couldn't cover.

A Final Piece of Help

By the time I graduated from college (with honors), I was working Mondays, Wednesdays, Fridays, and Saturdays at the tax office; Tuesday and Thursday evenings from 5pm-1am at the Games Room on campus; and I was a blackjack dealer Friday and Saturday nights.

In short, I was working almost 60 hours a week in three different jobs, commuting to campus every Tuesday and Thursday for my last twelve hours of classes, and ended up owing my parents a little more than $8000. [...]

A few months after all of that, my parents forgave my $8000 in loans as a late graduation present. I was really broke, but at least I didn't have any loans. As I said in the beginning, having no student loans was a mixture of work, luck — and help. (I know I'm lucky to have received the help from my parents.)

www.getrichslowly.org

1. Look at the cartoon and the title of the article. What do you expect the text to be about?

2. Read the text and say what you have understood.

3. a. Explain why the student says *"having no student loans was a mixture of work, luck — and help"* (l. 61-62).
b. How do you react to Crystal's story?

2 "I don't care what it costs"

video 2

A 2008 PBS report in UMass Boston.

LANGUAGE TOOLS

★ WORDS

Financing

- loan, al**low**ance, **scho**larship, grant

→ A scholarship can help you cover your class and living expenses.

- fee **wai**vers, **ex**em**p**tion, **dis**counts

→ Some students can benefit from fee waivers and pay less.

Facing difficulties

- pre**vent**, **hin**der, de**ter** sb. from...
- a pre**di**cament, a plight (= a very bad situation)

→ Some students are in a desperate plight.

- be faced with, be con**fron**ted to, cope with
- sur**mount** = over**come**

★ GRAMMAR → p. 23

Concession

→ No matter how hard it is, I will go to university.

1. **Watch the video** and say what you have understood.
2. Watch again, listen to the different testimonies and **identify**:
   - each student's situation,
   - what they are doing or have done about it,
   - how they feel about it.
3. **Discuss** what you have found out.

Recap → List the different ways students finance their studies. page 9

TRAINING TASK

Financing your studies

How would you choose to finance your studies (scholarship, loan, part time work...)?

Explain your choice, organising your arguments.

Academic and non-academic skills

"It's about academics, Coach."

"I could have gone to college on an athletic scholarship, but they found out I could read."

Jojo Johanssen is a senior student at Dupont University. He was admitted on account of his athletic skills[1].

PART 1 Here he was, at the heart of a great university, one of the five best-known people on the campus... Nobody, not the president of the university or anybody else, was nearly so recognizable or awesome as the starting five of the national champions. *Go go, Jojo.* Of course, Dupont was just a stop on the way to the final triumph, which was playing in *the League*[2]. In the meantime, being at Dupont was cool. Everybody was impressed that you were playing ball for Buster Roth. For that matter, everybody was impressed that you were even *attending Dupont*. The sweet irony was that he had wound up at a better university than Eric[3]. If the unthinkable happened and you didn't make it to the League, it was pretty good credentials just to be able to say you graduated from Dupont – assuming you managed to keep your grades above water and did graduate. Well, that was what tutors were for, wasn't it ?

Doubts began to form. What if something *did* happen? In high school, teachers would tell him that he had a perfectly good mind, but it wasn't going to do him any good if he didn't apply himself and develop it; and if he didn't, someday he'd regret it. He took it as an inside-out compliment. He didn't have to apply himself and develop his mind and all that stuff. He was of a higher order of student. He was a basketball star. The high school would make sure he had all the grades he needed to stay eligible. Which they did. Several times he got really interested in courses and did pretty well, but he was careful not to let on. One time he wrote a paper for history that the teacher liked so much he read part of it to the class. He could still feel how exciting and at the same time embarrassing that had been. Luckily, word of it never got beyond the classroom. [...]

A few weeks later, Jojo asks for a meeting with his coach.

PART 2 Buster Roth gave Jojo a kindly smile. [...]

"Okay, then... what, Jojo ?"

"It's about academics, Coach."

Coach's voice turned a bit stern. "What *about* academics, Jojo? What class? I've told you guys a hundred times, you don't let things *develop*. The first sign of some issue, you come to one of us. You don't let these damned things just drift along."

"It's nothing like that, Coach." Jojo was rubbing his hands so hard, Coach glanced at them. "It's – I guess – what I want to say is – I guess I just don't feel I'm getting enough out of it, that's all."

"Out of *what*, Jojo?" Coach had pulled his eyebrows together over his nose. Obviously he hadn't a clue as to what Jojo was trying to say.

"Out of the academics, Coach, out of my classes."

"*What* classes? You're not having any trouble passing, are you? You had a two-point-two grade point average last time I heard anything about it. So what's the problem, Jojo?"

1. College admissions requirements in the USA usually include athletic and/or artistic achievements.

2. "the League": here, refers to a basketball league, like the NBA.

3. Eric: Jojo's brother.

"Well..." said Jojo, struggling – he now had the fingers of both hands intertwined and thrust deep between his thighs, which caused his whole upper torso to hunch over – "like... like I'm taking this upper level French course for my language requirements?"

"Yeah..."

"And we read the books in English instead of French, that kind of thing."

"Mr Levin, right?"

Jojo nodded yes.

"He's terrific. He's a real friend of the program, Jojo. He understands the importance of athletics in higher education. [...]"

"But we do all our reading in English, Coach. I'm not really learning any French."

"So what? Whattaya wanna be, a language scholar?"

Tom Wolfe, *I am Charlotte Simmons* (2004)

1. **Look at the cartoon**: what does it tell you about sports in US universities?
2. **Read the introduction and part 1 of the text**. Say what you understand about Jojo's situation.
3. Read again and focus on the following sentences:
   - *"He was of a higher order of student"* (l. 20),
   - *"Luckily, word of it never got beyond the classroom."* (l. 26).

   What does it say about Jojo?
4. **Now read part 2** and explain what Jojo expects from the university and what the university expects from him. page 6
5. Read the whole text and explain what strikes you in Jojo's situation.

Recap → List the different skills taken into account for college admissions in the US and react. page 9

LANGUAGE TOOLS

★ **WORDS**

Non-academic skills

- athletic and artistic skills
- extra-curricular activities: volunteer work, social/community activities, tutoring...

TRAINING TASK

Extra-curricular activities

You are considering spending a year in an American university.

Browse the websites of the universities below to research the extra-curricular activities they offer:

- Princeton
- Austin
- San Diego
- The Art Institute of California

Then say briefly where you could or would like to apply and why.

↑ High school students cook and serve meals for the homeless in a soup kitchen, Colorado, USA.

The purpose of higher education

"What's the matter with that kid?"

The narrator remembers her older brother's first year at university, in the 1970's.

The hug I had given Chapter Eleven[1] in the summer of '72 turned out to be a kind of farewell, because when he returned home from college after his freshman year my brother had become another person. He'd grown his hair out (not as long as mine, but still). He'd started learning the guitar. Perched on his nose was a pair of granny glasses and instead of straight legs he now wore faded bell-bottom jeans. The members of my family have always had a knack for self-transformation. While I finished my first year at Baker and Inglis and began my second, while I went from being a seventh-grader to an alarmingly tall eighth-grader, Chapter Eleven, up at college, went from science geek to John Lennon look-alike.

He bought a motorcycle. He started meditating. He claimed to understand *2001: A Space Odyssey*, even the ending. But it wasn't until Chapter Eleven descended into the basement to play Ping-Pong with Milton[2] that I understood what was behind all this. We'd had a Ping-Pong table for years, but so far, no matter how much my brother or I practiced, we had never come close to beating Milton. [...] But that summer, something was different. When Milton used his extra-fast serve, Chapter Eleven returned it with a minimum of effort. When Milton employed the "English" he'd learned in the Navy, Chapter Eleven counter-spun. Even when Milton smashed a winner across the table, Chapter Eleven, with stupendous reflexes, sent it back where it came from. Milton began to sweat. His face turned red. Chapter Eleven remained cool. [...] "Go!" I cheered him on. "Beat Dad!" 12-12. 12-14. 14-15. 17-18. 18-21! Chapter Eleven had done it! He'd beaten Milton! [...]

"What's the matter with that kid?" I heard my father ask my mother through the wall separating our rooms. "Now he's talking about dropping out of engineering. Says it's too boring."

"It's just a stage. It'll pass."

"It better."

Shortly thereafter, Chapter Eleven had returned to college. He hadn't come back for Thanksgiving. And so, as Christmas of '73 approached, we all wondered what he would be like when we saw him again.

We quickly found out. As my father had feared, Chapter Eleven had scuttled his plans to become an engineer. Now, he informed us, he was majoring in anthropology.

As part of an assignment for one of his courses, Chapter Eleven conducted what he called "fieldwork" during most of that vacation. He carried a tape recorder around with him, recording everything we said. He took notes on our "ideation systems"[3] and "rituals of kin bonding". He said almost nothing to himself, claiming that he didn't want to influence the findings. Every now and then, however, while observing our extended family eat and joke and argue, Chapter Eleven would let out a laugh, a private Eureka that made him fall back in his chair and lift his Earth shoes[4] off the floor. Then he would lean forward and begin writing madly in his notebook.

As I've mentioned, my brother didn't pay much attention to me while we were growing up. That weekend, however, spurred on by his new mania for observation, Chapter Eleven took a new interest in me.

Jeffrey Eugenides, *Middlesex* (2003)

1. Chapter Eleven: the narrator's brother's nickname

2. Milton: the father

3. ideation systems: how ideas are formed in a given community

4. Earth shoes: developed by a yoga instructor, designed to mimic walking barefoot in the sand; part of the "casual revolution" started on campuses in the 1970s

↑ John Lennon in the 1970s.

1. **Read the title of the text**. Imagine who may be speaking and what the matter may be.
2. **Read the text** and say what you have understood. **Explain** the chronology of events.
3. **In groups**, read again and pick out information about:
   - Chapter Eleven's "self-transformation",
   - his parents' reactions,
   - the narrator's relationships with her brother.
4. **Share your findings** and **explain** how and why Chapter Eleven has changed.
5. What is the tone of the extract?

Recap → What different views of higher education are exposed in the text? page 9

LANGUAGE TOOLS

★ **WORDS**

Transformation

- **al**ter, go from... to... , turn into, grow, **mo**dify, switch, swap
- meta**mor**phosis, **ra**dical change, shift

Accomplishment

- a**chie**vement, **ful**fillment, per**for**mance
- reach a goal, at**tain**, **ca**rry out

★ **PRONUNCIATION** → p. 22

Pronouncing the letter <o>

→ college, diploma

TRAINING TASK

Two minutes to convince

"What are universities for?"

get a good job | meet new people | enrich your culture | ...

1. Make notes and organise your arguments; illustrate them with examples.

2. Give a lively talk to convince your classmates.

★ WORDS

❶ The cost of university

Study the chart below, then write at least five sentences discussing it.

Use some of the following words. Check their meanings in a dictionary if necessary.

Nouns: price, cost

Adjectives: expensive, costly, unaffordable, prohibitive

Verbs: devote, pay off, sacrifice, afford

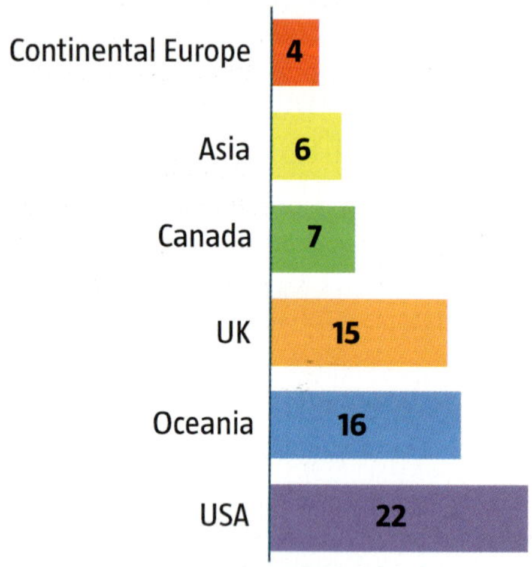

Average tuition fees per year around the world, in 2012 (€ '000)

❷ "Faux amis"

Using the context, choose the right expression. A dictionary may be useful.

1. I can't go to the movies. I'm studying because I'm *(passing/taking)* an exam tomorrow.
2. Well done! I was told you *(succeeded/passed)* your exam.
3. I got good *(notes/marks)* in my continuous assessment this year.
5. The teacher gave me a *(conference/lecture)* about my behaviour. I really felt embarrassed
6. My brother is being *(educated/brought up)* at Cambridge. He is studying English literature.

❸ Talking about higher education Bac

a. Complete this word map with the vocabulary you have learned in this chapter. Find other possible headings and related words.

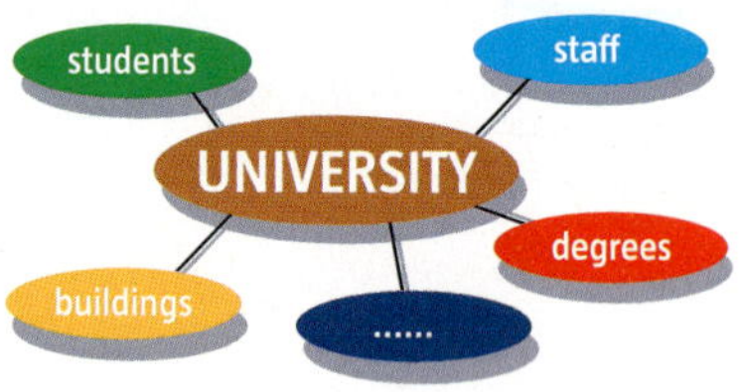

b. Use some of these words to talk briefly about higher education in the UK or the USA.

★ PRONUNCIATION

❹ Stressing prepositions (track 3)

Les prépositions peuvent se prononcer différemment selon qu'elles sont suivies ou non d'un complément.

Listen to the following sentences. What do you notice about the prepositions?

1. What are you dreaming of? Are you still dreaming of studying abroad?
2. We all come from Illinois. How about you? Where do you come from?
3. Who did you send your application forms to? Did you send them to the Head of the English department?
4. I'll tell you what I'm saving my money for. I'm saving it all for my gap year.
5. Your gap year! Who will you travel the world with? Don't tell me you're going with your flat-mate.

Practise in your workbook. page 7

❺ Pronouncing the letter <o> (track 4)

a. Listen to the pronounciation of the letter <o> in the following words. Classify them into five columns.

• college - support - lose - protest - dollars - vote - world - diploma - report - story - move - lord - work

b. Practise reading aloud the following words. Classify them according to the pronunciation of the letter <o>.

• proposal - Europe - government - old - job - New York - over - welcome - those - society - cost - vocation - politics - short - topic - post - profession - scholarship

c. Listen and check. (track 5)

★ GRAMMAR

What... is... / It is... that

Observe

1. **a.** This proposal will bring about a class divide.
b. *What this proposal will bring about is a class divide.*
2. **a.** The future of university education is being debated here.
b. *It is the future of university education which/that is being debated here.*

• Comparez les phrases 1a et 1b et les phrases 2a et 2b.
• Quelles nuances de sens apportent les phrases en italiques ?

→ Grammaire 19 p. 207

Practise

6 **Rewrite the following sentences.**
1. I would like to get a degree in Law. → *What...*
2. Only academic results should be taken into account. → *What...*
3. A demonstration is needed if we want the situation to change. → *What... / It is...*
4. This famous university will soon raise its tuition fees. → *What... / It is...*
5. The future of higher education lies in our hands. → *What... / It is...*

7 **You have just been accepted into a university in the UK where tuition fees are very expensive. Prepare your letter of application for a scholarship. Give at least four reasons why you deserve one.**

La concession

Observe

1. Even if you're a great player, you still have to study.
2. Although I struggled financially, I am proud to have graduated successfully.
3. No matter how hard I worked, I didn't get a decent scholarship.
4. Despite his results, he will not be accepted into this university.
5. In spite of her diplomas, she did not manage to find a job.

• Qu'apportent les parties soulignées ?
• Comparez la construction des phrases 1 et 2 avec celle de la phrase 3, puis des phrases 4 et 5.

→ Grammaire 21 p. 209-210

Practise

8 **Use the following elements to make sentences expressing concession.**
1. My parents - afford to pay for the tuition fees // my academic results - not satisfying.
2. Laura - work hard every day // Laura - not finance her studies.
3. John - talented and skilled // his college application - reject.
4. Mike - entitled to an athletic scholarship // Mike - decide not to go to university.
5. My cousin - graduate quickly // my cousin - not find any job as an engineer.

9 **You have been invited to a radio program about college admissions to a selective university. Explain how you got admitted in spite of the difficulties.**

"Can you tell us about your experience?"
"Well, though I wasn't sure I was good enough, I realised it would be a great opportunity to study there. So I sent my application despite the difficulties I knew I would face."
"What kind of difficulties did you face?"
"..."

More exercises in your Workbook → p. 8

Exposer un point de vue

Les conseils ci-dessous vous aideront à formuler votre opinion pour être clair et convaincant.

Entraînez-vous à présenter votre point de vue sur la question suivante :
Should universities use positive discrimination to increase diversity?

1 Rassemblez et organisez vos idées

Étapes	Conseils	Exemples		→ À vous
1. Définissez la problématique.	• Repérez **les mots clés**. • Assurez-vous de **leur sens** (cherchez des synonymes ou une explication). • **Reformulez** le sujet.	*→ universities, positive discrimination = affirmative action (AA)* *→ diversity = being different (age, gender, ethnicity, physical abilities...)*		**Reformulez le sujet ci-dessus avec vos propres mots.**
2. Rassemblez vos idées.	• **Mobilisez vos connaissances** (mots associés, avantages/inconvénients, causes/conséquences, exemples...) ; • **Notez vos idées** comme elles vous viennent. • **Complétez-les** par quelques recherches (internet, presse...).	*→ admission criteria* *→ Oxford and Cambridge: more than 50% students from private schools = unfair (depends on social background)* *→ grades/marks should be more important than anything else*		**Ajoutez vos idées sur la question.**
3. Classez vos idées.	• **Distinguez** : - avantages et inconvénients, - arguments et exemples. • **Clarifiez** votre opinion sur le sujet.	***For*** *Give poorer students equal opportunities: (e.g students who couldn't afford the best secondary schools)*	***Against*** *Unfair for bright students in case of quotas (e.g.: denied access even if they have better grades than some students coming from poor social background).*	**Classez vos idées : faites des regroupements.**
4. Organisez votre discours selon le point de vue que vous allez défendre.	• Commencez par présenter brièvement les **différents points de vue** possibles. • Donnez ensuite **votre opinion** en la justifiant.			**Préparez votre plan.**

❷ Préparez votre « brouillon d'oral »

Ne rédigez pas votre intervention : appuyez-vous sur des notes organisées (mots clés, signes, abréviations...).

Étapes	Conseils	Exemples
1. Préparez des notes précises pour... **- l'introduction,** **- la conclusion.**	• Posez la **problématique** et annoncez votre opinion. • Concluez en réaffirmant votre **opinion**.	→ *Some people think it is time to introduce affirmative action... / I'm not convinced.* → *Everything considered... ; Even if... I still consider... ; I personally think...*
2. Faites ressortir les différentes parties de votre exposé.	• Notez vos **grandes parties** en aérant vos notes. • Surlignez les **arguments** pour et contre avec des couleurs différentes. • Faites apparaître vos **transitions**.	→ *first of all...* → *AA: equality of opportunity* *- UK: schools = expensive* *- AA → helps poorer students* *AA: unfair for some students* *- limited number of places* → *Another point I'd like to make is that...; On the one hand, that's why, moreover... On the other hand / it can be argued that...*
3. Préparez-vous à prononcer votre intervention.	• Vérifiez et notez les **sons** et l'**accentuation** des mots qui vous posent problème.	→ *affirmative action* → *private* /ˈpraɪvɪt/

→ ***À vous***

Préparez votre brouillon d'oral en utilisant le plan élaboré en ❶.

❸ Lors de votre exposé

Maintenez l'attention de votre auditoire :

a. Regardez les personnes à qui vous vous adressez ;

b. Parlez assez fort, pas trop vite, et articulez ;

c. Accentuez les mots significatifs ;

d. N'hésitez pas à reformuler vos propos.

→ ***À vous***

Présentez votre point de vue sur la question en 2 minutes.

Le jour du Bac

Toutes séries

→ voir aussi *Entraînement Bac* p. 30 et p. 150

Lors de l'épreuve d'expression orale du baccalauréat, vous serez amené(e) à présenter **une notion** du programme étudiée en classe.

• Vous devrez présenter et expliquer **différents aspects** de cette notion à travers les thèmes étudiés en classe au cours de l'année.

• Vous pourrez également être amenés à exposer des **points de vue**, dont le vôtre.

• Exploitez certains de vos points de **manière partielle** pour pouvoir y revenir lors de la phase d'interaction avec l'examinateur (gardez certains exemples pour cette phase).

• **Soignez votre conclusion**, en évoquant un argument sur lequel vous voudriez revenir lors de la phase d'interaction.

FINAL TASKS

Motions

task 1

Speaking

Defend a motion about admission to university

COME AND HAVE YOUR SAY!

DEBATE

1 Everybody should be allowed to go to university without paying anything

2 Everybody should be allowed to go to university but it cannot be free

3 Only the best students should go to university - without paying anything

22 october • 18:00 to 19:00 • Clive Booth Hall

1. Get ready

- You will have 2 min to defend a motion.
- Discover the motion you have to defend.
- Think about the arguments you are going to use and prepare a draft.

2. Action!

- Present your opinion to the class.
- Speak from your notes and be convincing!

task 2

Reading

Match motions with people's opinions

- Your teacher will give you different people's opinions and different motions. Match the opinions with the right motions.

Bac

University of Arizona, USA

Compréhension de l'oral

Listen to a radio programme:

Is it worth going to college?

1. Listen to the document three times and take notes.

2. Write a report in French of what you have understood.

Expression orale

Oral presentation

1. Using what you have learnt about **higher education**, prepare notes explaining to what extent university can be seen as a **seat of power**. You can follow these guidelines:

- The university as an elite institution holding power.
- The power given to the individual: academic and non-academic skills.
- The power granted by education.

Illustrate your presentation with relevant examples you may know.

2. Give your oral presentation.

3. Be ready to discuss the topic with your teacher.

→ Aide

Utilisez la fiche *Recap* du workbook p. 9 ou sur www.didierpassword.fr pour préparer cette synthèse orale.

Compréhension de l'écrit

Study a set of documents

Your teacher will give you several documents. Read them carefully and answer the questions.

Expression écrite

Write two different texts

Using the elements given by your teacher, write:

1. A testimony

2. A comment to have your say

Good reads

How are things going?

The narrator, a brilliant student, has been summoned to Dean Caudwell's office. The scene is set in the 1950s.

"How are things going with your classwork?"

"I believe well, sir."

"You're getting all you hoped for from your courses?"

"Yes, sir."

This wasn't strictly speaking true. My professors were either too starchy or too folksy for my taste, and during these first months on campus, I hadn't as yet found any as spellbinding as those I'd had during my freshman year at Robert Treat. [...]

"You're socializing enough?" Caudwell asked. "You're getting around and meeting the other students?"

"Yes, sir."

I waited for him to ask me to list those I had met so far, expecting he would then record their names on the legal pad in front of him – which had my name written in his script across the top – and bring them into his office to find out if I'd been telling the truth. But his response was only to pour a glass of water from the pitcher on a small table behind his desk and hand it across the desk to me.

"Thank you, sir." [...]

"Then the only problem is that you seem to be having trouble settling into dormitory life," he said. "Is that so? As I said in my letter, I'm a bit concerned about your having already resided in three different dormitory rooms in just your first three weeks here. Tell me in your own words, what seems to be the trouble?"

The night before I had worked out an answer, knowing as I did that my moving was to be the meeting's main subject. Only now I couldn't remember what I'd planned to say.

"Could you repeat your question, sir?"

"Calm down, son," Caudwell said. "Try a little more water."

I did as he told me. I am going to be thrown out of school, I thought. For moving too many times I am going to be asked to leave Winesburg. That's how this is going to wind up. Thrown out, drafted, sent to Korea, and killed.

"What's the problem with your accommodation, Marcus?"

"In the room to which I was initially assigned" – yes, there they were, the words that I'd written out and memorized – "one of my three roommates was always playing the phonograph after I went to bed and I wasn't able to get my night's sleep. And I need to get my sleep in order to do my work. The situation was insupportable." I had decided at the last minute on "insupportable" instead of "insufferable," the adjective with which I'd rehearsed the previous night.

"But couldn't you sit down and work out a time for his playing the phonograph that was agreeable to the two of you?" Caudwell asked me. "You had to move out? There was not other choice?"

"Yes, I had to move out."

"No way of reaching a compromise."

"Not with him, sir." That's as far as I went, hoping that he might find me admirable for protecting Flusser from exposure by not mentioning his name.

"Are you often unable to reach a compromise with people with whom you don't see eye to eye with?"

"I wouldn't say 'often,' sir. I wouldn't say that anything like that has happened before."

"How about your second roommate? Living with him doesn't seem to appear to have worked out either. Am I correct?"

"Yes, sir."

"Why do you think it was so?"

"Our interests were incompatible."

"So there was no room for compromise there either."

"No, sir."

"And now you're living alone, I see. Living by yourself under the eaves in Neil Hall."

"This far into the semester, that was the only empty room I could find, sir."

"Drink some more water, Marcus. It'll help."

But my mouth was no longer dry. I was no longer sweating either. I was angered, in fact, by his saying "It'll help," when I considered myself over the worst of my nervousness and performing as well as anybody my age could be expected to in this situation. I was angered, I was humiliated, I was resentful, and I would not even look in the direction of the glass. Why should I have to go through this interrogation simply because I'd moved from one dormitory room to another to find the peace of mind I required to do my schoolwork? What business was it of his? Had he nothing better to do than interrogate me about my dormitory accommodations? I was a straight – A student – why wasn't that enough for all my unsatisfiable elders (by whom I meant two, the dean and my father?)

"What about the fraternity you're pledging? You're eating your meals there, I take it."

"I'm not pledging a fraternity, sir. I'm not interested in fraternity life."

"What would you say your interests are, then?"

"My studies, sir. Learning."

"That's admirable, to be sure. But nothing more? Have you socialized with anyone at all since you've come to Winesburg?"

"I work on weekends, sir. I work at the inn as a waiter in the taproom. It's necessary for me to work to assist my father in meeting my expenses, sir."

Philip Roth,
***Indignation* (2008)**

Philip Roth (born 1933)

One of America's most honoured writers. His Jewish upbringing in Newark (New Jersey) and his college days are the basis of many of his novels and other works. Roth received a Pulitzer Prize for his 1997 novel, American Pastoral, *which features his best-known character, Nathan Zuckerman.*

Expression orale (1)

Phase d'expression en continu

L'épreuve d'expression orale se déroule en deux temps :
une phase d'expression en continu, une phase d'interaction.

Séries ES, S et technologiques
« Le candidat tire au sort une des notions du programme étudiées dans l'année.
Après 10 minutes de préparation, il dispose d'abord de 5 minutes pour présenter cette notion. »

Série L
« Le candidat présente à l'examinateur la liste des notions du programme qu'il a étudiées dans l'année et les documents qui les ont illustrées. L'examinateur choisit l'une de ces notions.
Après 10 minutes de préparation, le candidat dispose d'abord de 10 minutes maximum pour présenter cette notion. »

Instructions officielles, B.O. du 24 nov. 2011

Avant l'épreuve

- Les neuf chapitres de votre manuel sont liés aux quatre notions au programme :

Notions	Chapitres
Mythes et héros	❹ *The Queen* .... p. 74 ❺ *War on screen* .... p. 96 ❽ *British characters* .... p. 152
Espaces et échanges	❷ *The new Americans* .... p. 32 ❼ *Museum restitution* .... p. 132
Lieux et formes du pouvoir	❶ *Going to university* .... p. 12 ❾ *News from the world* .... p. 170
L'idée de progrès	❸ *Tech-less world* .... p. 52 ❻ *Telecommuting* .... p. 114

- Pour chaque chapitre, dans le workbook ou sur www.didierpassword.fr, une fiche ***Recap*** Bac vous permettra de :
- **noter ce que vous avez appris,**
- **progresser dans la découverte de la problématique,**
- **établir le lien avec la notion du programme.**

- Remplissez ces fiches avec soin, elles vous aideront aussi à **faire des liens entre différents chapitres traitant une même notion.**

- **Tirez aussi partie de vos propres connaissances,** acquises en cours d'anglais (le programme de Première porte sur les mêmes notions), dans d'autres disciplines ou à travers votre expérience personnelle (films, livres, chansons, rencontres, voyages...).

Le jour du Bac

Préparez votre « brouillon d'oral »

• Une grande partie des 10 minutes dont vous disposez sera consacrée à la préparation de votre exposé. Vous n'oublierez pas de consacrer 2 ou 3 minutes à la préparation de l'interaction (voir *Entraînement Bac* p. 150).

• **Rassemblez vos connaissances**, vos idées et votre opinion sous forme de notes sur :
- les thèmes des chapitres étudiés et leur lien avec la notion,
- la notion elle-même.

• **Organisez vos notes**. Vous pourrez :
- soit partir du ou des thèmes et expliquer en quoi ils illustrent la notion,
- soit partir de la notion en général et l'illustrer par des exemples.

• **Préparez votre introduction** en fonction de votre plan, et soignez votre conclusion.

• **Notez quelques mots utiles** :
- pour structurer votre prise de parole,
- pour montrer les liens logiques,
- pour comparer,
- pour illustrer vos propos,
- pour expliquer ce que vous voulez dire.

Votre prestation

• **Retenez l'attention** de l'examinateur. Regardez-le et revenez sur vos propos pour les expliquer ou les illustrer d'un exemple si vous remarquez des signes d'incompréhension.

• **Indiquez votre opinion de manière succincte** afin de pouvoir y revenir lors de la phase d'interaction.

• **Donnez quelques exemples personnels** qui indiqueront l'intérêt que vous portez au sujet.

• **Parlez de manière audible** en soignant la prononciation : sons, mots accentués, intonation.

Exemples de notes pour un brouillon d'oral

Entraînez-vous à partir de la notion « Lieux et formes du pouvoir » *(Seats and forms of power)*.
Vous pouvez vous appuyer sur le chapitre 1 *Going to university* et éventuellement le chapitre 9 *News from the world*.

Seats and forms of power*: selection in university (chapter 1) – power of the press (chapter 9)*
→ *university education as a means of social integration / the changing newsroom as counterweight to established institutions / class action and the voice of the individual*
→ *the university as an elite institution holding power / the power of the press*

• *Students / pay high tuition fees*
→ *power of money / may seem unfair*

• *Tuition fees may limit access to university*
→ *a political decision*

• *Individual skills (academic and non academic) / to get a grant / access based on merit / power of each individual + possible to get a loan/a (part-time) job*
→ *students more responsible?*

• *Governments make decisions about the education system, for example, decide on students' general access to university / universities have their own specific requirements*

• *Education = an instrument of social change and personal development*
→ *social mobility / individual gain*
→ *enables people to understand what's going on, to have better jobs...*

• *Higher education matters to many people and so do fair admissions. The process of admission, which is widely debated, involves different people and institutions.*

• *to begin with, secondly, last but not least...*
• *as, since, as a result, even if...*
• *like, unlike, whereas...*
• *for example, for instance, such as...*
• *Indeed, as a matter of fact...*

UNIT 2 The new Americans

What do the new Americans aspire to?

← **Look** at the cover of *Time Magazine* and **comment** on it. What image does it give of America?

FINAL TASKS

P. 46

Talk show

Speaking
Take part in a radio programme about the new Americans

Listening
Guest selection for a talk show

CULTURE

- Learning about American immigration: present and past.
- Exploring the American Dream:
  - why it still appeals to the new Americans,
  - how they contribute to it.
- Social study: Fareed Zakaria, *"I still believe in the American Dream"*
- Literary works:
  - Chang Rae Lee, *Gesture Life*
  - Eavan Boland, *The Emigrant Irish*
  - Margaret Regan, *The Death of Josseline*

COMMUNICATION

- Understanding facts and feelings in personal testimonies.
- Understanding key information and comments in video documentaries.

Asking and answering questions about personal experiences.

- Understanding information and opinions in a press article.
- Understanding facts and feelings in personal testimonies and fictitious narratives.

TOOLS

★ **Words**
- Immigration
- Obstacles and success
- Work
- Feelings
- Integration
- Achievements
- Can-do spirit
- Prosperity / Want

★ **Pronunciation**
- Rhythm and weak forms
- Stress on compound nouns
- Words ending in *-ion*

★ **Grammar**
- *Want/would like/expect sb to...*
- *When/If...*

Bac

Stratégies
→ *Comprendre un monologue* p.44

Évaluation
→ *4 situations d'évaluation* p. 47

Destination America

1 A Nation of Nations

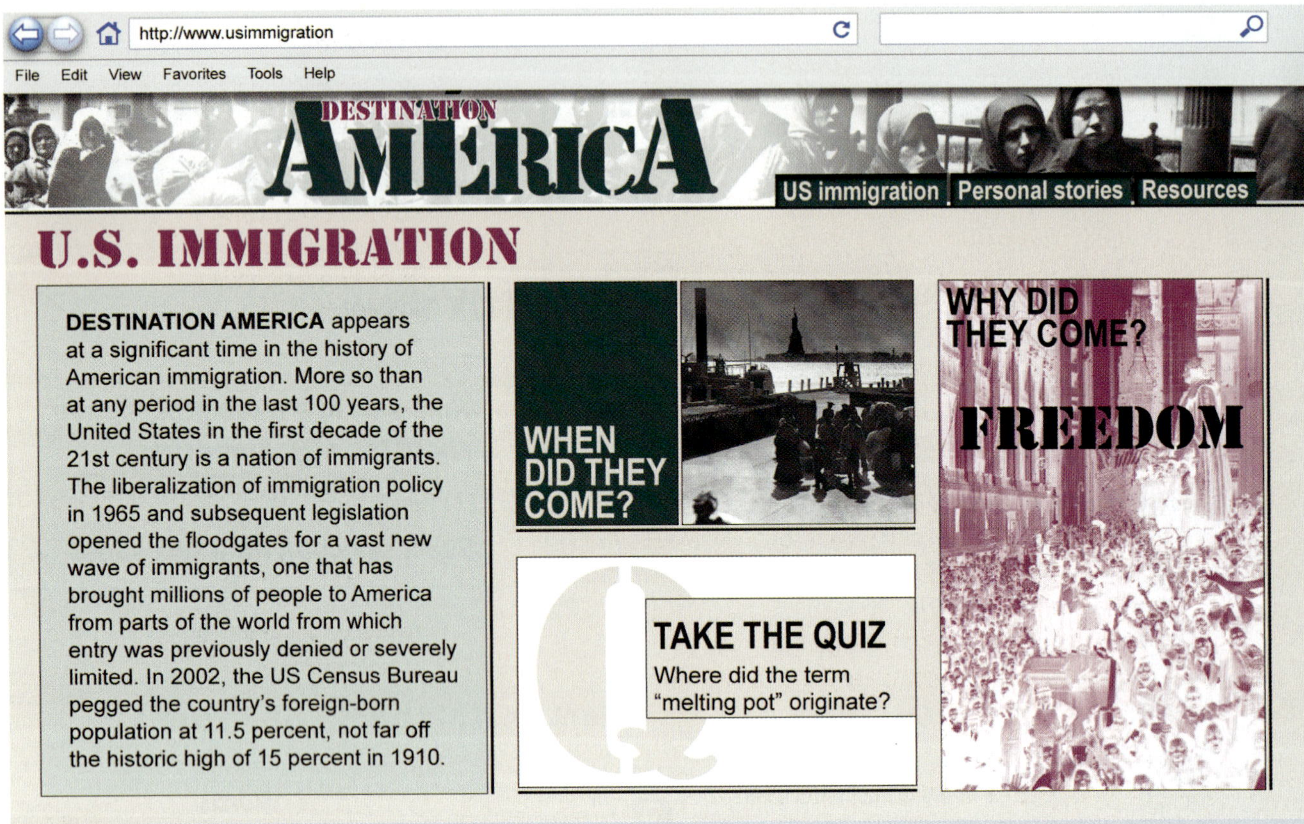

1. a. Scan the first page of the website above.
b. What information do you expect to find on the website?

2. Take the quiz and discuss what you have understood.
pages 14-15 or www.didierpassword.fr.

3. Discuss and comment on the charts below.
Practise saying the figures first:
→*Three million two hundred and ninety thousand from Mexico*

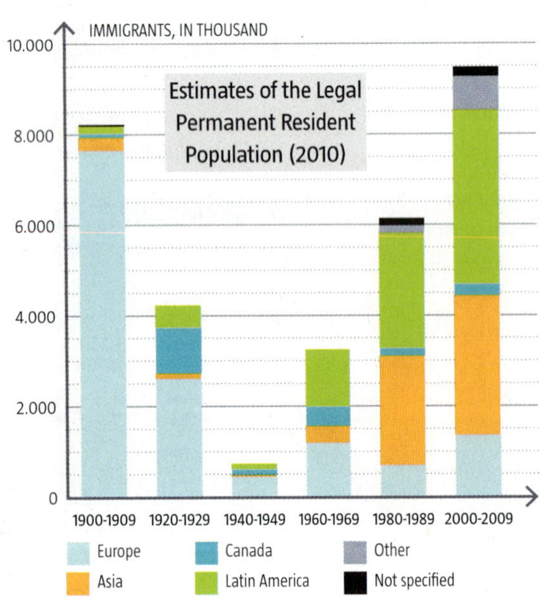

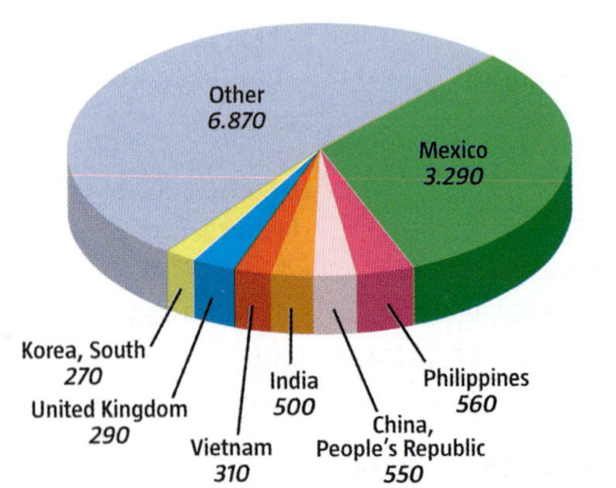

Country of birth of Legal Permanent Residents (2010), in thousand

2 Personal stories

track 8

Radio interviews

Fang Yi Sheu

Farah Naficy

1. What questions would you like to ask new immigrants to the USA?
2. **Listen**. Did you find answers to your questions?
3. **a. In groups**. Listen again and find out information about:
   - their countries of origin and the reasons why they came *(group 1)*,
   - their feelings *(group 2)*,
   b. Report your findings to the other groups.
   c. Fill the ID cards and compare the different stories.

page 12 or www.didierpassword.fr

Recap → Explain why America is still a destination for immigrants. page 19

LANGUAGE TOOLS

★ WORDS

Immigration
- **im**migrant, **fo**reigner, **ex**ile, **ref**ugee
- **na**tive **coun**try, **ho**meland, roots
- start from scratch
- **ha**ven, **ref**uge, **shel**ter, a**sy**lum

Obstacles and success
- **pre**judice, discrimi**na**tion ≠ inte**gra**tion
- hos**ti**le = un**wel**coming
- make **mo**ney
- ful**fil**/accomplish, a**chie**ve a dream

★ GRAMMAR → p. 43

Want, would like, expect sb to...

→ Farah's mother wanted her to become independent.

★ PRONUNCIATION → p. 42

Stress on compound nouns

→ **home**land, **birth**place

TRAINING TASK

A presentation leaflet

Make a presentation leaflet for the Ellis Island Immigration Museum.

1. a. Watch the video and make notes.
b. Organize your notes under these headings:
- Historical and Geographical data
- The Immigrants: Facts and Figures
- The Family History Centre

page 13 or www.didierpassword.fr

2. Group work.
Choose one of the categories above and complete the corresponding section of the leaflet.

video 3

In search of a better life

1 "A shot at the American Dream"

http://www.pbs.com

When I arrived in the US from the Carribean six years ago, I realized New York was not exactly what I had seen on TV.
As a child, I had spent most of my time watching American TV shows and I had imagined to find the same.
Never mind, I was glad to see the Statue of Liberty.
My family and I settled in Brooklyn. It was quite difficult at the beginning but now, we have perfectly adjusted to American life. I don't want to go back!

Kayla from Cuba

http://www.pbs.com

I am from Mexico City and I arrived in New York three years ago.
I wanted to go to college, graduate and find a challenging job. I have great ambitions.
Today, I'm working part-time in a Starbucks Café and I have integrated a prestigious university here.
After my graduation, I hope I will have a shot at the mythical American Dream.

Miguel from Mexico

1. **Read these posts** by two immigrants to the US. Identify the reason why they came and what happened to them.
2. **Say** to what extent they have fulfilled their dreams.

2 Immigrants hope their *American Dream* is not fading

track 9

A NPR Radio programme, 2009

1. **Before listening**, say what you expect this programme to be about.
2. **Listen** and find information about the different speakers.
3. Listen again and find out:
   - their origins,
   - their reasons for coming,
   - their feelings.
4. **Explain and discuss** their views on the American Dream.

LANGUAGE TOOLS

★ WORDS

Work
- a **me**nial job, an un**skil**led job
- **wa**ges, a **sa**lary, a well/**ba**dly-paid job
- a job oppor**tu**nity, a job **o**ffer, ap**ply** for a job

Feelings
- frus**tra**tion, doubt /daʊt/
- hope *(n.)* → **hope**ful *(adj.)*
- pride *(n.)* → proud /praʊd/ *(adj.)*
- disap**poin**ted, disil**lu**sioned
- **suf**fer from

★ GRAMMAR → p. 43

When/If...

→ When Miguel graduates he will have a shot at the American dream.

★ PRONUNCIATION → p. 42

Rhythm and weak forms

3 The "Dream Act"

Nelly Rodriguez, 18, from Wishata, Kansas, holds a sign during a rally on Capitol Hill, April 20, 2004, in Washington. Roughly 100 students, some facing deportation, staged a mock graduation ceremony Tuesday on the lawn of the Capitol. They were urging passage of the "Dream Act", a bill which would make easier for undocumented immigrants to attend college in the United States and eventually become citizens.

1. **Look** at the photo and **read** about Nelly Rodriguez. Identify the issue raised.
2. **Say** what these students are fighting for.
3. **Webquest**: do research on recent developments concerning the "Dream Act".

Recap → What obstacles and difficulties can new immigrants meet?

page 19

TRAINING TASK

Picture Commentary

American Gothic,
Painting by Grant Wood (1930)

Mexican American Gothic,
Photo by Santiago Forero (2010)

1. Do some research about *American Gothic* by Grant Wood.
2. Compare it with *Mexican American Gothic* by Santiago Forero.
3. Present what Santiago Forero's picture evokes to you.

Successful integration

1 "I wasn't *un*welcomed"

The narrator, of Asian origin, has settled in Bedley Run, not far from New York City.

PEOPLE KNOW ME HERE. It wasn't always so. But living thirty-odd years in the same place begins to show on a man. In the course of such time, without even realizing it, one takes on the characteristics of the locality, the color and stamp of the prevailing dress and gait and even speech – those gentle bells of the sidewalk passerby, their *How are yous* and *Hellos*. And in kind there is a gradual and accruing recognition of one's face, of being, as far as anyone can recall, from around here. There's no longer a lingering or vacant stare, and you can taste the small but unequalled pleasure that comes with being a familiar sight to the eyes. In my case, everyone here knows perfectly who I am. It's a simple determination. Whenever I step into a shop in the main part of the village, invariably someone will say, "Hey, it's good Doc Hata."

The sentiment, certainly, is very kind, and one I deeply appreciate. Here, fifty minutes north of the city, in a picturesque town that I will call Bedley Run, I somehow enjoy an almost Oriental veneration as an elder. I suppose the other older folks who live here receive their due share of generosity and respect, but it seems I alone rate the blustery* greeting, the special salutation. When I buy my paper each morning, the newsstand owner will say, with a tone feigning gravity, "Doctor Hata, I presume." And the young, bushy-eyebrowed woman at the deli, whose homebound mother I helped quite often in her final years, always reaches over the refrigerated glass counter and waves her plump hands and says, "Gonna have the usual, Doc?". She winks at me and makes sure to prepare my turkey breast sandwich herself, folding an extra wedge of pickle into the butcher paper. I realize that it's not just that I'm a friendly and outgoing silver-hair, and that I genuinely enjoy meeting people, but also because I've lived here as long as any, and my name, after all, is Japanese, a fact that seems both odd and delightful to people, as well as somehow town-affirming.

In my first years in Bedley Run, things were a bit different. [...]

When I first arrived in Bedleyville, few people seemed to notice me. Not that they were much different from those in the other towns, at least not intrinsically. Fundamentally, it seemed to me, the people in a particular area are given to a common set of conditions and influences, like the growth in a part of a forest. There may be many types of flora, but only the resident soil and climate provide for them, either richly or poorly or with indifference. I suppose it was because Bedleyville was still Bedleyville then, and not yet Bedley Run (though desperately wanting to be), and pretty much anybody new to town was seen as a positive addition to the census and tax base. It was 1963, and from what I'd seen during my brief travels in this country, everyone for the most part lived together, except, I suppose, for certain groups, such as the blacks, or the Chinese in the cities, who for one reason or another seemed to live apart. Still, I had assumed that once I settled someplace, I would be treated as those people were treated, and in fact I was fully prepared for it. But wherever I went – and in particular, here in Bedley Run – it seemed people took an odd interest in telling me that I wasn't *un*welcomed.

Chang Rae Lee, *Gesture Life* (1999)

* **blustery :** loud

1. a. **Read the title and the introduction**; explain the situation.
   b. **Read the text** and say what you have understood.
2. **Group work**. pages 14-15
   - **Read from line 1 to line 46** *(group 1)*.
   Highlight details about the narrator's daily routine and the people's reactions.
   - **Read from line 47 to the end** *(group 2)*.
   Highlight details about the narrator's arrival: the date, the town at the time, the people's attitudes towards him.
3. **Whole class**. **Discuss** the evolution in the narrator's situation. Why are the first words of this passage in capital letters?

LANGUAGE TOOLS

★ **WORDS**

Integration
- **in**tegrate, mix, blend in
- a**dapt**, ac**cus**tom, con**form**

Achievements
- will **po**wer, determi**na**tion
- **hard**working, am**bi**tious, **stead**fast
- oppor**tu**nity, chance, **o**pening
- be **ea**ger/**an**xious/keen

2 "Renewed hope"

video 4

A TV documentary about San Diego's Vietnamese community

1. **Watch the video** and pick out information about the Vietnamese community in San Diego.
2. How would you relate this video to the title of this page "successful integration"?

Recap → List the different ways of integrating into a new country. page 19

TRAINING TASK

Faces of America

Andrew Carnegie

Salma Hayek

Jerry Yang

1. Group work.
Here are three famous immigrants to the US.
Select one and research his/her life.
Use your ID cards
page 16 or www.didierpassword.fr

2. a. Interview the other groups about the celebrities they have chosen.
b. What do these people have in common?

Keeping the American Dream alive

"I still believe in the American Dream"

The American Dream for me, growing up in India in the 1970s, looked something like the opening credit of *Dallas*. The blockbuster TV series began with a kaleidoscope of big, brassy, sexy images – tracts of open land, shiny skyscrapers, fancy cars, cowboy businessmen and the very dreamy Victoria Principal. We watched bootlegged copies of the show, passed around on old Betamax cassettes. America seemed dazzling and larger than life, especially set against the stagnant backdrop of India in the 1970s. Everyone I knew was fascinated by the US, whether they admitted it or not. Politicians who denounced the country by day would go home in the evenings and plot to send their kids to college in "the States".

↑ Annual Sikh Day Parade in New York, April 2011

Of course, the 1970s were actually tough times in America – stagflation, malaise, the aftermath of Vietnam and Watergate – but they were brutal in the rest of the world. Hyperinflation racked most third-world countries; coups and martial law were familiar occurrences, even affecting staunchly democratic India, where emergency rule was enforced from 1975 to 1977. Set against this atmosphere of despair, the US looked like a shining city on a hill.

A few years later, when I got to America on a college scholarship, I realized that the real American Dream was somewhat different from *Dallas*. I visited college friends in their hometowns and was struck by the spacious suburban houses and the gleaming appliances – even when their parents had simple, modest jobs. The modern American Dream, for me, was this general prosperity and well-being for the average person. European civilization had produced the great cathedrals of the world. America had the two-car garage. And this middle-class contentment created a country of optimists. Compared with the fatalism that was pervasive in India those days, Americans had a sunny attitude toward life that was utterly refreshing.

But when I travel from America to India these days, as I did recently, it's as if the world has been turned upside down. Indians are brimming with hope and faith in the future. After centuries of stagnation, their economy is on the move, fueling animal spirits and ambition. The whole country feels as if it has been unlocked. Meanwhile, in the US, the mood is sour.

Americans are glum, dispirited and angry. Perhaps most troubling, Americans are strikingly fatalistic about their prospects. The can-do spirit is convinced that it can't. [...]

But there are reasons for optimism. The US faces huge challenges, but it also has enormous advantages. "I've always been bullish on America," says Cole's Kent. "It's the largest, richest market in the world. Look at the demographics alone. North America is the only part of the industrialized world that will be growing in people. It now has a higher rate than Mexico, for the first time in History." Or listen to Alcoa's German-born Klaus Kleinfeld, previously the head of Siemens: "I know the things that America has that are unique. The openness, the diversity, the dynamism – you don't have it anywhere else. If you keep all these things, build on them, I still believe in the American Dream."

The term *American Dream* was coined during the Great Depression. The historian James Truslow Adams published *The Epic of America* in 1931, in an atmosphere of even greater despair than today's. He wanted to call his book *The American Dream*, but his publishers objected. No one will pay $3.50 for a book about a "dream", they said. Still, Adams used the phrase so often that it entered in lexicon. The American Dream, he said, was of "a better, richer and happier life for all our citizens of every rank, which is the greatest contribution we have made to the thought and welfare of the world. That dream or hope has been present from the start. Ever since we became an independent nation, each generation has been an uprising of ordinary Americans to save the American Dream from the forces which appear to be overwhelming it."■

Fareed Zakaria, "How to restore the American Dream", *Time*, October 21, 2010

Fareed Zakaria
(born 1964)
Born in Mumbaï, India, and a Harvard graduate, he is currently a contributing editor at Time Magazine.

1. Discuss what the title of the article implies.

2. Read the article and tell the class what you have understood.

3. a. Read again down to line 82.
In groups, pick out information about:
- the journalist's vision of the American Dream...
  when he lived in India *(group 1)*;
  when he first visited the US *(group 2)*;
- his perception of today's situation *(group 3)*.

b. Share your findings and explain the changes.

4. Read from line 83 to the end and pick out the "reasons for optimism" (l. 83).

Recap → Explain why the American Dream is an enduring dream. page 19

LANGUAGE TOOLS

★ WORDS

Feelings
- hope, faith, prospect, reliance
- ambition, aspiration, drive
- fatalistic /feɪtəˈlɪstɪk/, despondent, discouraged

Can-do spirit
- energy, motivation
- challenge, stimulus, impetus

Prosperity ≠ want
- prosperous, affluent, well-to-do, well-off, destitute
- affluence ≠ need, lack

TRAINING TASK

Tweeting the Dream

Tweet contest: *"Can you define the American Dream in 140 characters or less?"*

1. In groups, discuss the definition of the American Dream.

2. On your own, tweet the dream.
Send it to the class and vote for the best tweet.

★ WORDS

❶ Feelings and reactions

a. Here is a list of adjectives:
• apprehensive, glad, optimistic, exultant, thrilled, hopeful, audacious, excited, anxious, delighted, buoyant, courageous, hesitant, cheerful, elated, worried, brave

Sort them out under these five headings:

excitement | apprehension | happiness | hope | courage

b. Use some of the adjectives above to talk about these people's feelings.

↑ Portrait of Mexican American family, California

← Italian emigrants, Ellis Island, around 1930

❷ The odd one out

a. In each of the following lists, find the odd one out:
1. asset - obstacle - hindrance - difficulty
2. native - local - national - foreign - domestic
3. divide - separate - integrate - isolate - detach
4. similar - remote - comparable - identical
5. tourists - travellers - immigrants - visitors
6. misunderstand - misinterpret - grasp - ignore

b. Complete with the words you have crossed out in *a*.

When settling in a ... country, speaking the language fluently is an ... when it comes to finding employment. ... sometimes find it difficult to ... because of their poor command of the language. That's why many of them take language classes. They know it will also help them to ... cultural habits that may be very ... from theirs.

❸ Talking about immigration

Bac

a. Find as many words as you can:
reasons for immigrating: war...
obstacles: language...
integrating: job...

b. Use some of these words to speak about immigration.

★ PRONUNCIATION

❹ Rhythm and weak forms

track 10

One [of the] reasons [why] we decided [that] we should move [to the] USA [was because of] economic hardship.

En anglais, certains mots appelés « formes faibles » ne sont pas accentués. Il s'agit souvent de mots grammaticaux. C'est l'alternance entre formes faibles (non accentuées) et formes fortes (accentuées) qui donne son rythme à l'anglais.

Practise in your workbook. page 17

❺ Stress on compound nouns

a. How would you pronounce these compound nouns? Which word would you stress more? Why?
• homeland, birthplace, Asian American, success story, will power, world stage, corporate world, high-tech engineer, real estate agent, lifestyle, school education, community center

b. Listen and check, then draw conclusions. track 11

c. Practise reading them aloud.

❻ Words ending in *-ion*

track 12

a. Listen and say which syllable is stressed in each word. What conclusions can you draw about the suffix *-ion*?

verbs	derived nouns
immigrate	immigration
expect	expectation
fascinate	fascination
starve	starvation
organize	organization
assimilate	assimilation
confront	confrontation
deport	deportation
integrate	integration
discriminate	discrimination
determine	determination

b. Practise pronouncing these words, paying particular attention to the stressed syllable.

★ GRAMMAR

Want/would like/expect sb to...

Observe

1. Ferdows Nafisy wants her daughters to become independent women.
2. Fang-Yi Sheu would like her parents to understand her.
3. Farah expects her children to adjust to American life.

• Observez les phrases ci-dessus.
Comparez leur sens et leur construction.
• Chacune de ces phrases contient deux verbes.
Comment expliquez-vous la forme du second verbe ?

→ Grammaire 21 p. 210

Practise

7 Using the elements below, imagine sentences expressing expectations.
a. Martin Matoda / recruiters / give him a job
b. Farah / Iranian women / be better recognized
c. Fang-Yi Sheu / Taiwanese dancers / develop modern dance in their homeland
d. Farah / fellow immigrants / integrate more easily

8 After getting your diploma, you have moved to the USA to study at university. When you arrive, the teachers tell you what they expect from the students and what they would like you to do. Imagine their speech.

When/If...

Observe

1. When/if Martin Matoda finds a job he likes, he will be able to settle and start a new life.
2. If/when the "Dream Act" is passed, it will be easier for undocumented students to attend college.
3. When he has graduated, Miguel will have a shot at the American Dream.

Comparez les phrases ci-dessus. Expliquez l'emploi des formes verbales soulignées.

→ Grammaire 20 p. 208 et 21 p. 210

Practise

9 Complete the following sentences.
a. They will leave their country if...
b. When they have become American citizens, ...
c. If locals and immigrants work together, ...
d. He will move to Silicon Valley when...
e. It will be easier for immigrants to integrate if...

10 You intend to move abroad. Write down a few lines saying what you will do when you are in your new country.
→ When I am there, ...
→ If ...

← Naturalization oath ceremony, Florida.

11 Look at the picture on the left. Write down a few lines about these people's projects.
→ When/If... I...

More exercises in your Workbook → p. 17-18

Comprendre un monologue

Dans un monologue, une personne s'exprime seule sans être interrompue. Son discours peut se construire au fur et à mesure de sa prise de parole (témoignage) ou avoir été préparé à l'avance (exposé).

1 Préparez-vous à l'écoute

Posez-vous des questions avant l'écoute. Même si les réponses que vous apportez sont multiples, elles vous aideront à mieux « entrer » dans le document.

Étapes	Indices	Exemples
1. Identifiez le contexte et la situation.	Un titre, une image, la source, les activités de classe qui ont précédé...	→ *Incredible India*
2. Posez-vous des questions sur...	• **le sujet** de la prise de parole.	→ L'Inde : on va sans doute présenter les atouts du pays dans le domaine économique, politique, artistique... ou raconter une expérience étonnante.
	• **le type de prise de parole** (bulletin d'informations, publicités, annonce radiophonique, témoignage, extrait de conférence ou de discours...) ;	→ Un documentaire informatif, une publicité, une conférence ?
	• **celui qui parle** (âge, homme/femme, fonction...).	→ Un habitant du pays ou un journaliste ?
	• **le but** de la prise de parole	→ Informer, expliquer, raconter, convaincre... ?
3. Faites des liens entre vos premières hypothèses et vos connaissances culturelles.	• Répertoriez rapidement ce que vous savez du sujet.	→ En quoi l'Inde est-elle un pays étonnant ? (traditions, culture, démographie, puissance économique, parfums, nourriture...)
	• Faites la liste des mots en lien avec la thématique et que vous êtes susceptible d'entendre.	→ *Taj Mahal, temples, architecture, colours, economic growth, Bollywood, a tourist destination, crowded...*

→ À vous

Préparez-vous à écouter le reportage radiophonique suivant :
New York Laundromat becomes an English classroom

A laundromat in New York →

2 Soyez actif lors de l'écoute

Lors d'écoutes successives vous pourrez vérifier vos hypothèses et effectuer des repérages.

Éléments à repérer	Objectifs
• **L'environnement sonore** (bruits de fond, musique) • **Qui parle ?**	• Identifier le type de prise de parole (témoignage, exposé, discours, publicité).
• **Le ton, l'intonation**	• Identifier les sentiments ou opinions.
• **Les mots qui se détachent** clairement : - les mots accentués ou prononcés plus lentement, - les mots répétés ou appartenant au même champ lexical, - les formes négatives.	• Déterminer le thème, les opinions et les arguments.
• **Les indicateurs de temps** : - les formes verbales (formes faibles) : temps, aspect, voix, - les marqueurs et adverbes de temps *(ten years ago, since then...)*, • **Les indicateurs de lieux** (noms propres, noms communs...), • **Les chiffres**, heures, dates (prononcés plus lentement), • Les éléments de **quantification** *(many, most, no...)*.	Situer, cerner ce dont on parle : • dans le temps, • dans l'espace, • d'un point de vue quantitatif.
• **Les articulateurs logiques** *(so, then, but, though, on the other hand...)* et **chronologiques** du discours *(first, after, before, last but not least...)*	• Comprendre la cohérence du discours et l'enchaînement des événements.

3 Reliez les éléments repérés pour construire le sens

a. Reliez les mots appartenant au même champ lexical et qui apparaissent à différents endroits du document (ex. : *India/Mumbai/... ; computer/industry/growth...*).
b. Compensez les mots que vous n'avez pas reconnus en vous appuyant sur la logique du discours et de la situation.
c. Répondez aux questions « **qui, quoi, où, quand, comment, pourquoi** ».

→ À vous

track 14

- **Écoutez au moins trois fois le reportage et recueillez le plus d'indices possibles.**
- **Reliez les éléments que vous avez repérés et préparez-vous à en rendre compte.**

Le jour du Bac

Séries ES, S et technologiques

→ voir aussi *Entraînement Bac* p. 50

- **Le titre du document** vous sera communiqué et ce document sera en lien avec une **notion** du programme : exploitez ces informations pour **émettre vos hypothèses**.
- Soyez prêt à tout écouter mais à ne pas tout comprendre : on vous demande d'extraire les **informations essentielles**, pas de rédiger un script.
- Vous disposerez de 3 écoutes successives : profitez de chacune d'entre elles pour **enrichir** progressivement **votre prise de notes** et affiner votre compréhension.
- Prenez des **notes brèves** et non rédigées afin de ne pas disperser votre attention.
- **Construisez du sens** en vous appuyant sur vos connaissances et votre bon sens.
- Vous disposerez de 10 minutes pour **rendre compte par écrit, en français**, de ce que vous avez compris.

FINAL TASKS

Talk Show

task 1

Speaking

Take part in a radio programme about the new Americans

• **Role Play**: your teacher will give you an ID card with the part you have to play: either a journalist, a guest, or a member of the audience.

1. Get ready

• As a journalist or a member of the audience: prepare some notes to present the programme and the questions you want to ask your guests.

• As a guest: complete your ID card with what you imagine about your character. Be ready to answer the journalist's or the audience's questions.

2. Action!

• Act out the talk show.

Carmen Alvarado
Hondurian

- Left Honduras in 2010
- Reason: join her husband
- Became an active member of Charity Action Against Hunger

Sangjay Lakshmi
Indian

- Left India in 2009
- Reason: work as a high tech engineer
- Became CEO of his company

Anna Lin Wu
Chinese

- Left China in 2007
- Reason: study at Yale.
- Graduated and found the job she wished for

task 2

Listening

Guest selection for a talk show

• Two journalists are preparing a TV programme about the new Americans. They have received several e-mails from people willing to take part in the show and tell their stories.

• Listen to the journalists' conversation: who did they select? Explain their choices.

Bac

Compréhension de l'oral

Listen to a testimony:

From illegal immigrant to world-known specialist

1. Listen to the document three times and take notes.

2. Write a report in French of what you have understood.

Expression orale

Oral presentation

1. Using what you have learnt about the **new Americans**, prepare notes explaining what part immigrants play in the **exchanges between countries**. You can follow these guidelines:

- The reasons why people emigrate and choose the United States as their destination.
- What they can achieve in the US.
- How they shape the American identity.

Illustrate your presentation with other relevant examples you may know.

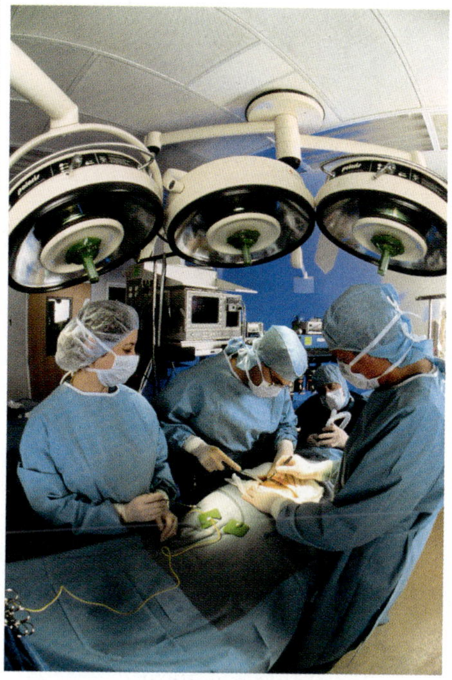

2. Give your oral presentation.

3. Be ready to discuss the topic with your teacher.

→ Aide

Utilisez la fiche *Recap* du workbook p. 19 ou sur www.didierpassword.fr pour préparer cette synthèse orale.

Compréhension de l'écrit

Study a set of documents

Your teacher will give you several documents. Read them carefully and answer the questions.

Expression écrite

Write two different texts

Using the elements given by your teacher, write:

1. A diary entry

2. A dialogue

Culture File

IMMIGRANT COMMUNITIES

In groups

1. Pick out one set of documents.
2. Carry out research about the immigrant community it refers to.

Whole class

3. Compare these immigrant communities.

← Annie Moore, first Irish emigrant processed at Ellis Island on Jan. 1, 1892

1 Irish: in the cities

Irish immigrants numbered about a million in the 1850s, following the potato famine.

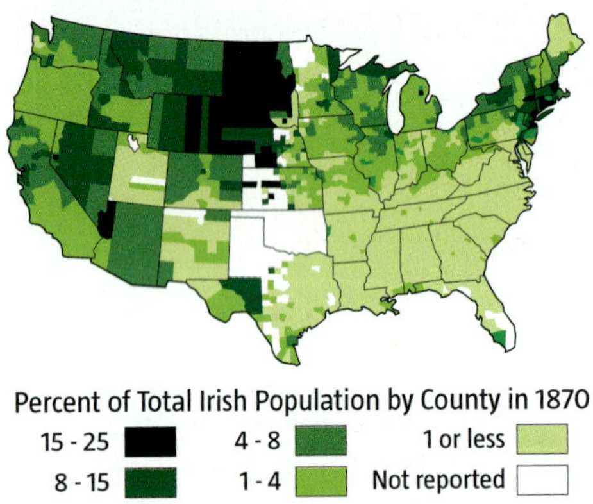

The Emigrant Irish

Like oil lamps, we put them out the back —
of our houses, of our minds. We had lights
better than, newer than and then
a time came, this time and now
we need them. Their dread, makeshift example:
they would have thrived on our necessities.
What they survived we could not even live.
By their lights now it is time to
imagine how they stood there, what they stood with,
that their possessions may become our power:
Cardboard. Iron. Their hardships parceled in them.
Patience. Fortitude. Long-suffering
in the bruise-colored dusk of the New World.
And all the old songs. And nothing to lose.

Eavan Boland (born 1944) *Irish poet*

2 Asians: in California

San Francisco Chinatown is the largest Chinatown outside Asia and the oldest in North America.

← Dragon Gate in San Francisco, Calif.

Poem written by a Chinese immigrant on the wall of the Angel Island immigration station c. 1920 →

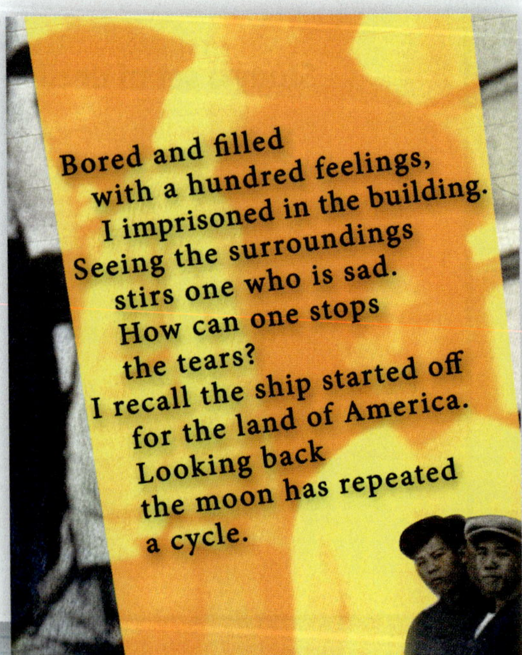

3 Latinos: crossing borderlands

Illegal immigrants near Sells, Arizona

Josseline shivered as she stepped over the stones and ducked under the mesquites. She was in Arizona, land of heat and sun, but on this late-January day in 2008, it was cold and damp. The temperature was in the 50s*, and the night before it had dropped to near freezing. A winter rain had fallen, and now the desert path was slippery and wet, even more treacherous that it had been before.

Josseline was seven miles north of the Mexican border, near the old ranching town of Arivaca. [...] It was a wonderland of cactus and mesquite, beautiful but dangerous, with trails threading through isolated canyons and up and down hills studded with rocks. She had to get through to this perilous place to get to her mother. A little girl with a big name – Josseline Jamileht Hernández Quinteros – she was five feet tall and a hundred pounds. At fourteen, young as she was, she had an important responsibility: it was her job to bring her little brother, age ten, safely to their mother in Los Angeles. The Hernández kids had never been away from home before, and already they'd been travelling for weeks. Now they were almost there, just days away from their mother's embrace. [...]

The group had crossed from El Salvador to Guatemala, then traveled two thousand miles from the southern tip of Mexico to the north. The trip had been arduous. They'd skimped on food, slept in buses or, when they were lucky in *casas de huespedes*, the cheap flophouses that cater to poor travelers. In Mexico the migrants feared the *federales*, the national police, and now, in the United States, they were trying to evade the Border Patrol, the dreaded *migra*.

But here in the borderlands they were in the hands of a professional. Like the thousands of other undocumented migrants pouring into Arizona – jumping over walls, trekking across mountains, hiking through deserts – the group had contacted with a coyote, a smuggler paid to spirit them over the international line. The coyote's fee, many thousands of dollars, was to pay for Josseline and her brother to be taken from El Savador all the way to their mother in Los Angeles. So far, everything had gone to plans. They had slipped over the border from Mexico, near Sasabe, twenty miles from here, and had spent a couple of days picking their way through this strange desert, where spiky cacti clawed at the skin and the rocky trail blistered the feet. The coyote insisted on fast pace. They still had a hike of twenty miles ahead of them, out to the northbound highway. [...]

Josseline (pronounced YO-suh-leen) pulled her two jackets closer in the cold. [...] She tried to pay attention to the twists and turns in the footpath, to obey the guide, to keep up with the group. But by the time they got to Cedar Canyon, she was lagging. She was beginning to feel sick.

Margaret Regan,
***The Death of Josseline* (2010)**

* 50s: about 10 degrees Celsius

Entraînement BAC

Compréhension de l'oral

Séries ES, S et technologiques

« • L'épreuve de compréhension de l'oral s'appuie sur un ou deux documents enregistrés, audio ou vidéo.
• Ces documents sont liés aux notions du programme mais non étudiés précédemment en classe.
Le titre de l'enregistrement est donné aux candidats.
• Il pourra s'agir de monologues, de dialogues, de discours, de discussions. Il pourra s'agir d'extraits d'émissions de radio, de documentaires, de films, de journaux télévisés.
• La durée de l'enregistrement n'excédera pas 1 min 30 pour l'ensemble des documents.
• Les candidats ont trois écoutes de l'enregistrement, séparées chacune d'une minute. Ils peuvent prendre des notes pendant chaque écoute. Ils disposent ensuite de 10 minutes pour rendre compte par écrit en français de ce qu'ils ont compris, sans exigence d'exhaustivité. »

Instructions officielles, B.O. du 24 nov. 2011

Le jour du BAC

- Vous pourrez être évalué(e) sur **un ou deux supports**.
- Cette épreuve n'est accompagnée d'aucune question en anglais : à vous de **construire le sens** à partir des éléments que vous comprendrez. Les conseils qui suivent vous y aideront.
- Rappelez-vous qu'il vous faut **saisir l'essentiel** et pas nécessairement tous les détails.
- Reliez toujours le **thème des documents** aux **notions** étudiées en classe.
- Vous rédigerez votre compte-rendu **en français**.

1. Compréhension orale à partir d'un document unique

Reportez-vous aux *Stratégies*, *Comprendre un monologue* p. 44, et *Comprendre un dialogue* p. 108, afin d'effectuer des repérages efficaces et mettre en lien les éléments pour faire du sens.

You are going to listen to a document entitled: ***Settling into a new life***

track 15

Reformulez le titre avec vos propres mots pour vous assurer de l'avoir bien compris et reliez-le à ce que vous avez étudié au cours de l'année.

Première écoute

- Concentrez-vous sur cette première écoute : ne prenez pas trop de notes afin de rester attentif.
- Profitez de la pause (1 min) pour noter (en français ou en anglais) tout ce que vous avez compris.
- Commencez à organiser votre prise de notes en vous posant des questions : vous pouvez faire un tableau.

Type de doc	...
Qui parle ?	...
De qui/de quoi ?	...
Où ?	...
Quand ?	...
Comment ?	...
Pourquoi ?	...
Qu'est ce qu'on en dit ? (événements, opinions, sentiments)	...

Deuxième et troisième écoutes

- Prenez des notes au fur et à mesure de l'écoute. Si un passage vous paraît particulièrement délicat, écoutez sans noter pour pouvoir vous concentrer.
- Complétez votre tableau au fur et à mesure lors des pauses entre les écoutes.

Phase de synthèse

- Vous disposez de 10 min pour finir d'organiser et de mettre en forme, en français, ce que vous avez compris.
- Vous pouvez faire des hypothèses de sens à partir des éléments que vous n'avez pas complètement compris : veillez toutefois à ce que ces hypothèses soient cohérentes par rapport à l'ensemble du document.
- Rédigez ensuite votre synthèse, en veillant à sa cohérence, à l'orthographe et à la présentation.

→ *Le document est ... / traite de.... Une, deux ... personnes sont interviewées/ témoignent/donnent leur opinion/font la promotion de.... Ces personnes évoquent... La scène se passe...*

2. Compréhension orale à partir de deux supports

You are going to listen to two documents entitled:
Becoming an American citizen

track 16

Les conseils donnés pour le document unique valent aussi pour la compréhension de deux documents.

- Lorsque deux documents sont annoncés, l'un sera de type dialogue, l'autre de type monologue.
- Un seul titre peut recouvrir les deux documents : vous pouvez ainsi vous faire une idée du thème qui les relie.

Si deux titres vous sont proposés, essayez de les relier à un thème commun :
Ex. : a. *Naturalization ceremony*
b. *"I'm an American now"*

→ vous pourrez déduire qu'il s'agit d'une cérémonie au cours de laquelle des immigrants acquièrent la citoyenneté américaine, et que l'un d'entre eux va témoigner.

- Prenez des notes séparées pour les deux documents, dans un tableau à deux colonnes.

	Doc 1	Doc 2
Type de doc	1 monologue	1 dialogue
Qui parle ?	...	...
De qui/de quoi ?	...	...
Où ?	...	...
Quand ?	...	...
Comment ?	...	...
Pourquoi ?	...	...
Qu'est ce qu'on en dit ? (événements, opinions, sentiments)	...	...

- Reliez les documents au moment de faire la synthèse :

→ fait-on référence à un même thème, un même événement, une même personne ?
→ les documents ont-ils le même but ?
→ les opinions développées sont-elles contradictoires et/ou complémentaires, les exemples différents ?

- Rédigez votre synthèse :

- soit en expliquant ce que vous avez compris de chacun des documents puis en les comparant ;
- soit en expliquant les liens, les complémentarités et les différences entre les deux documents.

UNIT 3 Tech-less world

↑ ***Man outside his yurt,*** Catskill, New York

How to live without technology?

Look at the photograph and **react**.
What forms of technology are most important to you?

FINAL TASKS

P. 66

Post-apocalyptic stories

Writing
Imagine a world without technology

Reading
Match book covers and blurbs

CULTURE

- Understanding the impact of technology on our daily lives.
- Exploring tech-less experiences:
  - as a personal choice,
  - as a consequence of a technological failure.
- Literary works:
  - S.M. Stirling, *Dies the Fire*
  - Paul Theroux, *The Mosquito Coast*
  - Jon Krakauer, *Into the Wild*

COMMUNICATION

- Describing and giving explanations about life without technology.
- Writing stories relating experiences and describing feelings and reactions.

Understanding facts and feelings in personal testimonies and fictitious narratives.

Presenting a personal experience.

TOOLS

Words
- Electricity cuts
- Discontent / Satisfaction
- Obstacle / Failure
- Dependence / Independence
- Deprivation
- Dislike
- Benevolence / Malevolence
- Success
- Abundance

Pronunciation
- Intonation in questions
- Intonation of lists

Grammar
- Present perfect + *since/for*
- *a/the/Ø*

BAC

Stratégies
→ *Rédiger un texte narratif* **p. 64**

Évaluation
→ *4 situations d'évaluation* **p. 67**

Blackouts: when the lights go off

1 Breaking News

video 5

Massive power outage affecting up to 2,000 people in Orange County, California, Sept 9, 2011

1. **Before watching the video**, say what kind of document you expect to see and what it may be about.
2. **Watch the video with the sound off** and list everything you can remember.
3. **In groups**. **Watch again with the sound on** and pick out information about:
   - the situation and its consequences *(group 1)*,
   - people's ways of coping *(group 2)*,
   - people's feelings *(group 3)*.
4. **Whole class**: summarize the situation.

← San Diego, Ca. Sept. 8, 2011. Workers serve pizza to customers after a massive blackout

LANGUAGE TOOLS

★ WORDS

Electricity cuts

- power **short**age /'ʃɔːtɪdʒ/, **black**out = power cut
- be... **black**ened, be in the dark
  be af**fec**ted by a power **out**age /ˈaʊtɪdʒ/

Discontent

- dis**sa**tisfied, **sul**ky, **an**gry, **wo**rried, dis**tur**bed, frus**tra**ted,

Satisfaction

- pleased, de**ligh**ted, thrilled, over**joy**ed, en**thra**lled /ɪn'θrɔːld/
- enthusi**as**tic /'ɪnˌθjuːzɪ'æstɪk/

★ PRONUNCIATION → p. 62

Intonation in questions

Intonation of lists

★ GRAMMAR → p. 63

Present perfect + since / for

→ They have been affected by a power outage for a week now.

2 Personal experiences of blackouts

There have been several electricity failures all over the world in the past years. Here are online posts relating people's personal experiences.

http://www.blackout

File Edit View Favorites Tools Help

Posted at 07:12 PM #1 — title: **New York blackout in August 2003** — Share

Elizabeth

After the power failed the streets were completely packed right in the middle of the afternoon. Nobody was doing any kind of work. Within minutes, hundreds of people in my neighbourhood of Brooklyn gathered outside. We read, talked, watched the rain and in the evening we could see all the stars in the sky. I just discovered how friendly our neighbours were and really I don't understand all the fuss about it.

Post Reply · Previous · Next

Posted at 08:02 PM #2 — title: **New York blackout in August 2003** — Share

Jordan

Well, I'm afraid we take everything for granted and we fail to see how dependant on electric devices we are. Like many people my commute home was a little longer than usual (six hours instead of 40 minutes) but everyone behaved so well! With nothing to do, like many others, we ended up in the street helping direct traffic. I have heard that restaurants were offering free drinks to the thousands of people who were walking home.

Post Reply · Previous · Next

Posted at 08:27 PM #3 — title: **Sao Paulo, Brazil blackout in November 2009** — Share

Marcelo Wong

I've been living in the city of Sao Paulo for 15 years. I've never seen the city in complete darkness, as it was last night. I had just left my shop when the street lights started to blink for a couple of seconds, then the whole city was plunged into darkness. As a result, the train service stopped, electric-powered buses stopped on the streets, affecting the traffic and also the traffic lights weren't working, leaving the city in a chaotic situation. People who were still in their offices were forced to get out of the buildings. One of my friends has kids on the 21st floor - he used a mobile phone to talk to them and comfort them as they were crying.

Post Reply · Previous · Next

Posted at 08:56 PM #4 — title: **Powercut chaos in Tauranga, New Zealand, February 12, 2011** — Share

Irving King

café owner

Power is the most essential thing for us. We need power to keep the food chilled or heated and if it doesn't work, we've got to throw all the food away. We can't use the till, that's electronic too, so we can't sell anything and we can't make coffee either. There's nothing you can do about things like this. It's just something you have to work through.

Post Reply · Previous · Next

1. In groups, read one of the posts above and pick out details about:
- the consequences of the blackout,
- the solutions people found,
- their feelings and reactions.

Report to the other groups.

2. Discuss what these accounts show about blackouts.

Recap → List the possible consequences of power cuts. page 24

TRAINING TASK

Voice-over

Prepare the soundtrack for a video.

1. Watch the video and jot down what happened to the man and what he may feel.

2. Discuss and organize your findings.

3. Then individually record your voice-over beginning with: *"Yesterday when I got home…".*

video 6

↑ What if petrol disappeared?

Tech-free days

Students unplug

Sunday October 10th, 2010

Students at Portland's Lincoln High School, experience life without technology

"Before we got fire, we used to talk to each other."

For four days this week, Elise Cramer didn't pick up her cell phone. The 17-year-old Lincoln High School senior didn't check Facebook or turn on the television, either. She and 53 other Lincoln students participated in a technology fast for the school week, which was shortened by a day. [...] Cramer coped better than one might expect for someone her age.

"It's liberating kind of," she said. "You're not connected, and you get to discover new things."

The challenge was the idea of English teacher Jordan Gutlerner, who asked junior and seniors in two periods to unplug all technological devices, including cell phones, computers, the Internet, video games and music-playing devices. The challenge was voluntary, but all but two students took part. [...] On the third day, the 20 students in one period shared varying responses to the assignment.

"I feel really anxious because I don't know if I'm missing something important," Amanda Schenberger said. "I keep thinking, 'I can't wait for this to end because I need to check my e-mail.' How many Facebook notifications am I going to have after this?" [...] Robert Paige said when his parents aren't home, he usually turns on the TV and all the lights for comfort. This week, he had to find other things to do.

"I just kind of sat and thought," he said. "I was thinking a lot about where we're going with the world... about technology and what impact it has on society."

Paige, an avid videographer, said it's been hard not to check Craigslist* for equipment deals. But he said the assignment has been eye-opening.

"Our generation has been exposed to the media way too early," Paige said. "I think that's degrading society to the point that we're not going to be able to recover. Technology is a great help, but we don't need it."

Elise Cramer said the assignment showed the importance people place on feeling wanted.

"We want people to reach out to us," she said. "Without that, I think you feel lonely. Being alone is not a bad thing, but we're never alone."

Cramer was among many who broke the fast for one reason or another. She checked e-mail for assignments. Paige kept in contact with his parents via cell phone, and he couldn't resist watching the latest episode of "Sons of Anarchy." Even Gutlerner slipped, ordering Chinese food from a cell phone.

"I think these devices are addictive," Gutlerner said. "Even people who aren't addicted to them are behaving as though they are."

On Friday, Gutlerner's students were allowed to boot up again. He said he assumes most will return to normal usage, but some vowed to change. Several said they were considering deactivating Facebook and MySpace accounts.

Gutlerner hopes the fast catches on with other Lincoln teachers. His students are considering challenging the rest of the school to unplug for a couple of days later this year.

Elise Cramer thinks it's a good lesson.

"You don't have to go live in the woods, but you have to be conscious about how you use these electronics," she said. "When people are educated about what they're doing, that's when they can make a personal decision to change." ■

Molly Hottle,
www.oregonlive.com

* **Craigslist**: online classified advertisements

1. **Before reading**: have a look at the title, the standfirst and the first paragraph.
Imagine what the text may deal with.

2. **Read the article** and say what you have understood.

3. **a.** Read again and pick out information about:
- the experience itself,
- the negative aspects of it,
- its positive sides.

b. Share your findings.

4. **Explain and illustrate** Elise Cramer's conclusion:
"You don't have to go live in the woods, but you have to be conscious about how you use these electronics," [...] "When people are educated about what they're doing, that's when they can make a personal decision to change." (l. 98-105)

Recap → Explain why tech-free day experiments are a challenge. page 24

LANGUAGE TOOLS

★ **WORDS**

Obstacle
- stop, pre**vent**, keep sbdy from + V-*ing* = **hin**der, im**pede**, thwart

→ The assignment thwarted all his plans about the weekend.

Failure
- fail to, be unsuc**cess**ful, try in vain, make nothing of

Dependence/Independence
- be de**pen**dent on, hooked on, ad**dict**ed to
- need, re**quire**, crave, can't do with**out**
- break out of, get rid of, give up, shake off the habit of

Deprivation
- go without, be de**pri**ved of, need, miss, re**frain** from doing something
- loss, lack, pri**va**tion, **hard**ship, fast

TRAINING TASK

Unplug!

How long will you resist without digital technology?
Try doing without it for a whole week-end!

1. Keep a diary report of what you do and how you feel.
Present your experience to the class (2 min).

2. Write a short paragraph explaining what this no-mobile/ no-computer/no- ... experience brought you (150 words).

↑ No-Tech Day is a challenge for gadget addicts to go without their tech toys for a day.

Go cold turkey = to suddenly and completely stop doing something you are addicted to

Dark times

Surviving

An unexplained phenomenon, called "the Change", has caused all energy or ignition powered machinery to stop working. All means of communication have ceased, water cannot be pumped, even guns cannot be fired. In this post-apocalyptic environment, Havel and a group of people are travelling in search of a place where to settle.

The tiny hamlet[1] sat at the junction of the Lochsa and the Clearwater[2]; in normal times it was a jumping off point for the wilderness areas around, and for white-water rafting. Now half a dozen of its residents stood across the roadway; three of them had hunting bows, the other axes or baseball bats.

Havel reined in his horse and flung up his right hand with the fist clenched. He could hear Angelica's whoa! to her team, and the hoof-falls of the rest behind him ceased, dying away to an occasional clop or a crunch as a horse shifted in place.

"Afternoon," he said.

"Afternoon," the burly middle-aged man who seemed to be the leader said. "Lot of road people already been through."

Road people? Havel thought. Then: *Well, yeah, there must have been millions caught away from home when the Change happened...* [...]

"I've got to warn you though, we don't have any food to spare. Barely enough for our own."

Havel nodded. He'd expected nothing different. This was hard country, well away from farming and ranching areas further west and south. The locals could probably survive on hunting and fishing until winter, but not many passersby could.

"We're fixed for now," he said. "Got plenty of meat."

Several of the men stiffened with suspicion. Already? Havel thought, and went on aloud: "Elk, venison and bear" — he touched the long wound that ran across his forehead and into his scalp — "which the bear brought on himself. We could trade some jerky[3] for flour or rice or beans."

The little band of townsfolk relaxed. Their leader looked at the swords the travelers all carried, and the bows. [...]

"You folks are together then? Looks like you're loaded for bear!"

That brought a few chuckles from his townsmen; Havel smiled thinly — it still hurt to move his face much "We ran into some survivalists, original-sovereign types. They seemed to think they could do anything they wanted, now that things are Changed. We're taking precautions to avoid another incident like that."

The leader's eyes took in their various bruises and contusions and spat eloquently. "Those crazy bastards? What happened?"

Havel shrugged. "Coyotes have to eat too, so we didn't bury the bodies," he said, and got another, louder chuckle. "We'd like to camp for a few days and work on our gear before we move on. We're heading towards Lewiston. If anyone wants to trade, we can do farrier work or such".

A nod, and the leader leaned on his axe. "We have a couple of horses that could use shoeing. Head on down that lane, there's a campground by the river and some cabins – use 'em if you want, but the plumbing's not working. There's some other folks who got caught on the road staying there, too."

S.M. Stirling, *Dies the Fire* (2005)

1. hamlet: very small village
2. Lochsa and Clearwater: rivers in Idaho
3. jerky: dry meat

LANGUAGE TOOLS

★ **WORDS**

Dislike

- turn pale, **shi**ver, flinch, wince, **re**coil from, shrink from ≠ leap for joy, **re**lish /ˈrelɪʃ/

→ When he saw the survivalists, he didn't even flinch.

→ She relishes freedom more than everything else.

Benevolence

- kind, **cha**ritable, hu**ma**ne /hjuːˈmeɪn/, **sym**pathizing, well-in**ten**tioned, com**pas**sionate

Malevolence

- **mer**ciless, harsh, **cold**-hearted, **trea**cherous /ˈtretʃərəs/, in**vi**dious, **ruth**less, **bar**barous, ma**li**cious

1. Have a look at the introduction and the illustration.
Imagine what the story will be about.

2. Read the text. Discuss what you have understood about the different characters and their situations.

3. a. In groups: read the text again and highlight details about:
- the hamlet and its residents *(group 1)*,
- the travellers *(group 2)*.

pages 20-21

b. Discuss your findings and draw conclusions about the group of people you have studied.
c. Report them back to the other group.

4. Whole class: compare both groups of people.

5. How do you understand the passage:
"We ran into some survivalists, original-sovereign types. They seemed to think they could do anything they wanted, now that things are Changed. We're taking precautions to avoid another incident like that." (l. 28-30)

6. Describe what the world is like after "the Change".

Recap → Explain the impact of "the Change" on individual and social behaviour. page 24

TRAINING TASK

An encounter

Imagine the meeting between Havel's group and the people from the campground down the river (l. 38-40).

1. a. In groups, list your ideas and plan your story.

Events | Places | Actions | Attitudes

b. Discuss and decide on the reactions you want to stress:

Trust | Fear | Discontent

2. On your own, write your story (150-200 words).

Better off

Building a new life

↑ Scene from *The Mosquito Coast*, directed by Peter Weir (1986)

Allie Fox, a brilliant inventor, has taken his family from Hatfield, Massuchussets, to a remote part of Honduras known as Jeronimo. Their story is narrated by his eldest son, Charlie.

It was plain from where we sat that Jeronimo was a success. We had defeated the mosquitoes, tamed the river, drained the swamp and irrigated the gardens. We had seen the worst of Honduras weather – the June floods, the September heat – and we had overcome both. We had just this moment withstood an earth tremor – nothing had shaken loose! We were organized, Father said. Our drinking water was purified in a distiller that ran from Fat Boy*'s fire-box. We had the only ice-making plant in Mosquitia, the only one of its kind in the world, and the capability, Father said, of making an ice-berg.

Down there were corn stalks, eight and a half feet high, and cobs a foot long – "So big, it only takes eleven of them to make a dozen." We had fresh fruit and vegetables and an incubator (Fat Boy's spare heat) for hatching eggs. "Control – that's the proof of civilization. Anyone can do something once, but repeating it and maintaining it – that's the true test". We grew rice, the most difficult of crops. We had a superior sewage system and shower apparatus. "We're clean!" An efficient windmill pump over-rode the water-wheel on the ice-making days. Most of the inventions had been made from local materials, and three new buildings were faced with Father's bamboo tiles. We had a chicken-run and two boats at the landing and the best flush toilets in Honduras. Jeronimo was a masterpiece of order –"appropriate technology", Father called it.

We produced more than we needed. The extra fish we caught swam in a tank Father named the 'Fish Farm'–his names were always a bit grander than the things themselves. We harvested more than we could eat, but the excess was not sold. Some of it he gave to people in return for work, but he never handed out any food to beggars. What he preferred to do was to cut the produce open – watermelons, say, or cucumbers or corn – and empty out the seed and dry them. He would give these to anyone who helped him. There was always work to do – he was determined to straighten the river and clear it of hyacinths. "It could take a lifetime," he said. "But I've got a lifetime – I'm not going anywhere!" River workers were rewarded with blocks of ice and bags of seeds. "Hybrids! Burpees! Wonder corn! Miracle beans! Sixty-day tomatoes!"

We were happy and hidden. All you could see of Jeronimo from the river was Fat Boy's square head and tin hat and the smoking chimney stack. [...]

It was now November, the weather like Hatfield in July, and Jeronimo was home.

Paul Theroux, *The Mosquito Coast* (1981)

*** Fat Boy:** a machine for making ice from fire, built by the father

1. **Read the introduction and take a look at the photograph**. Identify the place, the characters and the situation. Read the first sentence of the text and guess what it might be about.
2. **Read the whole text** and discuss what you have understood.
3. **a. In groups**, pick out:
   - the positive and negative aspects mentioned in § 1 *(group 1)*,
   - the inventions and their consequences on people's daily lives in § 2 *(group 2)*.

   b. Discuss your findings and draw conclusions about the family's experience in Jeronimo.
   c. Report them to the class.
4. **Whole class**. Read the text again, focusing on the father's words and attitudes. Draw conclusions about his personality, his role in this new society and the son's opinion of his father.
5. **Comment** on the last sentence of the text (l. 37-38)

LANGUAGE TOOLS

★ WORDS

Success

- be suc**cess**ful, **ma**nage to /ˈmænɪdʒ/, make the best of it, over**come**, make/do with, cope with, with**stand** /wɪðˈstænd/

→ The wooden bridge he has built withstands the strongest winds.

Abundance

- be **loa**ded with, be en**dowed** with /ɪnˈdaʊd/, have extra..., have one's fill, have in great sup**ply** /səˈplaɪ/
- a land of plenty

→ The land was well endowed with natural resources.

★ GRAMMAR → p. 63

a / the / Ø

→ Tech-less experience can teach us about the addictive habits of an individual.

Recap → Using what you have learnt and your own experience, explain why living in a tech-less world could be rewarding. page 24

TRAINING TASK

A postcard

Write Charlie's answer to a friend's postcard below (150 words).

HATFIELD MA.

Hi Charlie,
Can't join you on Facebook or by email so I'm having to fall back on snail mail and send you a postcard. How's the simple life in the jungle? It's probably just as well you can't see my new phone: it takes photos, surfs the net, stores music - you might just feel a teeny bit jealous!
Also - saw an AMAZING film in 3D! It's hard to explain, but you really feel like you're on a whole different planet. Which is pretty much the case for you, I suppose! What do you DO out there in the jungle? Hope this makes it to you and finds you well.
See ya
Xxx
Peter

A view of the Town Hall, Hatfield

★ WORDS

1 Feelings and attitudes

Look at this still from the film *Children of Men*. Write a short narrative describing the scene. Use words you have learnt in this chapter.

It's 2027 and people can no longer have children. A very young pregnant woman has been found and must be saved.

↑ Theo trying to help the young girl escape from a refugee camp.

2 Cause and consequence

a. **List connecting words expressing cause (*because*, etc.) or consequence (*so*, etc.).**

b. **Connect these pairs of sentences using words from your list. Try to use different link-words.**

1. Some kinds of technology are dangerous. / People would like to get rid of them.
2. There was a massive power outage. / Communities couldn't work as usual.
3. People are accustomed to using technological devices. / They don't trust their personal capabilities anymore.
4. Sheila's earliest customers could not buy her famous cupcakes. / The blackout had spread all over the Bay of Plenty.

3 Talking about progress Bac

a. **Read the following words and make sure you understand them:**

• enrichment - increase - downfall - update - decrease - crumbling - upgrade - betterment - deterioration - progress - regression - worsening - corruption

b. **Sort them out under two headings:**

improvement | degeneration

c. **Use them to talk about a tech-less world.**

★ PRONUNCIATION

4 Intonation in questions (track 17)

"Kevin, could you imagine a life without technology?"
"What do you mean, without technology?"
"Well, how would you react if you no longer had a car or a computer?"
"Are you joking? This is just unimaginable!"

a. **Listen to the questions above, say whether the intonation is rising (↗) or falling (↘), then conclude.**

→ In a Yes-No question, the intonation is usually...

→ In a Wh-question, the intonation is usually...

b. **Practise reading a dialogue aloud.** page 22

5 Intonation of lists

"With no electric devices, no TV, no cell phone, no computer, the only things we had to do was read books, watch the rain, sleep on the porch, and count stars."

L'intonation permet au locuteur d'indiquer si une liste est terminée ou pas.

a. **Listen to the sentence above and indicate when the intonation is rising or falling. What conclusions can you draw?** (track 18)

b. **Now practise pronouncing the following sentence with the right intonation.**

→ During the blackout, the train service stopped, the traffic lights went off, electric-powered buses stopped, people were forced to get back home, and children started panicking.

c. **Listen and compare.** (track 19)

★ GRAMMAR

Present Perfect + *since/for*

Observe

1. There has been no power around here since late this afternoon. It's a nightmare.
2. We've been eating cold food since electricity went off and we don't know when we will get it back.
3. Last time there was a power cut, buses and trains did not run for two days but we managed.
4. There has been no electricity for a whole week and now there's no more food in the shops.

• Qu'indiquent les compléments qui suivent la préposition *since* et ceux qui suivent la préposition *for* ? Concluez sur l'emploi de *since* et de *for*.
• Observez les formes verbales surlignées. Que pouvez-vous en dire ?
• Observez les phrases 3 et 4 et comparez les formes verbales surlignées. Que pouvez-vous en dire ?

→ Grammaire 14 p. 204

Practise

6 Complete the following sentences with the appropriate verbal form (preterit or present perfect) and the appropriate preposition (*for* or *since*). Justify your choice.

a. I *(repair)* my laptop twice ... I bought it!
b. We *(stay)* in complete darkness ... three long days. It was terrifying!
c. They *(rediscover)* the simple values of life ... the blackout.
d. She *(adopt)* new attitudes ... the state raised energy taxes. It is a good solution then!
e. The employees *(work)* with candles ... two days last week. ... the power went off, they *(lose)* all their data and are really worried.

7 A storm has damaged your area. There is no electricity anymore. Imagine a short narrative explaining what has happened and how you have adapted to the situation (60-80 words).

a/the/Ø

Observe

1. We were told that in the jungle there were Ø dangerous rivers and Ø terrible mosquitoes.
2. But we managed to defeat the mosquitoes and tame the rivers.
3. We also had Ø fresh fruits and Ø vegetables.
4. I particularly liked a fruit that looked like an apple.
5. The vegetables we grew were the best we had ever had and the fruit I preferred was very juicy.

Observez et comparez l'emploi des articles *a*, *Ø* et *the* dans les phrases 1 à 5. Notez vos conclusions dans un tableau comme ci-dessous.

	article associé à...		
	a	*the*	*Ø*
Nom indéfini singulier			
Nom défini singulier			
Nom indéfini pluriel			
Nom défini pluriel			
Sens générique			
Sens particulier			

→ Grammaire 4 p. 192

Practise

8 Complete the following sentences with *a*, *the* or *Ø*. Justify your answer.

a. In ... jungle, you find ... small houses but ... house we built was nice and roomy. It was ... house made of ... bamboo and ...liana.
b. ... food was hard to find and ... meat was scarce, but ...... meat we ate was very tasty.
c. We adopted ..... wild dog that we called "Roofy" because we found him on ... roof of ... house.
d. We often helped ... local population. It was ... fantastic experience, ... experience of our lives!

9 Translate the following sentences into English.

a. Il était difficile de trouver de l'eau mais les rivières étaient propres et l'eau qu'ils buvaient n'était pas polluée.
b. Les céréales étaient rares mais les habitants mangeaient souvent des fruits.
c. Allie étudiait les fleurs et la botanique. Les plantes qu'il trouvait ici étaient plus colorées.
d. Ils avaient construit un pont pour traverser le fleuve. Le pont était étroit mais utile.

More exercises in your Workbook → p. 22-23

Écrire un texte narratif

Lorsque vous racontez une histoire qui met en scène des personnages dans une situation particulière, votre récit doit être clair et vivant pour capter l'attention du lecteur.

1 Planifiez votre récit

Avant de rédiger, vous devrez faire des choix.

Éléments du récit			Conséquences sur la narration	Exemples
Qui ?	**Narrateur**	= un personnage de l'histoire →	• s'exprime à la première personne • peut exprimer ses sentiments • peut savoir ce que font et disent les autres personnages	→ *When the pilot appeared and talked to me, I was frightened...*
		= un personnage extérieur →	• histoire racontée à la 3e personne • peut savoir ce que font et pensent les personnages	→ *She was startled when the pilot talked to her...*
	Personnages	• identité (âge, sexe...), intérêts, motivations... • relations entre les personnages →	déterminent... - comportements/réactions - attitudes - sentiments	[Exemple dans le cas d'un enfant :] → *I started screaming when I heard the groan...* → *I immediately turned to my father who had always protected me.*
Où ?		→	Descriptions plausibles : en cohérence avec l'endroit où vous avez choisi de situer votre récit.	→ *I was in the heart of the jungle, and there, right in the middle of the river, was...*
Quand ?		→	Éléments du récit (lieux, objets, comportements...) : plausibles par rapport à l'époque que vous avez choisie.	→ *the Middle Ages:* *- no cars,* *- horses,* *- knights...*
Quoi ? circonstances, événements, actions		→	Organisation chronologique ou non du récit.	→ *There I was in the middle of this hamlet. A few hours before I had used my mobile...*

→ À vous

Planifiez le récit que vous ferez à partir du sujet suivant :
Imagine you have just travelled back in time. Write a story about your experience.

2 Rédigez votre récit

Points de vigilance	Conseils	Exemples
Cohérence du récit (→ Tenez bien compte des choix que vous avez effectués au départ)	• **Préservez l'unité thématique** : références au même champ lexical, synonymes, répétitions	→ *The people looked as if they were starving, they were very pale and skinny, food seemed to be scarce.*
	• **Préservez l'unité temporelle** récit raconté d'un point de vue présent (temps du présent, *here, yesterday...*) récit raconté d'un point de vue passé (temps du passé, *there, the day before...*)	→ *Here I am, in the time machine, ready...* → *There I was, ...*
Structuration du récit	• **Utilisez des marqueurs chronologiques** pour organiser les événements *(after, until, as soon as, when...)*	→ *As soon as the machine landed, I realized...*
	• **Alternez** les phases de narration et les phases de dialogue.	→ *Then I met a group of people and asked them "Could you tell me where I am?"*

3 Enrichissez votre texte, puis relisez-le

Pour rendre votre récit plus pittoresque et plus vivant :	Exemples	
	Texte « brut »	Texte enrichi
Décrivez pour permettre au lecteur de visualiser (verbes de perception, repères spatiaux...).	*I saw a group of people.*	→ *There, next to the hut, I saw a group of people.*
Donnez des détails : adjectifs, adverbes, relatives, explications.	*One of them came near to me.*	→ *A tall man holding a spear grabbed my hand.*
Ajoutez des éléments de comparaison.		→ *He looked like a giant.*
Choisissez des verbes indiquant les mouvements, attitudes, sentiments des personnages.		→ *I couldn't help shivering when I heard his voice.*
Varies les verbes introducteurs de dialogues *(shout, scream, inquire, snap back, whisper...)*	*"What are you doing here?" he said.*	→ *"What are you doing here?", he yelled.*

→ À vous

- **Rédigez le récit que vous avez planifié lors de l'étape 1 puis enrichissez-le.**
- **Relisez-vous en vérifiant le bon emploi des temps, l'orthographe et la ponctuation.**

Le jour du Bac

Toutes séries

→ voir aussi *Entraînement Bac* p. 72

- **Ne vous précipitez pas** dans la rédaction ! Laissez-vous le temps de bien comprendre le sujet. S'il est en lien avec le texte donné en compréhension écrite, appuyez-vous sur ce texte pour bien cerner la situation, les personnages, etc.
- Prenez le temps de faire un **brouillon**.
- **Organisez votre temps** afin de vous laisser la possibilité de relire et d'enrichir votre travail : un récit court mais clair et structuré sera plus agréable à lire qu'un long récit confus.

FINAL TASKS

Post apocalyptic stories

1

task 1

Writing

Imagine a world without technology

- Describe people's lives in a tech-les world.
Your teacher will give you a situation to start from.

1. Get ready

- **In groups**, list your ideas for a narrative: see ***Stratégies*** p. 64-65
- Organize your notes to plan a coherent story.

2. Action!

On your own: narrate the episode, including some dialogue.

task 2

Reading

Match book covers and blurbs

- Your teacher will give you 5 blurbs.
- Read them and match 4 of them with the corresponding covers on this page.

2

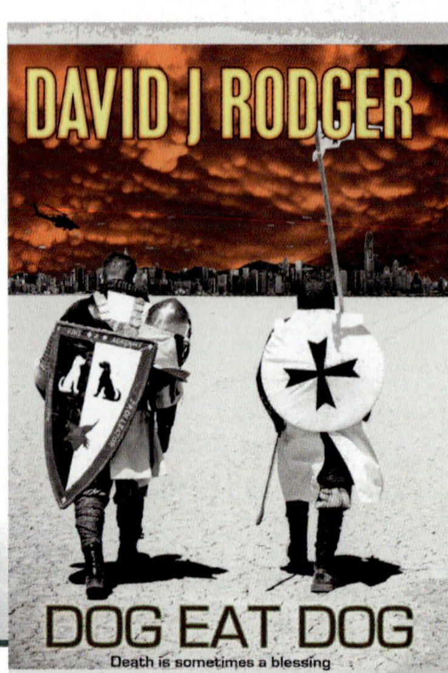

3

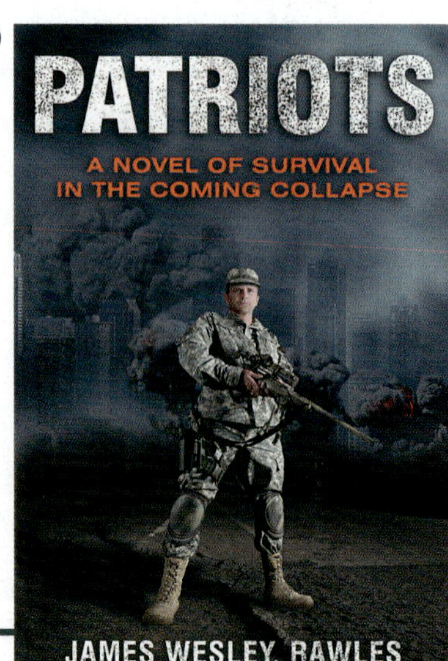

4

Bac

Compréhension de l'oral

Listen to a dialogue:

E-books readers: pros and cons

1. Listen to the document three times and take notes.

2. Write a report in French of what you have understood.

Expression orale

Oral presentation

1. Using what you have learnt about **the possible disappearance of technologies**, prepare notes explaining what going back to a tech-less world would imply for man. You can follow these guidelines:

- The different forms of technological progress.
- The impact on living conditions, and on personal and social relationships.

Illustrate your presentation with other relevant examples you may know.

2. Give your oral presentation.

3. Be ready to discuss the topic with your teacher.

→ Aide

Utilisez la fiche *Recap* du workbook p. 24 ou sur www.didierpassword.fr pour préparer cette synthèse orale.

Compréhension de l'écrit

Read a text

Your teacher will give you a text.
Read it carefully and answer the questions.

Expression écrite

Write two different texts

Using the elements given by your teacher, write:

1. Two e-mails

2. A conversation

Good reads

Into the Wild

Into the Wild ***is the real story of Christopher Mc Candless, who called himself Alexander Supertramp. After graduating, Alex decided to turn his back on his privileged life to go and live alone in the wilds of Alaska.***

In early April a long letter arrived in Franz's post-office box bearing a South Dakota postmark. "Hello Ron," it says,

Alex here. I have been working up here in Carthage South Dakota for nearly two weeks now. I arrived up here three days after we parted in Grand Junction, Colorado. I hope that you made it back to Salton City without too many problems. I enjoy working here and things are going well. The weather is not very bad and many days are surprisingly mild. Some of the farmers are even already going out into their fields. It must be getting rather hot down there in Southern California by now. I wonder if you ever got a chance to get out and see how many people showed up for the March 20 Rainbow gathering there at the hotsprings. It sounds like it might have been a lot of fun, but I don't think you really understand these kind of people very well.

I will not be here in South Dakota very much longer. My friend, Wayne, wants me to stay working at the grain elevator through May and then go combining with him the entire summer, but I have my soul set entirely on my Alaskan Odyssey and hope to be on my way no later than April 15. That means I will be leaving here before very long, so I need you to send any more mail I may have received to the return address listed below.

Ron, I really enjoy all the help you have given me and the times that we spent together. I hope that you will not be too depressed by our parting. It may be a very long time before we see each other again. But providing that I get through this Alaskan Deal in one piece you will be hearing from me again in the future. I'd like to repeat the advice I gave you before, in that I think you really should make a radical change in your lifestyle and begin to boldly do things which you may previously never have thought of doing, or been too hesitant to attempt. So many people live within unhappy circumstances and yet will not take the initiative to change their situation because they are conditioned to a life of security, conformity, and conservatism, all of which may appear to give one peace of mind, but in reality nothing is more damaging to the adventurous spirit within a man than a secure future. The very basic core of a man's living spirit is his passion for adventure. The joy of life comes from our encounters with new experiences, and hence there is no greater joy than to have an endlessly changing horizon, for each day to have a new and different sun.

If you want to get more out of life, Ron, you must lose your inclination for monotonous security and adopt a helter-skelter style of life that will at first appear to you to be crazy. But once you become accustomed to such a life you will see its full meaning and its incredible beauty. And so, Ron, in short, get out of Salton City and hit the Road. I guarantee you will be very glad you did. But I fear that you will ignore my advice. You think that I am stubborn, but you are even more stubborn than me. You had a wonderful chance on your drive back to see one of the greatest sights on earth, the Grand Canyon, something every American should see at least once in his life. But for some reason incomprehensible to me you wanted nothing but to bolt for home as quickly as possible, right back to the same situation which you see day after day after day. I fear you will follow this same inclination in the future and thus fail to discover all the wonderful things that God has placed around us to discover. Don't settle down and sit in one place. Move around, be nomadic, make each day a new horizon. You are still going to live a long time, Ron, and it would be a shame if you did not take the opportunity to revolutionize your life and move into an entirely new realm of experience.

You are wrong if you think Joy emanates only or principally from human relationships. God has placed it all around us. It is in everything and anything we might experience. We just have to have the courage to turn against our habitual lifestyle and engage in unconventional living.

My point is that you do not need me or anyone else around to bring this new kind of light in your life. It is simply waiting out there for you to grasp it, and all you have to do is reach for it. The only person you are fighting is yourself and your stubbornness to engage in new circumstances.

Ron, I really hope that as soon as you can you will get out of Salton City, put a little camper on the back of your pickup, and start seeing some of the great work that God has done here in the American West. You will see things and meet people and there is much to learn from them. And you must do it economy style, no motels, do your own cooking, as a general rule spend as little as possible and you will enjoy it much more immensely. I hope that the next time I see you, you will be a new man with a vast array of new adventures and experiences behind you. Don't hesitate or allow yourself to make excuses. Just get out and do it. Just get out and do it. You will be very, very glad that you did.

TAKE CARE RON,

ALEX

Please write back to: Alex McCandless
Madison, SD 57042

Jon Krakauer,
***Into the Wild* (1996)**

Jon Krakauer (born 1954)

an American writer primarily known for his writing about mountaineering, he is the author of best-selling non-fiction books such as Into the Wild, *published in 1996. The film inspired by the book was an instant success.*

Compréhension de l'écrit (1)

À partir d'un support unique

page 25

Séries ES, S, L et technologiques

« L'épreuve de compréhension de l'écrit prend appui sur un, deux ou trois documents qui peuvent relever de différents genres (extraits d'œuvres littéraires ou d'articles de presse notamment) ; ils peuvent être informatifs, descriptifs, narratifs ou argumentatifs. Ils renvoient à des notions du programme sans exiger des connaissances trop spécifiques. »

Instructions officielles, B.O. du 24 nov. 2011

George Weston was comfortable. It was a habit of his to be comfortable on Sunday afternoons. A good, hearty dinner below the hatches, a nice, soft, dilapidated couch on which to sprawl, a copy of *The Times*; slippered feet and shirtless chest, — how could anyone *help* but be comfortable?

He wasn't pleased, therefore, when his wife walked in. After ten years of married life, he still was so unutterably foolish as to love her, and there was no question that he was always glad to see her – still Sunday afternoons just after dinner were sacred to him and his idea of solid comfort was to be left in utter solitude for two or three hours.

Consequently, he fixed his eye firmly upon the latest reports of the Lefebre-Yoshida expedition to Mars (this one was to take off from Lunar Base and might actually succeed) and pretended she wasn't there.

Mrs Weston waited patiently for two minutes, then impatiently for two more, and finally broke the silence.

"George!"

"Hmpph?"

"George, I say! *Will* you put down that paper and look at me?"

The paper rustled to the floor and Weston turned a weary face toward his wife. "What is it, dear?"

"You know what it is, George. It's Gloria and that terrible machine."

"What terrible machine?"

"Now don't pretend you don't know what I'm talking about. It's that robot Gloria calls Robbie. He doesn't leave her for a moment".

"Well, why should he? He's not supposed to. And he certainly isn't a terrible machine. He's the best darn robot money can buy and I'm damned sure he set me back half a year's income. He's worth it, though – darn sight cleverer than half my office staff."

He made a move to pick up the paper again but his wife was quicker and snatched it away.

"You listen to me George. I won't have my daughter entrusted to a machine – and I don't care how clever it is. It has no soul, and no one knows what it may be thinking. A child just isn't *made* to be guarded by a thing of metal."

Weston frowned, "When did you decide this? He's been with Gloria two years now and I haven't seen you worry till now."

"It was different at first. It was a novelty; it took a load off me, and it was a fashionable thing to do; but now I don't know. The neighbors –"

"Well, what have the neighbors to do with it? Now, look. A robot is infinitely more to be trusted than a human nursemaid. Robbie was constructed for only one purpose really – to be the companion of a little child. His entire 'mentality' has been created for the purpose. He just can't help being faithful and loving and kind. He's a machine – *made so*. That's more than you can say for humans."

"But something might go wrong. Some – some –" Mrs Weston was a bit hazy about the insides of a robot, "some little jigger will come loose and the awful thing will go beserk and – and –" She couldn't bring herself to complete the quite obvious thought.

"Nonsense," Weston denied, with an involuntary nervous shiver. "That's completely ridiculous.

I. Asimov, *I, Robot* (1950)

Le jour du Bac

Le document

- **Faites-vous une idée du type de texte** auquel vous avez affaire (fiction, presse, essai, etc.), grâce à la source (auteur, provenance, date...) et à un rapide coup d'œil au texte (disposition, premières lignes, etc.).
- **Faites-vous une idée du thème** abordé à partir du type de texte, du titre, des éléments d'iconographie éventuels et de vos propres connaissances.
- Lisez le texte une première fois, lentement, et **soulignez** les noms des **personnages**, des **lieux** et les **marqueurs de temps**. Utilisez différentes couleurs pour retrouver plus rapidement les informations.
- **Notez** dans la marge ce que vous avez compris : thème général, idée principale d'un paragraphe, relations entre différents personnages, enchaînement des événements, etc.

Les questions

- Voir conseils donnés dans *Entraînement Bac* p. 94

Compréhension

1 When and where does the scene take place?

Repérez dans le texte les éléments qui se réfèrent explicitement ou implicitement au lieu ou au temps. Temps : *Sunday* ; à une époque future *(Lunar Base)*. Lieu : *The Times* (→ peut-être Angleterre, mais rien ne le confirme) ; planète Terre.

2 Who are the characters present and the characters mentioned? Give as many details as possible about each of them (name, relationships...).

Repérez les noms propres puis appuyez-vous sur les marques de ponctuation et les verbes introducteurs de dialogue pour savoir qui est présent physiquement, ou qui est mentionné dans les propos des personnages en présence.

3 Sum up in your own words the topic of the conversation (20 words).

in your own words : formulez la réponse avec vos propres mots, sans citer le texte. Respectez le nombre de mots demandé : 20 mots, c'est peu, alors allez à l'essentiel sans développer les détails.

4 Focus on George: say if the following statements are right or wrong. Justify by quoting from the text.

a. He isn't pleased to see his wife because he wants to leave her.
b. He refuses to spend money for his child.
c. He doesn't care about the neighbors' opinions.
d. He thinks only a parent is capable of looking after their child.

N'oubliez pas de répondre à la question vrai ou faux en prenant en compte tous les mots dans les énoncés proposés.
→ *George isn't pleased to see his wife* (vrai) *because he wants to leave her* (faux)

5 a. Describe the evolution of the woman's feelings towards Robbie. (30 words)
b. How does she account for it? (50 words)

Cette question vous invite à faire des comparaisons entre avant et maintenant : recherchez les points communs et les différences, que vous exprimerez dans votre réponse en utilisant des mots de liaison et des formes verbales appropriés (*at first, but now, used to, no longer...*).

6 Explain the man and the woman's feelings at the end of the text (between 100 and 130 words). Justify with two quotations.

Commencez par rechercher dans le texte des indicateurs de sentiments :
- dans les actions (verbes et adverbes),
- dans le dialogue.

Rédigez votre réponse sans oublier de citer deux passages qui vous paraissent illustrer votre propos.

Expression écrite

Séries ES, S, L et technologiques

« L'épreuve d'expression écrite est évaluée à l'aide d'une ou plusieurs tâches.

• À partir des indications données, le candidat rédige un ou plusieurs textes construits, prenant appui sur des événements, des faits ou des prises de position qu'il aura identifiés dans les documents servant de support à l'épreuve de la compréhension.

• Le candidat construit une argumentation personnelle à propos d'un thème en relation avec les documents servant de supports à l'évaluation de la compréhension de l'écrit ou à partir d'un nouveau document "tremplin" en relation thématique avec les documents-supports de la compréhension de l'écrit, et qui permet de contextualiser et de nourrir l'expression. »

Instructions officielles, B.O. du 24 nov. 2011

Le jour du Bac

Le sujet

- **Commencez** impérativement par l'épreuve de **compréhension de l'écrit** pour **entrer dans le thème**.
- Ce thème sera en lien plus ou moins étroit avec l'une des quatre grandes **notions du programme**.
- **Organisez votre temps** : la moitié du temps de l'épreuve écrite sera consacrée à l'expression.
- **Lisez tranquillement et plusieurs fois le sujet**, pour bien comprendre ce que l'on vous demande : le nombre de sujets à traiter, le type de sujet, le thème.
- **Reliez le thème** à ce que vous avez appris cette année.

Votre production

- **Faites un brouillon** que vous enrichirez progressivement : c'est indispensable !
- **Respectez le nombre de mots** indiqué.
- **Adaptez la mise en page** au type de sujet demandé (lettre, dialogue, journal intime, article, etc.), soignez l'écriture et la présentation.
- Prévoyez au moins dix minutes pour **vous relire**.

Les sujets qui vous sont proposés ci-dessous prennent appui sur l'épreuve de compréhension de l'écrit p. 70.

Expression

Choose one subject in each of the following sections.

Soyez particulièrement attentif aux consignes et au nombre de sujets à traiter (ici, deux sujets).

Section 1

Les trois sujets de cette section sont de type **narratif**. Reportez-vous aux *Stratégies* ***Écrire un texte narratif*** p. 64.

1 Imagine a continuation to the passage.

Pour écrire la suite d'un texte, faites le lien avec le passage étudié : ici, un dialogue narratif.

❷ **After her conversation with her husband, Mrs Weston decides to tell a friend about the incident. Write her letter.**

Soyez cohérent par rapport à la situation décrite dans le passage étudié.

❸ **Gloria has overheard her parents' conversation. Imagine her thoughts and feelings. Write her diary entry.**

• Lisez bien les termes de la question : ils vous indiquent la manière de traiter le sujet (*imagine* = écriture d'invention, *discuss* = introduction d'un point de vue argumentatif dans la narration etc.).

• Veillez à adapter la mise en page au type d'écrit attendu : lettre (sujet ❷), journal intime (sujet ❸).

Section 2

❹ ***"Life was much easier when apple and blackberry were just fruits"*. Explain what this sentence may mean. Illustrate your answer with examples.**

Dans les **sujets explicatifs** (❹ et ❺), on ne vous demande pas de prendre position mais d'expliquer un point de vue avec des faits, des exemples. Reportez-vous aux *Stratégies* ***Écrire un texte explicatif*** p. 162.

❺ **How important is technology to you?**

• Développez vos idée en vous appuyant sur des exemples précis (ex. Unit 3 *Tech-Less World*) ou des expériences personnelles.

• Les sujets ❻ ❼ ❽ ❾ font appel à vos **compétences d'argumentation** (le dernier sous la forme d'un dialogue). Reportez-vous aux *Stratégies* ***Écrire un texte argumentatif*** p. 182.

❻ **Some people think robots can replace man. Do you agree?**

Même si votre point de vue penche plus d'un côté que de l'autre, pesez le pour et le contre dans votre réponse : les deux parties ont forcément des arguments à faire valoir.

❼ **Discuss the following statement *"Technology brings more harm than good"*.**

❽ **Do you think the use of technology should be regulated?**

Évitez les plans binaires pour/contre, vous risquez de vous contredire alors que vous êtes censé(e) nuancer vos propos. Vous pouvez par exemple commencer par ce qui vous semble le plus évident, pour aller progressivement vers des arguments qui le sont moins.

❾ **Imagine you and one of your friend saw this poster. One of you approves of it, the other doesn't. Write the conversation.**

• Assurez-vous de bien comprendre le document « tremplin » et reliez-le à la thématique.

• Respectez la mise en forme du dialogue et veillez tout particulièrement à la ponctuation lors de la relecture.

UNIT 4 The Queen

↑ ***Reigning Queens: Elizabeth II of the United Kingdom,*** a screen print by Andy Warhol, 1985.

Who is behind the image?

← **Look** at the document. What image is given of the Queen of England? **Discuss** what you already know or would like to know about English Queens.

FINAL TASKS

P. 88

Royal stories

Writing
Write an episode in the life of a Queen

Reading
Re-order a narrative about a Queen

CULTURE	COMMUNICATION	TOOLS
• Learning about three Queens of England: - their reigns, - their public images, - their personal lives. • Literary works: - Alison Weir, *The Lady Elizabeth* - Shrabani Basu, *Victoria and Abdul* - Alan Bennett, *The Uncommon Reader* - William Shakespeare, *Henry VIII* - Charles Dickens, *Oliver Twist* - Queen Victoria's Diaries	• Writing a letter relating events and expressing feelings. • Writing a story including some dialogue. Understanding the main events, the characters' feelings and the points of view in a narrative. Giving a brief presentation of a person, a place or an event studied in class.	★ **Words** • Symbols of the monarchy • Political systems • Myths • Speech tags • Authority and ambition • Feelings • Duty • Leisure ★ **Pronunciation** • Tone units in long sentences • Stress on key information • Pronouncing *-ed* endings ★ **Grammar** • Reported speech • *Wish*

BAC

Stratégies
→ *Comprendre un texte narratif* **p. 86**

Évaluation
→ *4 situations d'évaluation* **p. 89**

A destiny out of the ordinary

← *Elizabeth I of England, the Armada Portrait*, c. 1588, attributed to George Gower

Elizabeth I — **Victoria**

- **1558** **Elizabeth I** ascends the throne
- **1564** Birth of Shakespeare
- **1583** Start of English empire with first American colony
- **1585** King Philip of Spain declares war on England
- **1588** Destruction of the Spanish Armada, King Philip's navy
- **1600** The British East India Company granted a 21 year monopoly on Indian trade
- **1837** Accession of **Victoria** to the throne.
  Dickens's *Oliver Twist* is published
- **1851** Crystal Palace: The Great Exhibition (the first World's Fair)
- **1858** India placed under direct rule of the British Crown
- **1863** First underground railway in London, now the world's largest city with 3 million people

1. Read the title and look at the paintings.
State your first impressions and discuss what strikes you most.

2. Before listening to the audioguides, list the information you expect to get from that type of document. Make a grid.

3. Listen to the audioguides: what have you understood?

4. Listen again.
a. For each painting, fill in your grid.
b. Share your findings.

5. Listen for further information and find common points and differences between the paintings and between the Queens.

6. Study the time line above. Find more common points and/or differences.

Recap → List elements which make the reigns of these three Queens remarkable. page 34

AudioGuides

track 21
Elizabeth I, the Virgin Queen (1533-1603)
Queen of England and Ireland,
from 1558 to 1603.

track 22
Queen Victoria (1819-1901)
Reigned from 1837 to 1901.
Queen of the United Kingdom of Great Britain and Ireland. Empress of India.
Head of the Church of England.

track 23
Elizabeth II (born in 1926)
Crowned in 1953.
Queen of the United Kingdom.
Supreme Governor of the Church of England. Symbolic Head of the Commonwealth.

↑ *Queen Victoria*, Franz Xaver Winterhalter, 1859

↑ *Queen Elizabeth II*, Pietro Annigoni, 1955

Elizabeth II

- **1877** Victoria becomes Empress of India
- **1901** London's population now 7 million
- **1952** Accession of **Elizabeth II** to the throne
- **1969** Troubles begin in Northern Ireland
- **1973** Britain joins the European Community
- **1994** Channel Tunnel opens
- **1998** Good Friday agreement brings peace to Northern Ireland
- **2002** Great Britain refuses to adopt the Euro

LANGUAGE TOOLS

★ WORDS

Symbols of the monarchy

- crown, throne, **sce**pter /ˈseptə/, orb = globe

Political systems and their heads

- **em**pire /ˈempaɪə/, **em**peror /ˈempərə/, **em**press
- consti**tu**tional **mo**narchy /ˈmɒnəkɪ/, king, queen, knight /naɪt/
- **par**liament /ˈpɑːləmənt/, prime /praɪm/ **mi**nister, **pre**sident
- rule, **go**vern, reign, head, lead, **ab**dicate

Myths

- **des**tiny, **ma**jesty, **glo**ry
- **i**con /ˈaɪkɒn/, **i**mage /ˈɪmɪdʒ/
- **my**thical, re**mar**kable

★ PRONUNCIATION → p. 84

Tone units in long sentences

TRAINING TASK

Audioguide

Prepare an audioguide telling a story about an event, place or person related to the Queens' reigns.

Group work

1. Research one of the topics below:

Walter Raleigh | Richmond Palace | Crystal Palace | the Channel Tunnel | the Commonwealth | British Raj

2. Write your information on a card and practise giving a presentation.

3. Record your audioguide.

A Queen's childhood

"Might I be Queen?"

The year is 1537.

"Wake up, my Lady Elizabeth, we have just received the most wonderful tidings!" exclaimed Lady Bryan, shaking her charge by the shoulder. Elizabeth rubbed her eyes, then opened them to see her governess beaming happily.

"England has a prince!" she cried. "Queen Jane has borne the King a son! A baby brother for you, child! Oh, this is a great day, for the King's Majesty and for us all!"

"A baby brother," echoed Elizabeth, wide awake now. At last, she would have someone to play with! He could come and live at Hatfield, this new brother, and...

"His name is Edward," Lady Bryan told her, "and he was born two days ago on the twelfth of October, the eve of St Edward the Confessor, a most auspicious day. Now we must make haste, my little lady, because we are summoned to court without delay. The King wishes you to play your part at the christening."

"Ohh!" Elizabeth was scrambling out of bed, bursting with elation. "What will I be doing?"

"You are to take part in the procession."

"Is that an important part?" asked the child.

"Very important, I believe," said Lady Bryan firmly, suppressing a smile. "Now, we must get you ready quickly!"

Once more, they found themselves in a litter trundling down the Great North Road. It had been ten months since Elizabeth had made her last journey to London for that magical Christmas, and that all seemed like an enchanted dream now. Life had quickly fallen back into the familiar pattern of lessons, meals, walks, rides and prayers, enlivened from time to time by letters and gifts from her father and her sister.

As they neared the City of London, they could hear a mighty pealing of joyful bells from all the churches. [...]

"God be praised, we are free from all threat of war!" Elizabeth heard a man cry.

"Why does he say that?" she enquired.

"Because the King now has a son to succeed him, and no man can challenge his right," Lady Bryan explained.

"You mean the Prince will be King one day?" Elizabeth asked.

She was beginning to realise that her new brother would be more than just a playmate.

"When God calls your royal father to Himself, which we must pray will not be for a long time."

"I do pray for that," Elizabeth said devoutly.

"And we must pray that God spares the Prince to us," Lady Bryan added.

"If He doesn't," said Elizabeth, considering, "might I be Queen?"

"Oh, no, sweeting, that could not be," cut in the governess hastily. "You and your sister are barred from the throne, and in any case, women do not rule kingdoms or men. Such a thing would be unnatural."

"I could learn," insisted Elizabeth. 'I should like to sit on a throne and order people about.'

"The very idea!" Lady Bryan laughed, for she could imagine Elizabeth doing just that. "We have a prince now, and more to follow, if God wills. I've no doubt that the King will in time find you a good husband, and that you shall be a godly wife and mother and not bother your head with ruling kingdoms!"

Elizabeth pulled a face. It would be much more fun to be Queen, she felt.

Alison Weir,
The Lady Elizabeth
(2008)

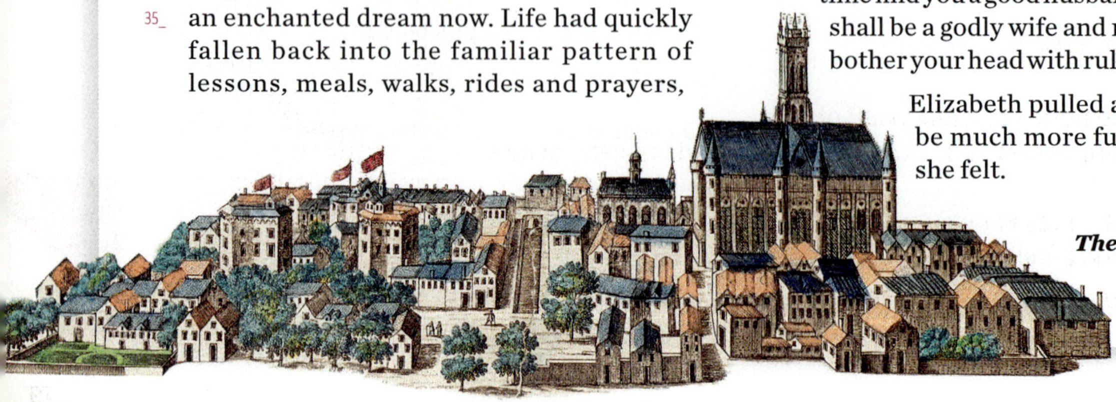

← Queen Elizabeth I, *Coronation portrait*, 1559

Henry VIII (1491-1547) became King in 1509

and married...

Catherine of Aragon	Ann Boleyn	Jane Seymour
in 1509 (repudiated in 1532)	in 1533 (beheaded in 1536)	in 1536 (died in childbirth)
mother of	*mother of*	*mother of*
Mary I (1516-1558) Queen from 1553 to 1558	**Elizabeth I** (1533-1603) Queen from 1558 to 1603	**Edward VI** (1537-1553) King from 1547 to 1553

1. **Before reading**, look at the title, the portrait above and the family tree. What questions spring to mind?
2. **Read the text** and discuss what you have understood.
3. **a. In groups**, read again and highlight information about:
   - the event mentioned and the changes it will provoke *(group 1)*,
   - the different characters' reactions *(group 2)*,
   - the succession rules in England at that time *(group 3)*.

   page 26

   b. Share your findings with your classmates.
4. **Comment** on lines 74-75: *"It would be much more fun to be Queen"*, and on Elizabeth's thoughts.

LANGUAGE TOOLS

★ WORDS

Speech tags
- say, tell, **an**swer, add, ex**claim**, sug**gest**
- ask = **won**der, in**quire** /ɪnˈkwaɪə/
- **whis**per = **mu**tter = **mur**mur

Authority and ambition
- am**bi**tion ≥ **po**wer **hun**ger, aspi**ra**tion

★ GRAMMAR → p. 85

Reported speech

→ She asked me if taking part in the procession was an important part.

Recap → After studying this text, what image do you have of Elizabeth? page 34

TRAINING TASK

Creative writing

↑ *Elizabeth I*, c. 1560

Rewrite the episode from a different point of view.
Lady Bryan, Elizabeth's governess, recounts this episode to a friend of hers.

In pairs:

1. Picture clearly who Lady Bryan is and how she is going to depict Elizabeth.
2. Imagine her friend's feelings and opinions about the child's personality.
3. Write their dialogue (varying the speech tags) and the narrative parts.

Duty and friendship

↑ Queen Victoria with Abdul Karim, c. 1885

1 Queen Victoria and Abdul

In 1887, Abdul Karim, an Indian Muslim, was engaged as a waiter at Buckingham Palace. He soon became one of Queen Victoria's closest friends and remained so until her death in 1901.

At her funeral procession in Windsor, Abdul Karim walked with the principal mourners. The elderly Queen had given this instruction herself, despite what she knew would be intense opposition from her family and Household. She had ensured her beloved Munshi[1] would be written into the history books.

But only days after the Queen's death, the Munshi was woken by the sound of loud banging on his door. [...] The King had ordered a raid on his house, demanding he hand over all the letters Victoria had written to him. [...]

As the 'Dear Abdul' letters burnt in the cold February air, the Munshi stood in silence. Without his Queen he was defenceless and alone. Postcards and letters from the Queen, dated from Windsor Castle, Balmoral, the Royal yacht *Victoria and Albert* and hotels across Europe, crackled in the flames. The Queen used to write to the Munshi every day, signing her letters variously as 'your dearest friend', 'your true friend', even 'your dearest mother'. [...] With Queen Victoria in her grave, the Establishment had come down hard and fast on the Munshi. King Edward VII asked him unceremoniously to pack his bags and return to India.

The fairytale — that had begun the day the young Abdul Karim had entered the Court in 1887 — was over.

Karim had been a gift from India to celebrate the Queen's Golden Jubilee. Strikingly dressed in a scarlet tunic and white turban, the handsome twenty-four-year-old youth had arrived from Agra, the home of the Taj Mahal — the world's most beautiful monument to love. Initially a servant waiting at the Queen's table, his rise through the ranks was swift. Within months he was cooking the Queen curries and, soon after, became her teacher or 'Munshi'. Whilst his colleague from India, Mohanuned Buksh, remained a waiter, Karim eventually became the Queen's highly decorated Indian secretary. He was also the lonely monarch's closest confidant [...].

If the Royal Household had hated Brown[2], they abhorred Karim, deeply suspicious of his influence over the Queen. These fears were strengthened by the increasingly violent calls for Indian independence that were filtering through to Court. But the Queen cared little for what others thought. She defended her 'Dear Munshi' relentlessly, handing him cottages in Windsor, Balmoral and Osborne and extensive lands in India. She insisted that he be treated on a par with the rest of her Household and had his portrait painted by the artists Swoboda and Angeli. [...] She praised him to her family and ministers. Throughout the last ten years of her life, Victoria stood like a rock by his side.

Shrabani Basu, *Victoria and Abdul, The True Story Of the Queen's Closest Confidant* (2010)

1. Munshi: Urdu word for secretary or teacher
2. John Brown: another personal servant and favourite of Queen Victoria

1. Read the titles and the introduction. Discuss the themes the text may explore.

2. a. Read the text and say what you have understood.
b. Find information about:
- the Queen's attitude,
- Abdul's situation and feelings before and after her death,
- the Household's attitude.
c. Share your findings.

3. Explain *"The fairytale — that had begun the day the young Abdul Karim had entered the Court in 1887 — was over."* (l. 20-21)

4. Discuss the reasons why Abdul is not *"written into the history books"*.

Abdul Karim in the 1880s.
"I am so very fond of him."
Queen Victoria, 1888, Balmoral →

2 The Queen and the commoner

track 24

An interview with Shrabani Basu, author of *Victoria and Abdul*

1. Before listening, list the questions you would like to ask Shrabani Basu.

2. Listen and discuss what you have understood.

3. a. In groups, listen again.
Pick out information about:
- the roles Abdul played for the Queen *(group 1)*,
- the Queen's behaviour towards him *(group 2)*,
- the Household's reactions *(group 3)*.
b. Share your findings with the class.

4. Comment on the different protagonists' reactions, stating their reasons.

Recap → To what extent can a Queen have friends of her own? page 34

LANGUAGE TOOLS

★ WORDS

Feelings
- **friend**ship, **ten**derness, af**fec**tion
- irri**ta**tion, im**pa**tience, an**noy**ance, exaspe**ra**tion, re**sent**ment, **an**ger, **out**rage /ˈaʊtreɪdʒ/, hos**ti**lity, bear a grudge

★ PRONUNCIATION → p. 84
Stress on key information

★ GRAMMAR → p. 85
Wish
→ They wish she hadn't engaged Abdul Karim as a secretary at Buckingham Palace.
→ I wish their letters were burnt.

TRAINING TASK

Letter to a friend

Princess Beatrice, Queen Victoria's youngest child, writes a letter to her friend, Lady Margaret, to tell her about a confrontation she had with Abdul. While showing due respect, she also mentions her frustration at her mother's behaviour.
page 27

The Queen and her people

"One has a duty to find out what people are like"

↑ Street Art.
May 2008, London.

Reading more and more, the Queen now drew her books from various libraries. In royal circles reading, or at any rate her reading, was not well looked on. [...]

Sir Kevin[1] was a graduate of the Harvard Business School and one of his publicly stated aims ("setting out our stall", as he put it) was to make the monarchy more accessible. The opening of Buckingham Palace to visitors had been a step down this road, as was the use of the garden for occasional concerts, pop and otherwise. The reading, though, made him uneasy.

"I feel, ma'am, that while not exactly elitist it sends the wrong message. It tends to exclude."

"Exclude? Surely most people can read?"

"They can read, ma'am, but I'm not sure that they do."

"Then, Sir Kevin, I am setting them a good example."

She smiled sweetly. [...]

"It's important", said Sir Kevin, "that Your Majesty should stay focused."

"When you say 'stay focused', Sir Kevin, I suppose you mean one should keep one's eye on the ball. Well, I've had my eye on the ball for more than fifty years so I think these days one is allowed the occasional glance to the boundary." She felt that her metaphor had probably slipped a little there, not, though, that Sir Kevin noticed.

"I can understand", he said, "Your Majesty's need to pass the time."

"Pass the time?" said the Queen. "Books are not about passing the time. They're about other lives. Other worlds. Far from wanting time to pass, Sir Kevin, one just wishes one had more of it. If one wanted to pass the time one could go to New Zealand".

[...] Sir Kevin retired hurt. Still, he had made a point and he would have been gratified to know that it left the Queen troubled, and wondering why it was that at this particular time in her life she had suddenly felt the pull of books. Where had this appetite come from? Few people, after all, had seen more of the world than she had. There was scarcely a country she had not visited, a notability she had not met. Herself part of the panoply of the world, why now was she intrigued by books which, whatever else they might be, were just a reflection of the world or a version of it? Books? She had seen the real thing.

"I read, I think," she said to Norman[2], "because one has a duty to find out what people are like," a trite enough remark of which Norman took not much notice, feeling himself under no such obligation and reading purely for pleasure, not enlightenment, though part of the pleasure was the enlightenment, he could see that. But duty did not come into it.

To someone with the background of the Queen, though, pleasure had always taken second place to duty. If she could feel she had a duty to read then she could set about it with a clear conscience, with the pleasure, if pleasure there was, incidental. But why did it take possession of her now? This she did not

1. Sir Kevin: the Queen's private secretary from New Zealand

2. Norman: a kitchen hand who recommends novels to the Queen discuss with Norman, as she felt it had to do with who she was and the position she occupied.

The appeal of reading, she thought, lay in its indifference: there was something lofty about literature. Books did not care who was reading them or whether one read them or not. All readers were equal, herself included. Literature, she thought, is a commonwealth; letters a republic. Actually she had heard this phrase, the republic of letters, used before, at graduation ceremonies, honorary degrees and the like, though without knowing quite what it meant. At that time talk of a republic of any sort she had thought mildly insulting and in her actual presence tactless to say the least. It was only now she understood what it meant. Books did not defer. All readers were equal, and this took her back to the beginning of her life. As a girl, one of her greatest thrills had been on VE[3] night, when she and her sister had slipped out of the gates and mingled unrecognised with the crowds. There was something of that, she felt, to reading. It was anonymous; it was shared; it was common. And she who had led a life apart now found that she craved it. Here in these pages and between these covers she could go unrecognised.

Alan Bennett, *The Uncommon Reader* (2007)

3. VE: victory in Europe (8 May 1945)

1. **Look at the picture and the titles** on p. 82: how can you link them all?
2. **a. Read the text** and say what you have understood.
   b. Highlight information about:
   - reading as seen by Sir Kevin and royal circles,
   - the reasons why the Queen took up reading,
   - the thoughts the Queen has about duty and pleasure.

   pages 28-29
3. **Explain** how literature relates the Queen to her people.
4. What image of the Queen do you get after reading this narrative?

LANGUAGE TOOLS

★ **WORDS**

Duty
- stay **fo**cused /ˈfəʊkəst/
- feel bound to, be **un**der an obli**ga**tion to, ful**fil** one's com**mit**ments

Leisure
- for **plea**sure
- en**joy**
- **ho**bby, **pas**time, enter**tain**ment, a**mu**sement, recre**a**tion, dis**trac**tion

Recap → Why would a Queen wish to 'go unrecognised'? page 34

TRAINING TASK

Narrative dialogue

Another fancy takes the Queen:
→ *The Queen wants to go shopping on her own,*
→ *The Queen wants to take more holidays,*
→ *etc.*

Choose one or imagine one and write her conversation with Sir Kevin, adding narrative parts.
- Picture clearly who Sir Kevin is.
- Imitate the tone of the extract.

★ WORDS

❶ Politics

a. Classify the words below under each heading (some words may fit under several headings).

Monarchy	Republic	Dictatorship	Democracy
...	...	...	...

Nouns: queen, democrat, tyrant, king, empress, despot, emperor, president
Verbs: reign, govern, oppress, preside, rule
Adjectives: dictatorial, presidential, monarchic, republican, despotic, imperial

b. Suggest other words for each heading.

❷ Intentions, moods and feelings

a. In each of the following lists, find the odd one out. Use a dictionary if necessary.

1. answer, reply, retort, warn, snap back
2. whisper, mutter, murmur, exclaim, mumble
3. yell, shout, scream, holler, sigh
4. add, acknowledge, admit, confess, accept
5. beg, insist, implore, refuse, demand
6. state, say, tell, utter, question
7. repent, deplore, regret, lament, offer

b. Be ready to justify your choice in English.

❸ Talking about remarkable figures Bac

a. Find at least three words you can classify under each of the following headings:

myth | prestige | extraordinary | mundane

b. Talk about one of the three Queens, using some of the words you have found.

★ PRONUNCIATION

❹ Tone units in long sentences (track 25)

...this most realistic portrait of henry the eighth / is perhaps the earliest image of the king / painted by hans holbein the younger / a german artist and printmaker

Lorsqu'on lit à voix haute une description composée de phrases longues, il est nécessaire d'effectuer des pauses qui permettent de ponctuer le texte et de lui donner sens.

a. Here is the script of a passage from an audioguide describing a portrait of Henry VIII. (track 26)
Listen and find out where the tone units are.

In this beautifully detailed portrait of Henry the eighth the king's figure and magnificent clothes are proof of his authority however Holbein's portrait is not especially flattering as Henry appears on the defensive suspicious and quite unapproachable.

b. Listen again and practise reading the passage aloud.

❺ Stress on key information (track 27)

abdul karim was one of queen victoria's closest confidants despite the attempts by the royal family to stop their relationship.

Lorsqu'on présente des faits, on accentue plus fortement les mots qui véhiculent les informations essentielles.

Practise in your workbook. (page 30)

❻ Pronouncing *-ed* endings (track 28)

a. Listen to the following words:

• painted - attributed - reigned - suggested - married - placed - carved - depicted - used - appreciated - commissioned - embroidered - furred - pictured - died - refused - received - profiled - determined - conveyed - confirmed

b. How many different pronunciations of the *-ed* ending have you heard? Classify the words in columns and draw conclusions on how to pronounce *-ed* endings.

c. Practise pronouncing the words above.

★ GRAMMAR

Reported speech

Observe

1. "His name is Edward," Lady Bryan told her, "and he was born two days ago on the twelfth of October [...]. Now we must make haste, my little lady, because we are summoned to court without delay. The King wishes you to play your part at the christening."

2. Lady Bryan told her that his name was Edward, and that he had been born two days before on the twelfth of October. Now they had to make haste because they were summoned to court without delay. The king wished her to play her part at the christening.

Lorsqu'on passe du style direct au style indirect, et inversement, des changements s'opèrent : décrivez-les.

→ Grammaire ⑱ p. 207

Practise

7 Report the following conversation:

"What will I be doing?" asked Elizabeth.
"You are to take part in the procession",
Lady Bryan answered.
"Is that an important part?"
"Very important, I believe," said Lady Bryan firmly, suppressing a smile. "Now, we must get you ready quickly!"

8 Imagine and report the conversation William and Kate had before getting married.

→ *Kate wanted to know what her life would be like after her marriage. She asked William...*

Wish

Observe

1. Queen Victoria's family did not like Abdul Karim.
a. They wished he had never come to England.
b. They wished Victoria were more sensible.

2. After Queen Victoria's death, her son forced Abdul Karim to go back to India.
a. He wished his mother had listened to him.
b. He wished Karim's family did not see him as a tyrant.

• Observez les formes verbales soulignées. Ont-elles une valeur temporelle ?
• Les formes verbales des phrases 1a et 1b expriment-elles la même idée ?
• Concluez sur la valeur du verbe *wish* et des formes verbales qui lui sont associées.

→ Grammaire ⑳ p. 209

Practise

9 Use the elements below to write sentences expressing wishes or regrets.

a. Queen Elizabeth's family often appears in celebrity magazines.
→ *Queen Elizabeth...*

b. After Lady Diana's death, many journalists felt they had gone too far.
→ *They...*

c. When King Edward VIII said he wanted to marry Wallis Simpson, his Prime Minister expressed strong objection.
→ *The King...*
→ *The Prime Minister...*

10 Imagine 5 sentences Queen Elizabeth I, Queen Victoria or Queen Elizabeth II could have written to express their wishes and regrets.

More exercises in your Workbook → p. 30-32

Comprendre un texte narratif

Dans un texte narratif, un narrateur fait le récit d'une histoire, et met en scène des personnages dans une situation particulière.

1536

On a hot, still morning in July, the Lady Mary, daughter to King Henry the Eighth, arrived at the great country palace of Hatfield, trotting into the courtyard on a white palfrey followed by four gentlemen, two ladies-in-waiting, and a female fool.

As soon as she had dismounted, she stooped to kiss the small girl who was waiting to greet her, whose nurse had just reminded her to sketch a wobbly curtsy to the older sister she had not seen for many months. The child was solemn-faced, fair-skinned, and freckled, with long tendrils of burnished red hair escaping from the embroidered white coif that was tied beneath her chin.

"My, you have grown, sweeting!" Mary exclaimed in her gruff voice, stroking Elizabeth's hair and straightening her silver pendant. "You're nearly three now, aren't you?" Elizabeth stared back, unsure of this richly dressed lady with the sad face and skinny body. Mary was not beautiful like Elizabeth's mother: Mary had a snub nose and a downturned mouth, and although her hair was red like Elizabeth and their father's, it was thin and frizzy. And of course, Mary was very old — all of twenty years, she had been told.

"I have brought you gifts, Sister," Mary said, smiling.

Alison Weir, *The Lady Elizabeth* (2008)

1 Préparez-vous à faire du texte une lecture active

Pour « entrer » dans le texte et le comprendre plus facilement, faites-vous une toute première idée de ce que vous allez lire.

Étapes	Exemples
1. Repérez • les éléments périphériques (titre, source, illustration...), • la mise en page (paragraphes, présence de dialogues), • les indications particulières (mots en italiques, en gras, mots détachés).	→ *The Lady Elizabeth - 2008* → *Dialogues = plusieurs personnages* → *1536 : date à laquelle se situe le récit*
2. À partir des éléments repérés, anticipez le thème ou le sujet du texte en vous appuyant sur vos connaissances et votre imagination.	**On peut supposer ici :** • que le texte, publié en 2008, raconte un événement qui se déroule en 1536 et porte sur quelqu'un qui s'appelle Lady Elizabeth, • que cette personne est noble, royale *(Lady)*, • qu'elle va parler à quelqu'un / que des personnes vont parler d'elle.
3. Faites des liens entre vos premières hypothèses et vos connaissances culturelles.	→ Lady Elizabeth *(s'agit-il d'Elizabeth I ?)* → 1536 *(cour d'Angleterre au début du 16e siècle).*

→ À vous

Préparez-vous à faire une lecture active d'un texte sur page 33
ou ▶ www.didierpassword.fr

2 Lisez le texte et identifiez la situation

Identifier	Conseils	Exemples
Époque	• Repérez dates, détails vestimentaires, moyens de transport… • Utilisez vos connaissances de l'époque et du contexte pour inférer le sens de certains mots.	→ *1536 - white coif - the Lady Mary, daughter to King Henry the Eighth* → *palfrey* associé à *trotting* (déplacement à cheval) → *ladies-in-waiting* (dames de compagnie)
Lieux	Repérez noms communs et noms propres.	→ *great country palace, Hatfield*
Personnages mentionnés et personnages principaux	• Repérez noms propres, noms communs, référents et identifiez qui renvoie à qui. N'hésitez pas à surligner les renvois à chacun des personnages par des couleurs différentes. • Visualisez, à l'aide du surlignage, qui sont les personnages principaux: ceux dont l'apparence physique, les actions, les pensées, les réactions sont développés. • Clarifiez leurs relations à l'aide d'un petit croquis. • Identifiez leurs sentiments, leur attitude réciproque et ce qu'ils se disent à l'aide des réseaux lexicaux.	→ *The Lady Mary… followed by four gentlemen, two ladies-in-waiting, and a female fool* → *the small girl… reminded her… she had not seen for many months. - you have grown sweeting* → *The child was solemn-faced, fair-skinned, and freckled, with long tendrils of burnished red hair.* *Mary* ← *sisters* → *Elizabeth* *father* / *father* *Henry the 8th* → *Mary : kiss, sweeting, stroke, smile* = certaine tendresse à l'égard de l'enfant
Narrateur	Le narrateur est-il un des personnages de l'histoire ou est-il extérieur ? - cherchez des *"I"* dans le texte, - lisez attentivement les passages descriptifs pour vérifier qu'il s'agit bien d'un narrateur extérieur.	→ *"I have brought you gifts, Sister," Mary said, smiling* (= Ici *"I"* renvoie à *Mary*) → *Mary had a snub nose and a downturned mouth, and although her hair was red like Elizabeth and their father's, it was thin and frizzy* Le narrateur n'est donc pas dans l'histoire.
Événements	• Repérez les différentes actions (verbes). • Reconstruisez l'enchaînement des événements en vous appuyant sur le temps des verbes, les connecteurs logiques et chronologiques.	→ *Mary arrived - dismounted - stooped to kiss the small girl.* → *As soon as she had dismounted, she stooped…*

→ À vous

Identifiez la situation dans le texte sur pages 32-33 **ou** ▶ www.didierpassword.fr

Le jour du Bac

Toutes séries

→ voir aussi *Entraînement Bac* p. 92

• Avant de lire le texte, **prenez connaissance des questions** : elles vous aideront à anticiper.

• Dès la première lecture du texte, essayez de **visualiser la situation** dans son ensemble sans prendre en compte tous les détails. N'hésitez pas à résumer la situation et à reformuler ce que vous avez compris.

• Appuyez-vous sur cette situation pour **inférer le sens des mots** ou des passages qui vous posent problème.

FINAL TASKS

Royal stories

task 1

Writing

Write an episode in the life of a Queen

1. Get ready

You will start from a situation your teacher will give you (see examples below).
- Make sure you understand the situation.
- Imagine the protagonists' reactions and feelings.

2. Action!

- Narrate the episode, including some dialogue. Don't forget to show the person behind the image.

↑ Catherine, Duchess of Cambridge, and Queen Elisabeth II, July 2011

Situation 1

Queen finds prowler at her bedside

An intruder at Buckingham Palace got into the Queen's bedroom last night. Michael Fagan sat on the Queen's bed for ten minutes and she engaged him in conversation. Eventually she found an excuse to fetch a footman, on duty in the corridor outside, and the prowler was detained.

***Daily Mirror*, 9 July 1982**

Suggested start

→ *On July, 8th, 1982, an intruder managed to get into Buckingham palace and into the Queen's bedroom. When the Queen saw him, she...*

Situation 2

Duchess of Cambridge invited to Balmoral so Queen can "get to know her better"

The Duchess of Cambridge married William, the Queen's grandson, in April 2011. William, Prince Charles's elder son, is second in line to the throne.

***The Telegraph*, 17 July 2011**

Suggested start

→ *William and Kate were invited to stay at the family castle in Scotland. On their first evening, they had tea with the Queen and...*

task 2

Reading

Re-order a narrative about a Queen

Your teacher will give you a text which has been jumbled up. Re-order it.

Bac

Compréhension de l'oral

Listen to a testimony:
Her Majesty

1. Listen to the document three times and take notes.
2. Write a report in French of what you have understood.

Expression orale

Oral presentation

1. Using what you have learnt about the three Queens prepare notes explaining to what extent they can be seen as **symbolic figures**.

You can follow these guidelines:
- Their private and public images.
- What they embody or symbolize.

Illustrate your presentation with relevant examples you may know.

2. Give your oral presentation.
3. Be ready to discuss the topic with your teacher.

→ ***Aide***

Utilisez la fiche *Recap* du workbook p. 34 ou sur www.didierpassword.fr pour préparer cette synthèse orale.

Compréhension de l'écrit

Study a set of documents

Your teacher will give you several documents.

Read them carefully and answer the questions.

Expression écrite

Write two different texts

Using the elements given by your teacher, write:

1. A diary entry
2. A comment on an online forum

Culture File

AUTHORS AND QUEENS

Pick out one of these documents.

In groups

1. Read or watch it. Discuss what you have learned about the Queen.
2. Jot down a few notes to share your findings with the class.

Whole class

3. Discuss the way the queens are portrayed.

1 Shakespeare & Elizabeth I

The play* Henry VIII *tells of the intrigues that took place during the first part of Henry's reign. Here Thomas Cranmer, the Archbishop of Canterbury, speaks of Elizabeth, Henry VIII's newborn child.

CRANMER

She shall be loved and fear'd: her own shall bless her;
Her foes[1] shake like a field of beaten corn,
And hang their heads with sorrow: good grows with her:
In her days every man shall eat in safety,
Under his own vine, what he plants; and sing
The merry songs of peace to all his neighbours:
God shall be truly known; and those about her
From her shall read the perfect ways of honour,
And by those claim their greatness, not by blood.
Nor shall this peace sleep with her: but as when
The bird of wonder dies, the maiden phoenix,
Her ashes[2] new create another heir,
As great in admiration as herself;
So shall she leave her blessedness to one,
When heaven shall call her from this cloud of darkness,
Who from the sacred ashes of her honour
Shall star-like rise, as great in fame as she was,
And so stand fix'd: peace, plenty, love, truth, terror,
That were the servants to this chosen infant,
Shall then be his, and like a vine grow to him:
Wherever the bright sun of heaven shall shine,
His honour and the greatness of his name
Shall be, and make new nations: he shall flourish,
And, like a mountain cedar, reach his branches
To all the plains about him: our children's children
Shall see this, and bless heaven.

William Shakespeare, *Henry VIII*
(first performed between 1612 and 1613)

↑ Ann Boleyn and Henry VIII, Shakespeare's Globe Theatre, London (2010)

1. foes: enemies
2. ashes: what remains after something has been burnt

William Shakespeare (1564-1616)

Regarded as the greatest writer in the English language, he was a prolific playwright and poet. His plays are performed more often than those of any other author.

2 Charles Dickens & Victoria

Oliver Twist, a poor orphan who endures a miserable life in a workhouse, has been punished for asking for more food.

He only cried bitterly all day; and, when the long, dismal night came on, spread his little hands before his eyes to shut out the darkness, and crouching in the corner, tried to sleep [...].

Let it not be supposed by the enemies of 'the system,' that, during the period of his solitary incarceration, Oliver was denied the benefit of exercise, the pleasure of society, or the advantages of religious consolation. As for exercise, it was nice cold weather, and he was allowed to perform his ablutions every morning under the pump, in a stone yard, in the presence of Mr. Bumble[1], who prevented his catching cold, and caused a tingling sensation to pervade his frame, by repeated applications of the cane. As for society, he was carried every other day into the hall where the boys dined, and there sociably flogged[2] as a public warning and example. And so far from being denied the advantages of religious consolation, he was kicked into the same apartment every evening at prayer-time, and there permitted to listen to, and console his mind with, a general supplication of the boys, containing a special clause, therein inserted by authority of the board, in which they entreated to be made good, virtuous, contented, and obedient, and to be guarded from the sins and vices of Oliver Twist.

Charles Dickens, *Oliver Twist* (1838)

1. Mr Bumble: the person whose job is to keep order in the workhouse
2. flog: beat somebody with a whip or stick

Queen Victoria's diaries

(30 December 1838) "Talked of *Oliver Twist*, which I must say is excessively interesting..."

(1 January 1839) "Talked to [Lord Melbourne*] of my getting on with *Oliver Twist*; of the description of 'squalid vice' in it; of the accounts of starvation in the Workhouses and Schools, Mr Dickens gives in his books. Lord M. says, in many schools they give children the worst things to eat, and bad beer, to save expense; told him Mamma admonished me for reading light books." [Two days later, Victoria persuaded Lord Melbourne to read *Oliver Twist*.]

(7 April 1839) "Lord M. was talking of some dish or other, and alluded to something in *Oliver Twist*; he read half of the 1st vol. at Panshanger. 'It's all among Workhouses, and Coffin Makers, and Pickpockets,' he said; 'I don't like that low debasing view of mankind.' We defended *Oliver Twist* very much, but in vain."

*Prime Minister from 1834 to 1841

↑ Child laborers carrying clay in an English brickyard, 1871

Charles Dickens (1812-1870)

One of the most renowned and acclaimed English writers. Most of his novels continue to entertain and provoke thought. His writings are charged with indignation at the social conditions and hypocrisy of 19th century England.

3 Elizabeth II & cinema

Directed by Stephen Frears, *The Queen* achieved immense critical acclaim and box office success and won awards.

You can watch the trailer on:
www.imdb.com/video/screenplay/vi3253862681/

*An English film director, **Stephen Frears** (born in 1941) became famous in 1985 with his production of* My Beautiful Launderette. *He has since directed a number of successful films in both Britain and America.*

Entraînement Bac

Compréhension de l'écrit (2)

À partir de supports multiples

Séries ES, S, L et technologiques

« L'épreuve de compréhension de l'écrit prend appui sur un, deux ou trois documents en langue étrangère et peut comporter des éléments d'iconographie. Ces documents renvoient à des notions du programme du cycle terminal sans exiger des connaissances trop spécifiques. »

Instructions officielles, B.O. du 24 nov. 2011

Document 1 page 35

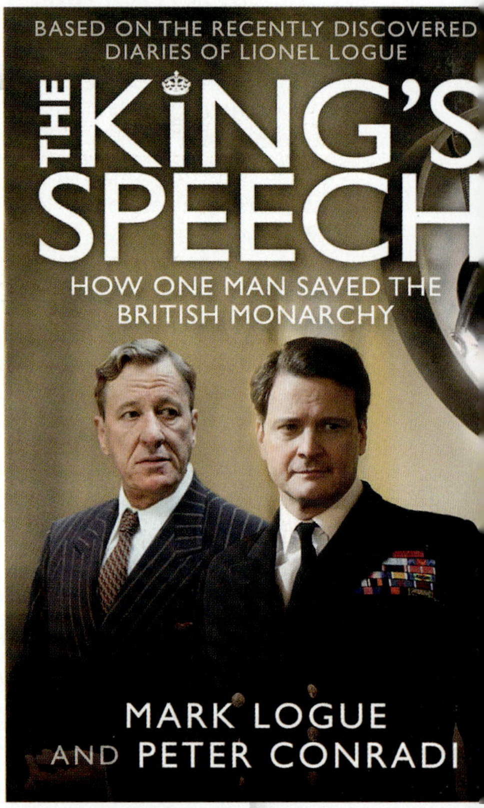

Albert Frederick Arthur George, King of the United Kingdom and the British Dominions and the last Emperor of India, woke up with a start. It was just after 3 a.m. The bedroom in Buckingham Palace he had occupied since becoming monarch five months earlier was normally a haven of peace and quiet in the heart of London, but on this particular morning his slumbers had been rudely interrupted by the crackle of loudspeakers being tested outside on Constitution Hill. "One of them might have been in our room," he wrote in his diary. And then, just when he thought he might finally be able to go back to sleep, the marching bands and troops started up.

It was 12 May 1937, and the forty-one-year-old king was about to face one of the greatest – and most nerve-racking – days of his life: his coronation. [...]

As the hours ticked by and the streets of London began to fill with crowds of well-wishers, many of whom had slept on camp beds, [...] the King had a 'sinking feeling' inside and could eat no breakfast. "I knew that I was to spend a most trying day and to go through the most important ceremony in my life", he wrote in his diary that evening. "The hours of waiting before leaving for Westminster Abbey were the most nerve racking." [...]

To be at the centre of such a ceremony – all the while balancing an ancient 7lb crown on his head – would have been a huge ordeal for anyone, but the King had particular reason to view what was in store for him with trepidation: plagued since childhood by a series of medical ailments, he also suffered from a debilitating stammer. Embarrassing enough in small gatherings, it turned public speaking into a major ordeal. The King, in the words of America's *Time Magazine*, was the 'most famed contemporary stammerer' in the world, joining a roll call of prominent names stretching back to antiquity that included Aesop, Aristotle, Demosthenes, Virgil, Erasmus and Darwin.

Worse, in the weeks running up to the coronation, the King had been forced to endure a whispering campaign about his health, stirred up by supporters of his embittered elder brother, who was now living in exile in France. The new King, it was rumoured, was in such poor physical state that he would not be able to endure the coronation ceremony, let alone discharge his functions as sovereign.

Mark Logue and Peter Conradi,
***The King's Speech: how one man saved the British Monarchy* (2010)**

Document 2 page 36

The king's speech

The real story

The story of the stuttering sovereign: the epic events that inspired the Oscar-tipped film, 'The King's Speech'

↑ A staged photograph of George VI announcing the declaration of war to the nation in September 1939

There are many forms of irony – verbal, dramatic, situational and so on – but the one that surely applied to King George VI was the irony of fate. It was as if the gods, or Fates, were amusing themselves by toying with his mind, mocking his failings, reminding him that he was very much a mortal. It was, after all, almost impossible for him to pronounce the letter 'k', thanks to his debilitating nervous stammer. A cruel fate for a king.

Even crueller, his reign coincided with a revolution in mass communication. For the first time in British history, subjects could listen to their monarch addressing them through their wireless sets, as if he were with them in their living rooms.

But the technology didn't allow George VI to pre-record his broadcasts, as would be the case for the generations that followed. When he addressed the nation, it had to be done through a live microphone, without editing, an agony for a stammerer.

The layers of irony did not end there. Because he had been told that cigarettes might help with his stammer, George VI chain-smoked – and he consequently died of lung cancer at the age of 56 in 1952. And the greatest irony of all? This vulnerable and stammering king proved to be exactly the right man at the right time.

The stammering that defined him, and the courage with which he tried to beat it, came to symbolise the vulnerability of the British people as they stood alone against the Nazi tyranny that had the rest of Europe in its grip. A certain solidarity between monarch and subject emerged, especially when George VI overruled requests from the government that he and his family relocate to the safety of Canada. ■

By Nigel Farndale,
telegraph.co.uk,
05 Jan 2011

Le jour du Bac

Les documents

- **Faites-vous une idée des types de textes** auxquels vous avez affaire (fiction, presse, essai, etc.), grâce à la source (auteur, provenance, date...), et à un rapide coup d'œil aux textes (disposition, premières lignes, etc.).
- **Faites-vous une idée du thème** abordé à partir des types de textes, des titres, des éléments d'iconographie éventuels et de vos propres connaissances.
- **Lisez les textes** une première fois, lentement, et **soulignez** les **noms des personnages**, les **noms de lieux** et les **marqueurs de temps.** N'hésitez pas à utiliser des couleurs différentes, cela vous aidera à retrouver les informations plus vite dans le texte.
- **Notez dans la marge** ce que vous avez compris : thème général, idée principale d'un paragraphe, relations entre différents personnages, enchaînement des événements, etc.
- **Faites des liens entre les différents documents** : par exemple, parle-t-on d'un même personnage, d'un même événement ou d'un même thème ? Développe-t-on une opinion, des exemples, un point de vue différents ou complémentaires ?
- Si vous rencontrez une difficulté de compréhension dans un document, **recherchez dans les autres documents** un élément susceptible de vous éclairer.

Les questions

- **Lisez toutes les questions** pour vous faire une idée de ce que l'on vous demande.
- **Commencez alors à répondre aux questions dans l'ordre**, en utilisant tous les documents. N'hésitez pas à passer à la question suivante si vous voyez que vous « bloquez » : vous y reviendrez plus tard.

Compréhension

1 a. **Who are the different documents about?**
(full name - public name - status)
Answer in one sentence.

On peut vous demander de répondre avec vos propres mots :
→ faites des phrases complètes mais simples qui montrent que vous avez compris ;
→ si on vous demande une phrase, n'en écrivez pas plus, vous perdrez du temps inutilement !

b. **Pick out important events in this person's life and then organize his biography:**

Date of birth: ....

....

....

....

....

- Lisez attentivement les consignes ; celle-ci exige une réponse en deux temps :
→ *pick out* vous indique qu'il faut relever dans le texte les groupes de mots qui renvoient à des événements importants de la vie du personnage ;
→ *and then* indique la deuxième partie de la consigne qui s'appuie sur le relevé.
- Le nombre de lignes de pointillés vous indique le nombre d'éléments à repérer.

2 **a. Read document 1, lines 25-26:** *("he also suffered from a debilitating stammer. Embarrassing enough in small gatherings, it turned public speaking into a major ordeal")* **and document 2, lines 11-16** *("It was, after all, almost impossible for him to pronounce the letter 'k', thanks to his debilitating nervous stammer")* **and explain in your own words what this person's problem was. Answer in one sentence.**

> • Appuyez-vous sur le contexte et sur tous les documents qui vous sont fournis pour déduire le sens des mots que vous ne connaissez pas : par exemple rapprochez *stammer* (doc 1, l. 26) de *public speaking* et de *impossible for him to pronounce the letter "k"* (doc 2, l. 13).
> • *Explain in your own words:* par exemple *he did not speak well / he couldn't pronounce some letters / he couldn't speak in public / he suffered from a serious speech defect.*

b. In which specific circumstance was it a real problem for him? Pick out a sentence in document 2.

c. Explain why technology was no help to him, by quoting document 2.

> Attention, pour cette explication on vous demande de prélever un élément du texte (mot, expression, phrase).

3 **Read these statements about this man and decide if they are right or wrong.**

Justify with a quotation from the documents. Indicate which document and the lines.

a. As a child he was healthy. *(1 quotation)*
b. He had no reason to worry about the coronation ceremony. *(2 quotations)*
c. Some people thought he was not cut out for the job. *(1 quotation)*
d. His elder brother supported him. *(1 quotation)*
e. He was a courageous man. *(2 quotations)*

> • N'oubliez pas de répondre à la question (vrai ou faux) avant de citer le texte.
> • *"Justify with a quotation":*
> → cherchez dans les documents une ou deux phrases, groupes de mots ou mots qui expriment la même idée ;
> → soyez le/la plus précis(e) possible et citez le texte correctement (guillemets, numéro du texte et numéros de ligne).

4 *"I knew that I was to spend a most trying day and to go through the most important ceremony in my life". (doc 1, line 18-19)*
Identify who is speaking and explain this person's state of mind. Answer in 40 words.

> Les référents des pronoms personnels ne sont pas toujours explicites, il faut identifier le contexte et la situation pour les repérer.

5 **Compare the two portraits of the man in documents 1 and 2. Answer in 40 words.**

> • Cette question vous invite à faire des comparaisons, c'est-à-dire à pointer les similitudes et les différences, que vous exprimerez dans votre réponse en utilisant les mots de liaison appropriés *(both, like, whereas, contrary to, unlike...)*
> • Respectez le nombre de mots que l'on vous demande d'utiliser à 10 % près (il y a environ 10 mots par ligne).

6 **The portraits in documents 1 and 2 are written from two different points of view. Match the following adjectives with the corresponding portrait.**
public - private - historical

UNIT 5 War on screen

↑ ***Tigerland,*** directed by Joel Schumacher, 2000

How are soldiers portrayed in American war films?

← **Look** at this film poster. What image of soldiers does it convey? **Discuss** what you know about war films.

FINAL TASKS

P. 110

Film reviews

Writing
Write a war film review

Listening
Match war film reviews and posters

CULTURE

- Learning about 20th century US involvement in wars:
  - World War II,
  - the Vietnam war,
  - the Gulf wars.
- Studying the representation of soldiers in war films.
- Cinema:
  - Randall Wallace, *We Were Soldiers*
  - Steven Spielberg, *Saving Private Ryan*
  - Ted Kotcheff, *First Blood*
- Literary works:
  - Larry Heinemann, *Black Virgin Mountain*
  - Rupert Morgan, *"Same place, same story, different millenia"*
  - Edwin Brock, *"Five Ways to Kill a Man"*
  - William Butler Yeats, *"Death"*

COMMUNICATION

- Understanding specific information and explanations in interviews and film reviews.
- Understanding events and feelings in trailers and film extracts.

Writing film reviews.

- Presenting and talking about films.
- Expressing one's opinion.

TOOLS

Words
- Talking about films
- Soldiers
- On screen portrayal
- Trauma
- Cruelty
- Disillusionment

Pronunciation
- Stressing derived adjectives
- Intonation and contrast

Grammar
- Passive forms
- Using nouns as adjectives

Bac

Stratégies
→ *Comprendre un dialogue ou une discussion* p. 108

Évaluation
→ *4 situations d'évaluation* p. 111

War films

1 They were soldiers...

video 7

A trailer for the film *We Were Soldiers*, directed by Randall Wallace, 2002

1. **Before watching**: what do you expect a war film trailer to show?
2. **Watch the trailer**: is it what you expected?
3. a. Watch the trailer again and **note**:
   - relevant information (characters, place, action),
   - how soldiers are portrayed,
   - how "war" is defined by the characters, images and music.

   b. **Share your findings** with the class.
4. **Discuss** if this portrayal of war and soldiers is typical of most US war films.
5. Would you want to watch the film? Give your reasons.

2 Talking about war films

track 30

1. **Before listening**: judging by the title, what do you expect to hear?
2. **Listen to the conversation** and discuss what you have understood.
3. a. Listen again and **identify**:
   - the speakers' opinions,
   - the reasons and the examples they give.

   b. **Share your findings**.
4. **How about you?** Tell the class why you like or don't like watching war films.

Recap → Recap war films' main characteristics. page 42

Black Hawk Down
Ridley Scott (2001)

Glory
Edward Zwick (1989)

LANGUAGE TOOLS

★ WORDS

Films

- di**rect**, shoot
- star *(v.)*, play in
- **mo**vie, **fea**ture **film**, **mo**tion **pic**ture
- plot, **sto**ryline, script
- **view**er, **mo**viegoer, **au**dience

Talking about films

- por**tray**, de**pict**, show
- **tou**ching, **sen**sitive, **mo**ving
- pro**vo**cative, **cha**llenging, contro**ver**sial
- pre**dic**table, **cli**ché **rid**den
- patri**o**tic, **flag**-waving, chauvi**nis**tic

Soldiers

- brave, cou**ra**geous, tough /tʌf/
- weak, frail, **cow**ardly, **fear**ful, dis**cou**raged

★ PRONUNCIATION → p. 106

Intonation and contrast

★ GRAMMAR → p. 107

Passive forms

→ The film was well received by the public and was awarded 5 Oscars.

The Dirty Dozen
Robert Aldrich (1967)

TRAINING TASK

Talking about a war film

1. Group work. Select one of the three film posters above, then go on IMDB.com to research the film. Make notes about:
- the war it deals with,
- the storyline and the main characters,
- the director and actors,
- the public reception of the film,
- the trailer.

2. Present the film you have chosen to the class.

WW2: guts and glory

WORLD WAR 2: 1941-1945

US involvement

- **1941:** most European countries, except Great Britain, occupied by Germany.
- **Dec 1941:** Japanese attack on Pearl Harbor, Hawaii brings the USA into WW2
- **6th June 1944:** "D Day": American and British troops land in France and advance toward Berlin.
- **May 8, 1945:** Armistice.
- **August 1945:** Japan surrenders after the USA drops atomic bombs on Hiroshima and on Nagasaki.

Number of US soldiers involved 16,100,000
US casualties: 405,400 - Total casualties: 60,000,000

1 A film poster

1. **Look at the film poster** and date the film, explaining your reasons.
2. **Discuss** how the soldiers are portrayed.
3. Use the poster to **imagine the plot** and narrate it orally.

2 Saving Private Ryan

video 8

An extract from *Saving Private Ryan*, directed by Steven Spielberg (1998)

LANGUAGE TOOLS

★ WORDS

Soldiers

- **pri**vate *(n.)*: a soldier of the lower rank ≠ officer
- pla**toon**, **re**giment
- **vet**(eran) /ˈvet[rən]/
- **mi**litary e**quip**ment / gear *(fam.)*: **hel**mets, **u**niforms, **wea**pons...
- res**pect**ful, o**be**dient, **well**-trained, **du**tiful, **lo**yal
- **pa**triotic, **de**dicated, **glo**rious, **self**-sacrificing

On screen portrayal

- **glo**rify, **ma**gnify, **en**hance, **em**phasize

1. **Watch the opening scene** of the film: how do the sound and pictures make you feel?
2. **Say** who the various people must be.
3. **Imagine** what the old man is thinking.
4. What image of soldiers does the scene give?

3 Film reviews

❶ http://www.imdb.com

Saving Private Ryan (1998)

Excellent despite some Spielberg slips into sentiment, 11 September 2002

Author: filmfanfrank **from Birmingham, UK**

During the WW2 Normandy landings, two brothers are killed. In another part of the world, another of the Ryan brothers is killed in action, leaving their mother with one remaining son and three telegrams due to be delivered. A group of courageous men, led by Captain Miller, set out to reach Private Ryan not only to break him the news but to safely return him back to the US.

What can I say — it is an excellent film despite some minor flaws. The plot is based on a real life situation during WW2 — already brought to screen in 1944 war film *The Fighting Sullivans* — and allows for us to follow a group of heroic men as they take part in the horrors (and humanity) of war. This is the film's strength and it is never stronger than in the first 25 minutes and, to a lesser extent, the final 20 minutes. The opening of the Normandy landing is simply pure emotional power and is really well done — it is so powerful that the actual plot itself is a bit of a letdown. [...]

It also sinks into sentiment a tad too often. For example Ryan's mother belongs to this kind of idealized vision of middle America that is Spielberg's. Also there is a little too much use of gawkish dialogue as well — although it's hard to criticise the death scenes for being emotional, because they should be. [...]

Overall it is excellent despite some stereotyping, US flag waving and the usual Spielberg love of sentimentality. Even if the actual plot is flimsy Spielberg expertly puts us as close to experiencing the horrors and the humanity within war as I hope we'll ever be.

❷ http://www.imdb.com

Patton (1970)

Viewed in Context, 29 February 2004

Author: moviemadmaddie **from Chicago, IL**

Patton tells the tale of General George S. Patton, famous tank commander of World War II. The film begins with Patton's career in North Africa and progresses through the invasion of Germany and the fall of the Third Reich.

The film was truly a shock to the system when it was released. The United States was still in the thick of the Vietnam war, and the country was extremely polarized between the hawks and the doves*. Then along comes *Patton*, with a portrayal of a rebellious General who was always being put in his place by the establishment — even though he was, of course, a major establishment figure (generals aren't usually the most liberal or progressive types). [...]

And that is why *Patton* works — you have an unambiguous war against an unambiguous evil — Nazi Germany. Whereas Vietnam might have been a tough conflict for even its supporters to explain, WWII was quite simple — we were the good guys, and they WERE the bad guys. And so you COULD root for the US Army and Patton without feeling a tinge of guilt.

* In this context, the "hawks" are the people who support war while the "doves" are the people who are opposed to it.

1. **Read the two reviews** and highlight information about:
   - the soldiers,
   - the viewers' general opinions. pages 37-38
2. Read again and study **how the reviews are built**.
3. **React**: which of these films would you rather see?

Recap → List the elements that are necessary in a film review. page 42

TRAINING TASK

A director's choices

Imagine you are Spielberg's assistant director: you have been asked to explain his choices in the opening scene of *Saving Private Ryan*. Prepare and record your commentary.

The Vietnam War: fallen heroes

VIETNAM WAR: 1955-1975

US involvement

- **1945:** Vietnam, a French colony since the end of the 19th century, declares its independence.
- **1954:** France, which has fought to maintain colonial rule, is defeated → Vietnam divides into two, North Vietnam being communist.
- **1963-1975:** increasing number of US troops deployed to prevent a communist takeover of South Vietnam.
- **April 1975:** North Vietnamese troops enter Saigon (South Vietnam) and oust American troops.

The Vietnam war is the longest the US has ever fought and one that indelibly marks American consciousness.

Number of US soldiers: 8,744,000 - US casualties: 58,200 - Vietnamese casualties: 2,000,000

1 "The first casualty of war"

1. **Look at this poster** and list the elements showing this is a war film poster.
2. **Discuss** what the soldier's posture may mean.
3. **Read the tagline**. Explain how you understand it, and try to relate it to the picture.

2 "It wasn't my war"

video 9

An extract from *First Blood*, directed by Ted Kotcheff (1982)

← Sylvester Stallone as John Rambo in *First Blood*

After being chased by the police, John Rambo has finally hidden in a building which is now surrounded.

1. **Watch the scene**. Say what you have understood. Then, find out about:
   - the possible relationship between the characters,
   - what happened to the young man,
   - his feelings then,
   - his life and his feelings now.
2. **Discuss** the image which is given of the soldier.
3. **Link** this scene to the *Platoon* poster above.

3 "John Wayne Dies"

Larry Heinemann (born 1944) served in Vietnam in the late 1960s.* Black Virgin Mountain *chronicles his return trips to Vietnam several years after the war.

In Vietnam, to be called a "John Wayne" was a flat-out insult. Boyhood hero as verb: to *John Wayne* it, to *pull* a "John Wayne," was strictly for the ticket-punching lifers[1], the Boy Scouts, and the other assorted hot-dog, hero wannabes – the guys who had watched way too much television. You want somebody to take a mess of hand grenades and assault that bunker up the slope yonder? Well, sir, get John. He's just that big a fool, right down to pulling the pins[2] with his teeth; dead already, went the running gag, but too dumb to lie down.

John Wayne's real name was Marion Michael Morrison, and the man, the husband and father, the actor, was likely as friendly and likable and generous and gregarious as the day is long. But "John Wayne," the big-screen Technicolor postwar film persona and pop culture legend I grew up with, was something altogether different. His 1968 film *The Green Berets* is especially patronizing and insulting, though screamingly funny in a gallows[3]-humor sort of way, right up to and including the closing image when he stands with his arm around a young Vietnamese lad at the very edge of what we are to suppose is the South China Sea, facing east, watching the sun "go down."

In the late spring of 1979, I was driving home one night and happened to catch the *Chicago Sun-Times* headline in a street-corner vending machine out of the corner of my eye: JOHN WAYNE DIES. I started giggling, then laughing, then roaring with laughter. "John Wayne," the larger-than-life Hollywood character, the very beans of testosterone-poisoned, cartoon-macho movie bullshit, was dead; finally, and thank God. I laughed so hard that tears came to my eyes and I had to pull to the curb.

Larry Heinemann, *Black Virgin Mountain: A Return to Vietnam* (2005)

John Wayne (1907-1979)
An American film actor, director and producer who appeared in more than 200 films. He mostly played imposing characters in westerns and war films, and remains a symbol of masculinity and one of America's favorite film stars.

1. ticket-punching lifers: military men who were decorated in Vietnam and thus got a "ticket" home as a reward
2. pins: what soldiers pull to detonate grenades
3. gallows: *gibet, potence*

1. **Read the information** about John Wayne and the introduction to the text. Imagine why Larry Heinemann wrote about John Wayne.
2. **Read the text** and say what you have understood. pages 38-39
3. a. **Explain** how Larry Heinemann felt about John Wayne.
   b. **Comment** on the last two sentences (l. 20-23).

Recap → To what extent may Vietnam veterans be seen as "fallen heroes"? page 42

LANGUAGE TOOLS

★ WORDS

Trauma
- **suff**er
- pain, angst, an**xi**ety
- **des**perate, de**pres**sed, low, down
- **hope**less, **help**less, **pow**erless

Cruelty
- **cru**el, **heart**less, **ruth**less, **pi**tiless, **cold**-hearted

★ GRAMMAR → p. 107

Using nouns as adjectives
→ "But *John Wayne*, the big-screen Technicolor postwar film persona and pop culture legend I grew up with, was something altogether different."

TRAINING TASK

A discussion board

This is an amazing scene, which isn't surprising when you think how talented an actor Stallone is. Besides, thanks to Rambo's final speech, soldiers are given back their humanity.

Here is a viewer's comment about the final scene of *First Blood* on a discussion board. Write your own contribution to react to it.

video 9

The Gulf Wars: existential crisis

"Same place, same story, different millennia"

Writer and film reviewer Rupert Morgan reflects on war and war films.

On the 1st May, 1945, the German forces surrendered in Italy, effectively ending the Second World War. The man they surrendered to was called General Sir William Morgan. My grandfather. War held no mystery for him – he'd known the absolute horror of the trenches as a young man in World War I and been a part of the Manhattan Project to develop the atomic bomb. He had no regrets, sure that what he had done was right and necessary, and even said that some of the best days of his life had been in the Somme, when the combat was the most bloody and intense.

I do not know if today's soldiers have such moral clarity about our contemporary wars. Certainly the cinematic representation of war has changed from the heroic to the tragic, the entire focus now being on amorality, trauma and the dehumanisation of combatants.

The moral case for the first Iraq War was supposedly impeccable, having been backed by a UN mandate, but *Three Kings*[1] was a film that took a satirical view, effectively saying that it was about economics and oil. George Clooney leads a trio of American soldiers who try to steal a secret cache of gold that Saddam Hussein is supposed to have hidden in a nearby village. They are not liberators or representatives of democracy and freedom, but men motivated by personal gain – in which they represent the USA as a nation. *Three Kings* seemed a modern take on war, but in the past, of course, the promise of riches was always a soldier's primary motive: victorious armies plundered conquered lands. Clooney is an American in Iraq, but he could be a Macedonian in Mesopotamia – same place, same story, different millennia.

Jarhead[2] deals with the same war, but focuses on the futility the soldiers feel because it is a combat almost entirely fought from the air. The whole film is suffused with a sense of surreal absurdity – the soldiers are in a featureless desert, with nobody to fight and little sense of why they are there. They come to suffer from a kind of existential crisis whereby they are desperate to kill someone simply to feel their lives have a purpose. *Jarhead* demonstrates the old maxim that war is boredom punctuated by moments of absolute terror, but it also says something important that it is easy to forget –a man joins the army because he wants to experience combat.

This is brilliantly evoked in Kathryn Bigelow's *The Hurt Locker*, which focuses on a bomb-disposal expert in Baghdad during the second Iraq War. He is a man who knows that each day may be his last and has learned to master his fear. An incredibly tense film, it makes you understand how a soldier can become addicted to the adrenalin that only war can offer, and be unable to return to the safety of civilian life.

I often ask myself if my grandfather, who I knew as a humorous old man who spent his days salmon fishing in Scotland, would recognise the soldiers in these films. I suspect he would. But I think he'd say the wars are not good ones.

Rupert Morgan (2011)

1. directed by David O. Russell (1999)
2. directed by Sam Mendes (2005)

↑ Scene from *The Hurt Locker*, Kathryn Bigelow (2008)

GULF WARS
1990-1991 / 2003-2011

US involvement

- **1990:** Iraq invades neighboring Kuwait. Operation Desert Storm (a US-led alliance of 32 countries) forces Iraq to leave Kuwait.
- **March 2003:** American, British and other troops invade Iraq on the grounds that the country has weapons of mass destruction (none are found). Iraqi dictator Saddam Hussein is deposed, leading to chaos and sectarian violence. The US maintains a force of 39,000 troops in Iraq to "advise and assist".
- **December 2011:** all US troops withdrawn from Iraq.

1. **Read the title and the introduction**: what do you expect the text will be about?
2. **Read the text**: note the title, setting, plot, and tone of each film discussed.
3. a. **Highlight information** about:
   - the soldiers in the various films,
   - the soldiers in the various wars. page 40

   b. **Find out and discuss** the common points and differences.
4. **Identify** the special relationship between the narrator and war, and discuss its impact on the tone of the text.

Recap → Discuss the evolution in the cinematic portrayal of soldiers. page 42

track 31

TRAINING TASK

Preparing a review

Listen to director Sam Mendes talking about his film, *Jarhead* (2005). Take notes that you think would be useful to write a review of that film.
Compare with your classmates and explain your choices.

LANGUAGE TOOLS

★ **WORDS**

Disillusionment

- frus**tra**ted, disap**poin**ted, **use**less
- disil**lu**sioned, disen**chan**ted, de**ceived**

★ WORDS

❶ Nouns as verbs: verbing up!

a. Match each verb with its definition:

Verbs	Definitions
1. Hoover	a. Use a web search engine
2. Xerox	b. Use a social network
3. Google	c. Use a vacuum cleaner
4. Facebook	d. Use a photocopying machine

b. Find other verbs created to name actions linked to technological advances.

c. In the following sentences, how do you understand the underlined words?

1. HENRY IV: My gracious uncle—
   EDMUND OF LANGLEY: Tut, tut! Grace me no grace, nor uncle me no uncle: I am no traitor's uncle.
   (William Shakespeare, *Richard II*, 1595)
2. Don't darling me. Just stop bossing me!
3. In Vietnam, many soldiers knew they could not John Wayne it.
4. He got his face Michael Jacksoned.
5. She spent the whole party Lady Gagaing.
6. The champion glided off, Batmanning through the crowd toward the start line.
7. LILY: Don't Ted-out about it.
   TED: Did you just use my name as a verb ?
   BARNEY: Oh, yeah, we do that behind your back. Ted-out: to overthink. Also see Ted-up. Ted-up: to overthink with disastrous consequences. For example, "Billy Tedded-up when he..."
   TED: All right, I get it!
   ("Matchmaker", *How I met your Mother*, 2005)

d. Now, try! Think of famous people and try to make your own name-based verbs.

❷ Talking about heroes Bac

a. Spot the odd one in each series:

1. brave - bold - courageous - fearful - daredevil
2. loyal - unreliable - faithful - dependable - trustworthy
3. heartless - ruthless - cold-hearted - sensitive
4. charismatic - dull - impressive - dazzling

b. Talk about the action film heroes you admired when you were younger or admire now.

★ PRONUNCIATION

❸ Stressing derived adjectives

track 32

a. Listen to these nouns and their derived adjectives. Pick out the stressed syllable for each of them.

1. power → powerful - respect → respectful - duty → dutiful
2. pity → pitiless - hope → hopeless - power → powerless
3. origin → original - emotion → emotional
4. real → realistic - hero → heroic - poet → poetic
5. rebel → rebellious - courage → courageous
6. Vietnam → Vietnamese - Japan → Japanese

b. Draw conclusions about the different suffixes. Practise reading the adjectives aloud.

❹ Intonation and contrast

track 33

- *I haven't seen it, but my brother has.*
- *All war films are the same to me.*
- *Oh come on, there are many sorts of war films!*

Lorsqu'un locuteur veut insister sur un point particulier ou montrer son désaccord, il accentue plus fortement certains éléments.

Practise in your workbook. page 41

★ GRAMMAR

Passive forms

Observe

1. The US government trained their soldiers into war machines. However, in the film, soldiers are portrayed as kind fathers and romantic husbands.
2. The film was well received by the public though it is showing the horrors of war too crudely.
3. Even if most citizens may consider war as a necessary evil, fighting should not be shown as something positive.

• **Comparez les formes verbales surlignées en bleu et celles en rose. En quoi diffèrent-elles ?**
• **Pourquoi l'énonciateur choisit-il une forme plutôt qu'une autre ? Concluez.**

g → Grammaire ⑲ p. 207-208

Practise

5 **Put the verbs between brackets in the appropriate form.**

a. When the war against Iraq *(declare)*, a lot of soldiers *(force)* to fight even if they *(prefer)* to stay home. Hundreds of civilians *(injure)* and most militaries *(not consider)* as heroes.

b. A few years ago, the US government *(send)* troops to maintain peace in Afghanistan but many soldiers *(kill)* during the fights. By 2013, the troops *(bring back)* into the country.

c. When the Vietnam war *(end)* in April 1975, American soldiers *(ship)* back home. Some *(admire)* for their courage but many *(feel)* they *(regard)* as losers.

6 **Think of a war studied in your History course, and present it briefly. Explain what happened to the soldiers and civilians involved in the conflict.**

Using nouns as adjectives

Observe

1. "The Green Berets" is a war film.
2. "The Green Berets" is a John Wayne war film.
3. "The Green Berets" is a technicolor John Wayne war film.
4. "The Green Berets" is a 1965 technicolor John Wayne war film.
5. "The Green Berets" is a propaganda 1965 technicolor John Wayne war film.

• **Quelle est la nature des mots soulignés dans ces phrases ? Pour chacun des groupes de mots, quel est le mot noyau ? Où est-il placé ?**
• **Quelle est la fonction des autres mots soulignés ? Pourquoi, d'après vous, sont-ils placés dans cet ordre ? Concluez.**

Practise

7 **Place the words between brackets in the right order to make meaningful sentences.**

From Here to Eternity is a novel/war/1951/James Jones
→ *From Here to Eternity* is a 1951 James Jones war novel.

a. *Scream* is a ... film (horror/1996/Wes Craven)
b. *As you like it* is a ... play (Shakespeare/comedy/1599)
c. *Parachutes* is a ... album (music/2000/Coldplay/rock)
d. *Friends* is a ... program (TV/Warner Bros/teenager)

8 **Imagine 3 sentences with nouns used as adjectives to describe the documents below.**

More exercises in your Workbook → p. 41

❶ 1945

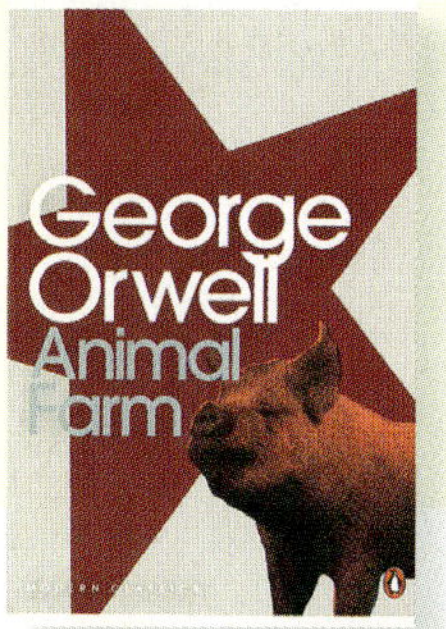

❷ 1976

❸ 2002

Comprendre un dialogue ou une discussion

Lorsque vous écoutez plusieurs personnes qui discutent, votre objectif est de comprendre l'essentiel des messages transmis en reliant ce que disent les uns et les autres.

1 Préparez-vous à l'écoute

Utilisez les éléments fournis pour formuler des hypothèses, aussi larges que possible.

Étapes	Indices	Exemple
1. Identifiez le contexte et la situation.	Un titre, une image, le lieu ou la date de la conversation, la source…	→ *A radio report: Women in Business.*
2. Posez-vous des questions et faites des hypothèses sur…	• **le thème de la conversation** • **le type d'échange** (dialogue informel, interview, débat, pièce de théâtre, film…) • **les interlocuteurs** (âge, sexe, fonction, rôle…) • **le but de la conversation**	→ interviews, concernant les femmes au travail, leur place dans la société → un ou plusieurs journalistes, des femmes, éventuellement leurs employeurs, des responsables politiques… → informer, expliquer, raconter, convaincre…
3. Croisez vos hypothèses et vos connaissances culturelles.	Faites la liste des mots en lien avec la thématique et que vous êtes susceptible d'entendre.	→ *job, workplace, responsibility, discrimination, money/salary, etc.*

→ À vous

Faites des hypothèses, les plus larges possibles, à partir de ces titres d'émissions :

radio 1	radio 2	radio 3
21:00 Hollywood and the Pentagon	**18:30** Have your say! Should monarchy stay?	**18:30** Film of the week: *Suspicion*

2 Vérifiez vos hypothèses

La première écoute doit vous permettre d'apporter des réponses à vos questions.

Éléments à repérer	Objectifs
• **L'environnement sonore** • **Les voix** (leur nombre, homme/femme, enfant/adulte…) • **Les noms propres** • **Les mots** que vous avez anticipés ou que vous connaissez • **L'alternance questions/réponses - accord/désaccord**	• Situer la scène • Identifier les interlocuteurs • Identifier le thème de la conversation • Identifier le type d'échanges

→ À vous

Hollywood and the Pentagon track 35

Écoutez une première fois l'enregistrement et vérifiez vos hypothèses.

3 Affinez vos repérages

Lors d'écoutes successives, vous pourrez recueillir et prendre en notes de nouveaux indices pour affiner votre compréhension. Tirez parti des répétitions et des reformulations, plus fréquentes à l'oral qu'à l'écrit.

Éléments à repérer	Objectifs
	Identifier le contenu informatif du document
• **Qui dit quoi** →	• Déterminer la fonction et le rôle des interlocuteurs
• Les **mots répétés** ou qui appartiennent au **même champ lexical** →	• Identifier l'objet des échanges et préciser le contexte
• **Les mots accentués** • **Les formes négatives** (toujours accentuées) • **Les modaux** quand ils sont accentués *(can, must, may, will...)* →	• Déterminer ce qui est important pour le locuteur : opinion, accord, désaccord, argument.
	Identifier l'attitude des locuteurs
• **L'intonation, le ton** →	• Ton (positif, critique, neutre, humoristique...) • Point de vue (accord, désaccord...) • Sentiments (colère, joie, doute, ironie, tristesse...)
• **Les pauses, les relances** *(you see, don't you think... what about... what I mean...)* →	• Intentions (affirmation, demande d'accord...)

→ À vous

Ré-écoutez l'enregistrement et faites une liste des éléments que vous avez saisis.

track 35

4 Reliez les éléments repérés pour faire du sens

a. Organisez vos notes pour mettre en relation les éléments repérés : de quoi parle-t-on, qui dit quoi, comment et pourquoi ?

b. Utilisez votre bon sens et partez de ce que vous avez compris pour compenser ce que vous n'avez pas reconnu à l'écoute.

→ À vous

Mettez en relation les éléments repérés précédemment et résumez ce que vous avez compris.

Le jour du Bac

Séries ES, S et technologiques

→ voir aussi *Entraînement Bac* p. 50

• Le titre du document vous sera communiqué et ce document sera **en lien avec une des notions** du programme : exploitez ces informations pour émettre vos hypothèses.

• Vous disposerez de 3 écoutes successives : profitez de chacune d'elles pour **enrichir progressivement votre prise de notes**, l'organiser et affiner votre compréhension.

• Essayez de mémoriser le plus d'informations possible.

• Prenez des **notes succinctes**, tout en continuant à écouter.

• Appuyez-vous sur **l'entourage immédiat** des formes qui vous posent problème pour mieux les saisir (sens, catégorie grammaticale).

• Il vous sera demandé, à partir des notes prises lors de l'écoute, d'en faire une restitution par écrit et en français.

• Rédigez cette restitution de manière simple et claire.

Final Tasks

Film reviews

task 1

Writing

Write a war film review

- Write a war film review to be posted on a blog.

You can either choose one of the following, or any other you may have seen.

- *The Thin Red Line*
- *Casualties of War*
- *Apocalypse Now*
- *Starship Troopers*

task 2

Listening

Match film reviews and posters

- Listen to four radio film reviews and match three of them with the corresponding posters on this page.

Bac

Compréhension de l'oral

Listen to an interview:

The Army and the film industry

1. Listen to the document three times and take notes.

2. Write a report in French of what you have understood.

The Pentagon

Expression orale

Oral presentation

1. Using what you have learnt about **American war films**, prepare notes explaining to what extent soldiers can be seen as **heroic figures**.

You can follow these guidelines:

- How soldiers in various wars are represented on screen.
- To what extent do these portraits reflect American attitudes towards different wars.
- Why American soldiers can be seen as emblematic figures.

Illustrate your presentation with relevant examples you may know.

2. Give your oral presentation.

3. Be ready to discuss the topic with your teacher.

→ ***Aide***

Utilisez la fiche *Recap* du workbook p. 42 ou sur www.didierpassword.fr pour préparer cette synthèse orale.

Compréhension de l'écrit

Study a set of documents

Your teacher will give you several documents.

Read them carefully and answer the questions.

Expression écrite

Write two different texts

Using the elements given by your teacher, write:

1. A continuation to the text

2. A contribution to an online forum

Culture File

WAR IN OTHER FORMS OF ART

In groups

1. Choose a document and say what aspects of war it depicts and what the artist's vision of war is.

Whole class

2. Compare the different documents and discuss to what extent each form of art helps convey its message.

1 Poems

Five Ways to Kill a Man

There are many cumbersome ways to kill a man.
You can make him carry a plank of wood
to the top of a hill and nail him to it.
To do this properly you require a crowd of people
wearing sandals, a cock that crows, a cloak
to dissect, a sponge, some vinegar and one
man to hammer the nails home.

Or you can take a length of steel,
shaped and chased in a traditional way,
and attempt to pierce the metal cage he wears.
But for this you need white horses,
English trees, men with bows and arrows,
at least two flags, a prince, and a
castle to hold your banquet in.

Dispensing with nobility, you may, if the wind
allows, blow gas at him. But then you need
a mile of mud sliced through with ditches,
not to mention black boots, bomb craters,
more mud, a plague of rats, a dozen songs
and some round hats made of steel.

In an age of aeroplanes, you may fly
miles above your victim and dispose of him by
pressing one small switch. All you then
require is an ocean to separate you, two
systems of government, a nation's scientists,
several factories, a psychopath and
land that no-one needs for several years.

These are, as I began, cumbersome ways to kill a man.
Simpler, direct, and much more neat is to see
that he is living somewhere in the middle
of the twentieth century, and leave him there.

Edwin Brock (1927-1997), British poet

Death

Nor dread nor hope attend
A dying animal;
A man awaits his end
Dreading and hoping all;
Many times he died,
Many times rose again.
A great man in his pride
Confronting murderous men
Casts derision upon
Supersession of breath;
He knows death to the bone
Man has created death.

William Butler Yeats (1865-1939), Irish poet

2 A song

Civil war

[...]
And I don't need your civil war
It feeds the rich while it buries the poor
Your power hungry sellin' soldiers
In a human grocery store
Ain't that fresh
I don't need your civil war

Look at the shoes you're filling
Look at the blood we're spilling
Look at the world we're killing
The way we've always done before

Look in the doubt we've wallowed
Look at the leaders we've followed
Look at the lies we've swallowed
And I don't want to hear no more

↑ Axl Rose, lead singer for Guns N' Roses, 1993

My hands are tied
For all I've seen has changed my mind
But still the wars go on as the years go by
With no love of God or human rights
'Cause all these dreams are swept aside
By bloody hands of the hypnotized
Who carry the cross of homicide
And history bears the scars of our civil wars
[...]

A song by Guns N' Roses (1991)

3 War comics

↓ The covers of two of the many war comics that were published and widely read during WW2.

UNIT 6 Telecommuting

↑ A telecommuter, enjoying flexibility in working hours and location

Is telecommuting improving our lives?

← **Look** at the photo, its caption and the question above.
Discuss the meaning of the word "telecommuting" and give examples.
Say what you think about it.

FINAL TASKS

P. 128

Promotional campaign

Speaking
Advocate telecommuting

Reading
Identify the target

CULTURE

- Discovering the workplace.
- Discussing the issue of telecommuting.

- Social study:
  - T. Johnson and R. Spitzman, *"Will work from home"*

- Literary works:
  - Joshua Ferris, *Then We Came to the End*
  - Lauren Weisberger, *The Devil Wears Prada*

COMMUNICATION

- Understanding facts and arguments in press articles and personal essays.
- Understanding explicit and implicit meaning in a narrative passage.

Presenting the issue of telecommuting, stating opinions and arguing.

Identifying the main points and opinions in a video and in a radio programme.

TOOLS

★ Words
- At work
- Statistics
- Business
- Work efficiency
- Relationships
- Feelings/personal reactions
- Decision making

★ Pronunciation
- Stressing personal arguments
- Stressing quantities

★ Grammar
- *Modals*
- *Make/have/let someone do sth*

BAC

Stratégies
→ *Lire un texte argumentatif* p. 126

Évaluation
→ *4 situations d'évaluation* p. 129

New trends

1 A virtual company

track 36

A radio programme about telecommuting, Feb 2010

1. **Before listening** to the radio programme, say what you expect to hear.
2. **Listen** and say what you have understood about telecommuting and Laura Schoppe.
3. **Listen again. In groups,** focus on:
   - Laura Schoppe's company, Fuentek *(group 1)*,
   - the advantages of telecommuting *(group 2)*,
   - telecommuting trends *(group 3)*.
4. **React** to this report.

2 Telecommute Nation

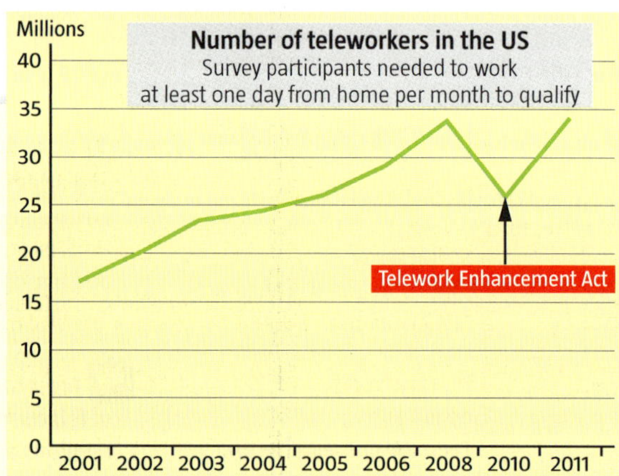

More than 34 million people – equal to the population of Texas and Pennsylvania combined – work from home occasionally. Twice as many could if they wanted. In the next few years, maybe they will.

You know, this would be a good day to work from home. The heat index is 114 degrees[1] today in Washington, D.C. I have to walk half-an-hour to and from work to an office with no better Internet than my living room. Everything I need to write I can fit into a laptop bag, or on a couch.

So why am I writing this article from the desk at *The Atlantic's* office?

Telecommuting, or working from home, is one of those trends that most people talk about as much in the future tense as the present. Only one in twenty formally employed Americans works consistently from home, but the fact that so many of us *could* work fills demographers' eyes with visions of empty cubicles[2] and broadband-blazing living rooms.

Fully 75% of the workforce will be mobile by 2012, the research firm IDC predicted in 2008. Not to be outdone, the Information Technology and Innovation Foundation predicted in 2009 that the number of jobs filled by telecommuters would grow nearly four-fold before 2020. Other studies hold that half of all jobs are receptive to telework, including the vast majority of information technology positions.

That's a lot of stats. In a nutshell: half of us[3] could work remotely if we wanted. Far less do. Why?

Derek Thompson, *The Atlantic*, July 22, 2011

1. about 45 °C
2. cubicles: open space office

3. "half of us" = half of American people with a job

1. **Look at the photo** on the right and read the standfirst of the article p. 116. How can you relate them?
2. **Read the article** and say what you have understood.
3. **a.** Read the article again and **highlight**:
   - information about the writer,
   - statistics about telecommuting.

   page 43

   b. Explain the writer's point.
4. To what extent does the graph illustrate the article? **Discuss** the possible reasons for the trends mentioned in the article.

↑ President Obama signs the Telework Enhancement Act (9 Dec 2010). This law requires the Federal government agencies to maximise the use of flexible work arrangements for their employees.

Recap → Summarize teleworking trends in the US.

page 50

LANGUAGE TOOLS

★ WORDS

At work

- **work**place, **off**ice, home
- staff, **man**ager, boss, ex**ec**utive, CEO (chief executive officer), em**ploy**ers, em**ploy**ees
- flexi**bil**ity: possibility to work either part time or full time; **fle**xible, **sche**dule /ˈʃedjuːl/ *or* /ˈskedjuːl/
- have time off, take a leave, a **ho**liday
- work from home, **te**lework, telecom**mu**te

Statistics

- grow fast, in**crea**se
- an **up**ward trend, a surge, a drop (of about ...% in ...)
- de**crea**se, slow down, drop
- fast, tre**men**dously, **slow**ly, **slight**ly
- **re**gular, slow, dra**ma**tic

★ GRAMMAR → p. 125

Modals

→ Half of us could work remotely if we wanted to.

★ PRONUNCIATION → p. 124

Stressing quantities

→ More than 34 million people work from home occasionally.

TRAINING TASK

Reading the news

**Home working:
Why can't everyone telework?**

The UK government is suggesting people work from home to avoid travel chaos around the 2012 Olympics, but why hasn't teleworking already taken off, asks Tom de Castella.

BBC News magazine, June 2, 2011

2012: Will Information Technology chiefs of staff be more open to telecommuting?

Increasingly [...] more and more companies are making the option available to employees.

Sujit John, Jan 3, 2012
The Times of India

Work-from-home programs still elude smaller workplaces

Although a lot of large companies have some sort of work-from-home program, the concept is still largely absent from many smaller workplaces. Nonetheless, telecommuting is catching on.

Globe and Mail Canada, Sep. 29, 2011

1. Read these headlines.

2. In groups.

a. Discuss their meanings and the possible contents of the corresponding articles.

b. Organise your findings and compare them with the trends in the USA.

Economic opportunities

1 A new business universe

The "Big Bang"

In a perfect world, we'd all sleep late, stay in our pajamas on days we're worn out, and have the time to do exactly what we want. We'd never punch a time clock, attend another meeting, or pick up fast food on the way home from a Little League game[1]. We'd have prepared a fresh salad, pasta sauce, and cupcakes in advance, because we'd have the time. But real life isn't always conducive to such. Instead, we're late to the meeting, we are probably going to miss the first four innings of the game, and afterward, it'll be burgers or pizza. Why can't we turn that luxury-of-time fantasy into a reality?

Um... wait, we can. Suddenly the choices we have to work from home, to set our own schedules, to be our own boss and call the shots are exploding. To borrow from science, what we're seeing is the equivalent of a "Big Bang", and we are dealing with an enormous money-making opportunity. There's a whole new business universe out there, and it's changing the way many women and men work and live.

The myth is that homemakers eat bonbons, watch soaps[2] and take care of the kids. The reality is that there's a new revolution of people staying home these days and they are doing a lot more than folding laundry; they are moms and dads, new grads and grandparents, skilled professionals, and high powered executives.

These individuals are finding more energy, more time, more ways to make money, and yes, they are doing it their way. So, if working from home is where your heart is, you are in the right place. It's definitely the right time. [...]

"Is it really possible? Can I really stay at home and make money?" We've heard that question asked by thousands of women and men across the country. Our resounding answer is "Yes!". This is the perfect time because the world is growing and changing. It's less restrictive and more inclusive, less traditional and more innovative. [...]

Not only has the Internet revolutionized the way we work and live, but it has created an alternative job market, new job descriptions and new opportunities. Think Chefs only work in restaurants? Meet Jennifer Beisser, CEO of ChefsLine, a business that supplies "on demand culinary advice for busy cooks". Clients find the service online, but they use the phone line to connect with a chef who will share personalised advice, step-by-step cooking instructions, and those little touches that can turn an ordinary dinner into fine cuisine. That chef who is providing the advice is doing so from his or her own home. [...]

Are you ready to rocket?

Want to explore today's work-from-home job market? It's fast, easy, and so much bigger than you can imagine. Just let your fingers do the walking... across your keyboard. There's no limit to your reach. The world is your oyster. ■

T. Johnson and R. Spitzman, *Will Work from Home* (2008)

1. Little League Baseball organizes youth baseball games. - **2. soaps** (*abbr.* soap operas): popular TV series.

1. Before reading: how do you relate "A new business universe" and the advert above?

2. Read the text and explain what you have understood about the "Big Bang" and its consequences.

3. Read the text again.

a. Define the "revolution" referred to in line 34.

b. Identify the writers' opinion on teleworking; highlight the arguments and examples given.

pages 44-45

c. Discuss the purpose of the text.

4. Comment on the last sentence: *"The world is your oyster"*.

2 "I got nothing done today"

track 37

A lecture by Jason Fried, a young web entrepreneur

Opinion poll
Q: What benefits is your company realizing from telecommuting?

Greater worker productivity	67%
Access to more qualified staff	39%
Improves employee retention	37%
Improves employee health	25%
Reduced highway use	18%
Environmental benefits	17%

1. Before listening, discuss who might have said *"I got nothing done today"* and why.

2. Listen to Jason Fried and say what you have understood.

3. a. Listen again and focus on his description of:
- a day at the office,
- the impact on the employees' feelings and productivity.

b. Summarize Jason Fried's opinion.

4. Study the opinion poll above. To what extent does it illustrate Jason Fried's point?

Recap → What is the economic impact of teleworking? page 50

LANGUAGE TOOLS

★ WORDS

Business
- help/boost **bus**iness, de**vel**op oppor**tu**nities, ex**pand**
- earn **mo**ney, make **mo**ney, earn a **li**ving /ˈlɪvɪŋ/
- save **mo**ney, cut costs
- **wa**ges, **sa**lary, **in**come

Work efficiency
- pro**duc**tive, **fo**cused, ener**ge**tic, com**mit**ted
- **in**novative, cre**a**tive
- **trust**worthy, re**li**able, **care**less, de**pen**dable ≠ unre**li**able
- **heal**thy ≠ un**heal**thy, stressed
- **be**nefit

→ I'll certainly benefit from the situation but it will benefit the company too.

★ GRAMMAR → p. 125

Make/have/let someone do sth

★ PRONUNCIATION → p. 124

Stressing personal arguments

TRAINING TASK

Argue your case!

You want to convince your employer to let you work from home.

1. In groups: find at least three arguments and illustrate them with examples.

2. Argue your case, emphasizing the important points.

Different relationships

Office life

↑ Still from the TV series *The Office*, 2010

The narrator remembers his working days in a white-collar[1] office.

We were fractious[2] and overpaid. Our mornings lacked promise. [...] Most of us liked most everyone, a few of us hated specific individuals, one or two people loved everyone and everything. [...] Karen Woo always had something new to tell us and we hated her guts for it. She would start talking and our eyes would glaze over. Might it be true, as we sometimes feared, on the commute home, that we were callous, unfeeling individuals, incapable of sympathy, and full of spite toward people for no reason other than their proximity or familiarity? We had these sudden revelations that employment, the daily nine-to-five, was driving us far from our better selves. Should we quit? Would that solve it? Or were those qualities innate, dooming us to nastiness and paucity[3] of spirit? We hoped not. [...]

In those days it wasn't rare for someone to push someone else down the hall really fast in a swivel chair. Games aside, we spent most of our time inside long silent pauses as we bent over our individual desks, working on some task at hand, lost to it – until Benny, bored, came and stood in the doorway. "What are you up to?" he'd ask.

It could have been any of us. "Working" was the usual reply.

Then Benny would tap his topaz class ring on the doorway and drift away.

How we hated our coffee mugs! Our mouse pads, our desk clocks, our daily calendars, the contents of our desk drawers. Even the photos of our loved ones taped to our computer monitors for uplift and support turned into cloying[4] reminders of time served. But when we got a new office, a bigger office, and we brought everything with us into the new office, how we loved everything all over again, and thought hard about where to place things, and looked with satisfaction at the end of the day at how well our old things looked in this new, improved, important space. There was no doubt in our minds just then that we had made all the right decisions, whereas most days we were men and women of two minds. Everywhere we looked, in the hallways and bathrooms, the coffee bar and the cafeteria, the lobbies and the print stations, there we were with our two minds. [...]

Some days we met in the kitchen [...] to eat lunch. There was only room for eight at the table. If all the seats were full, Jim Jackers would have to eat his sandwich from the sink and try to engage from over in that direction. It was fortunate for us in that he could pass us a spoon or a packet of salt if we needed it.

"It is really irritating," Tom Mota said to the table, "to work with irritating people."

"Screw you, Tom," Marta replied. [...]

We had visceral, rich memories of dull, interminable hours. Then a day would pass in perfect harmony with our projects, our family members, and our co-workers, and we couldn't believe we were getting paid for this.

Joshua Ferris,
***Then We Came to the End* (2007)**

1. white collar: office worker (≠ blue collar: workers involved in manual, industrial jobs)
2. fractious: irritable - **3. paucity:** poverty - **4. cloying:** nauseating

1. Look at the photograph and the title of the text p. 120: what do they evoke to you?

2. Read the text. Say what you have understood and discuss who the narrator may be.

3. a. Pick out particular office situations as described in the text. In pairs, choose one and get ready to talk about it.
b. Discuss what they reveal about office workers' conditions and relationships.

4. a. Explain line 51: *"Most days we were men and women of two minds"*.
b. Explain the use of "we" throughout the text.

5. Look at the two cartoons below: **discuss** their meanings and explain how they can relate to the text.

Recap → List the advantages and drawbacks of telecommuting in terms of personal and social relationships.

page 50

TELEWORKING WAS THE DEATH OF THE OFFICE PARTY

LANGUAGE TOOLS

★ WORDS

Relationships

- have **per**sonal rel**a**tionships, make friends
- be on good/bad/**friend**ly terms with, get al**o**ng with
- have fun with, bel**ong** to a group, share ≠ feel **lo**nely
- chat, **go**ssip, joke
- to**ge**ther ≠ al**one**
- **co**lleagues, **co**-workers

TRAINING TASK

Have your say!

Participate in an online survey about E-learning: *Would you like to study online?*

Post your answer, organizing your arguments.

Does it suit everyone?

1 "Not commuting is driving me crazy"

http://topics.telecommuting-ask-annie

File Edit View Favorites Tools Help

e-mail to Annie By **Harried Homebody** – June 11, 2010

Dear Annie: I'm in an awkward situation that reminds me of Oscar Wilde's famous remark about the two tragedies in life. ("One is not getting what you want, and the other is getting it.")

I'm a graphic designer at a large ad agency, and for years I made the long trek every day from a distant suburb to my office in a major city. I have two school-age children and assorted pets and relatives hanging around, and I was leaving so early in the morning and getting home so late at night that I never saw my family.

After much arguing, wheedling, and cajoling, I finally convinced my boss that – thanks in large part to all the gee-whiz technology we have now – I could work at home and be even more productive than I already was. He reluctantly agreed to let me do it.

That was about six months ago and I realized after a few weeks that it was a mistake. My productivity hasn't suffered, but it's driving me crazy to be home all day, putting up with endless distractions. I also miss my colleagues.

The funny thing is, my boss thinks this arrangement is working out so well that he already turned my old office into a second conference room. If I go back to him now and say I want to come back to work at the office, I'm going to feel like an idiot. What should I do?

Recommend

Sign up for the Ask Annie e-mail answer

Talkback – Annie's answer

Dear H.H.: If it's any consolation, you're not the only one struggling with this dilemma. "Everybody who doesn't work from home thinks it sounds like heaven, so people are often embarrassed to admit that they find it very difficult," observes anthropologist and urban planner Ziona Strelitz. [...]

About 42 million people, or roughly one-third of the U.S. workforce, now works from home at least one or two days a week. Some firms encourage employees to do so to save overhead costs, while many employees (you, for instance) telecommute hoping to advance their careers without sacrificing time with their families. Yet in researching a study on work-life balance, Strelitz found that full-time telecommuting isn't always a panacea. "Large numbers of people want and need an office to go to," she says.

What's so great about going to an office? Lots of things, as you've discovered. First, most workplaces don't feature barking dogs, importunate relatives, or offspring who urgently need a ride to soccer practice just when you've got a deadline looming.

More important, "most employees want a workplace for its stimulus, its implicit messages of professionalism and being 'at work,'" Strelitz notes. "In addition, you get access to a wide range of skills, ideas and personalities. People working together energize each other." [...]

One thing you probably miss is the chance to bounce ideas off colleagues in casual conversation. Strelitz's study found that people who work in an office tend to have influential mentors, and to be offered valuable opportunities that arise from being seen around the place, something people who work from home miss out on.

Full-time telecommuters in this economy may also fear that "out of sight, out of mind" makes their jobs less secure. Whether or not that's true, the worry is an added source of a stress at a time when most people already have more than enough.

Moreover, working alongside others can offer another real benefit - a sense of camaraderie. In survey after survey, employees give something like "I like the people I work with" as the main reason they are satisfied with their jobs.

Strelitz knows how draining a long commute can be: she used to commute an hour and a half each way between Princeton, N.J., and New York City. But her research suggests that, as you've found out, working at home can be just as exasperating in its own way, since, she says, "multitasking personal and work responsibilities is usually difficult, if not impossible."

So what should you do? First, stop feeling like an idiot: The problems you've encountered are perfectly normal. Second, swallow your pride and tell your boss you want to come back to the fold.

1. **Have a quick look at the document** p. 122 and say what you expect to read.
2. **Read Harried Homebody's e-mail**. Say what you have understood about her present and past situations. page 45
3. **Explain** the opening paragaph of her e-mail.
4. **Read Annie's answer**: what is her attitude to Harried?
5. Read Annie's answer again. **Pick out** the advantages and drawbacks of working in an office according to Ziona Strelitz.
6. **Explain** why "telecommuting isn't always a panacea".

2 The pros and cons of telecommuting

video 10

Mr Flexible Job, May 2011

LANGUAGE TOOLS

★ WORDS

Feelings/personal reactions
- feel em**ba**rrassed, **aw**kward, un**ea**sy ≠ enthusi**a**stic, thrilled a**bout**
- suit /suːt/, fit, **sui**table ≠ un**sui**table

Decision making
- choice, **o**ption, al**ter**native
- be of two minds about, **he**sitate, con**si**der, toy with the i**de**a

→ It was a difficult decision to make.

1. **Look at the title**: what can you guess about the video?
2. **Watch the video** and say what you have understood.
3. Watch again. **In groups** pick out:
   - the pros of telecommuting *(group 1)*,
   - the cons of telecommuting *(group 2)*.
4. Which argument did you find the most convincing? Explain why.

Recap → Explain why telecommuting does not necessarily suit everyone. Give examples. page 50

TRAINING TASK

Circular debate

Telecommuting should be a right for all employees.

Group work

Find arguments in favour of or against the motion:
- one person gives an argument for *(group 1)*,
- somebody reacts, giving an argument against *(group 2)*,
- and so on.

★ WORDS

❶ Linking and organizing your ideas

Use the following link words to complete the sentences below:
• while - for instance - despite - that's why - and yet - although

1. ... a lot of people could work from home if they wanted, not many do.
2. Laura works from home on Wednesdays, ... you did not find her at her office when you called last Wednesday.
3. Teleworking has been around for years in the US, ... in France the concept is still largely absent from many workplaces.
4. Telecommuting benefits the environment, ... it reduces pollution and fuel consumption.
5. Harried really wanted to work from home, ... now that she does she misses her colleagues.
6. ... the fact that I could be even more productive if I worked from home, my boss is very reluctant to let me do it.

❷ Describing changes

a. Link adjectives to nouns in order to find as many expressions as possible.

adjectives	nouns
fresh, dramatic, slow, effective, quick, slight, impressive, striking, sudden, constant, regular, eventful, tremendous, sharp	shift, trend, transition, adaptation, evolution, improvement, effect, revolution, start, increase, drop

→ *a slight improvement*

b. Use some of these expressions to depict changes that have taken place since the IT revolution.

❸ Talking about telecommuting

Bac

a. In the following list, sort out the words referring to the positive/the negative aspects of telecommuting.
• suit, deprive, fit, ineffective, useful, hamper, appropriate, inadequate, discourage, allow, adapted, hinder, prevent, stimulate, convenient, encourage, hold back, help, deter, unsuitable

b. Use them to talk about telecommuting.

★ PRONUNCIATION

❹ Stressing personal arguments

track 38

You can't ask people to be creative and efficient in just fifteen minutes. I certainly need long, uninterrupted periods of time to process information and consider suitable solutions to a problem.

Pour insister sur certains arguments, le locuteur peut choisir d'accentuer plus fortement certains mots.

a. Listen to the following passage. Say which arguments are emphasized.

track 39

Is it really possible? Can I really stay at home and make money? Yes! This is the perfect time because the world is growing and changing. It's less restrictive and more inclusive, less traditional and more innovative. Not only has the Internet revolutionized the way we work and live, but it has created an alternative job market, new job descriptions and new opportunities.

b. Compare with your classmates, then listen again and check.

c. Practise reading the passage aloud.

❺ Stressing quantities

track 40

More than 34 million people work from home occasionally and twice as many could in the next few years. Telecommuting is one of those trends that most people talk about as much in the future tense as the present.

Les quantifieurs sont toujours accentués car ils apportent des informations essentielles.

a. Listen to the following sentences, paying attention to the way quantifiers are stressed. Practise reading them aloud.

track 41

1. Only one in twenty formally employed Americans works from home, but the fact that so many of us could do so is an interesting perspective.
2. That's a lot of stats. In a nutshell: half of us could work remotely if we wanted. Far less do.
3. Although a lot of large companies have some sort of work-from-home program, the concept is still largely absent from many smaller workplaces.

b. Practise in your workbook. pages 46-47

★ GRAMMAR

Modals

Observe

a. All the surveys show that in the US, IT employees may work from home but only if their bosses agree.
b. Not everyone can telework today as most employers still refuse this possibility.
c. Workers should adopt more flexible working times if they want to increase their production.
d. Small businesses must adapt to current trends if they want to survive.

1. American workers may all telework one day, who knows?
2. Telecommuting could become a real revolution if most people accept it.
3. Staying at the office only a few days a week should become common soon.
4. Obliging a whole team to work from home must be hard to impose.

Que pouvez-vous dire du sens des modaux dans les phrases *a, b, c, d* et dans les phrases *1, 2, 3, 4* ? Comparez puis concluez.

→ Grammaire ⑬ p. 201

Practise

6 Rewrite the following sentences using a modal.

1. I advise your employees to work from home. → *Your employees...*
2. The trainees are allowed to leave earlier. → *The trainees...*
3. Telecommuting is now a possibility for most employees. → *Now most employees...*
4. Chief executives are obliged to work more efficiently. → *Chief executives...*

7 Classify these headlines according to the meanings of the modals used.

Can't allocate enough time for work? Then this is the right job for you!
Telecommuting may not change your life dramatically, but still, why not try it?
Today's workers must adapt or quit!
A bachelor's degree in nursing can help you become a medical telecommuter.
Always dreamt of working from home? Now you may!
Afraid of working from home? You shouldn't!
Why it must be so hard to work in and out...

Make/have/let somebody do sth

Observe

1. My boss lets me work from home one day a week, which is a great opportunity for me. But he often makes me work on Saturdays and I can't stand it.
2. Telecommuting makes people more responsible because they must keep to their schedules.
3. Our chief executive has us attend many conferences. We feel it's a waste of time but if we tell him he'll make us go or quit.
4. She wants to quit her job as a public relations assistant because her boss has her serve coffee during meetings. But she also lets her work from home when it's possible and never makes her work late in the evening. So it's not that bad, don't you think?

Observez les formes verbales soulignées. Quelles différences de sens expriment-elles?

→ Grammaire ㉒ p. 210

Practise

8 Rewrite the following sentences using the appropriate structures.

1. Our employer obliged us to go to that international meeting.
2. My boss allowed me to work from home.
3. His manager has accepted his decision to work part-time: he is so glad!
4. I organize teleconferencing because the client asked me to, but I prefer proper meetings.
5. Although I was really hot, I had to close the window because my colleague had a cold.
6. The CEO asked us to meet our partners abroad and we did so.

9 An employee writes a letter to his trade union to complain about his working conditions. He explains what the boss obliges him to do and then lists what he and his workmates would like the boss to let them do.

More exercises in your Workbook → p. 47

Comprendre un texte argumentatif

Dans un texte argumentatif l'auteur, le narrateur, ou l'un des personnages exprime son opinion et la justifie.

Choice of a lifestyle

For my job, I work two days a week in an office, and the rest of the time from home. To me, this offers a perfect balance between having a job and maintaining a happy personal life.

On the one hand, when I am at home I work at my own rhythm. If I have errands to run, or shopping to do, or the kids to pick up from school, I can do it and still find time to get my job done. That, to me, is an invaluable freedom. On the other hand, some things are best discussed in person with one's colleagues, so those two other days are welcome.

When I do go into the office, however, I always notice how much less stressed I am than many of my colleagues, despite having the same amount of work as them. What is stressing them, I therefore conclude, is not the work itself, but the way they are working. Because they are always in the office, and have no time for other things, their entire life is under pressure.

My situation, nevertheless, has involved other kinds of sacrifice. In our society, we are encouraged to measure success in two ways – salary and job title. My conscious choice was to measure my success *not* by salary or position but by my lifestyle. Not everyone will agree with me, but I know which I think is the most important.

Rupert Morgan (2012)

1 Préparez-vous à une lecture active

Faites-vous rapidement une première idée du thème et de la problématique du texte ci-dessus.

Étapes	Exemples
1. Repérez et lisez : • **les éléments périphériques** (titre, source, illustration...) pour avoir une idée du thème, • **la mise en page** (paragraphes, présence de dialogue...), • **le début des paragraphes** pour repérer les champs lexicaux.	→ *Choice of a lifestyle – 2012* = plusieurs styles de vie possibles → plusieurs paragraphes = plusieurs idées développées = plusieurs éléments de réponse à la problématique → *job, work, office, home*
2. À partir des éléments repérés, anticipez le thème et la problématique.	• thème : choix de vie • quelle place pour le travail dans la vie ? À la maison ou au bureau ?
3. Faites des liens entre vos premières hypothèses et votre connaissance du sujet.	→ avantages et inconvénients du travail au bureau / à la maison ; télétravail

→ À vous

Préparez-vous à faire une lecture active d'un texte : pages 48-49
ou ▶ www.didierpassword.fr

2 Identifiez les opinions et leurs justifications

Lisez le texte *Choice of a lifestyle* et appuyez-vous sur le repérage de certains éléments :

Éléments à repérer	Exemples
Les opinions • les éléments indiquant clairement que l'auteur exprime son opinion	→ *To me, I think, my choice...*
• les termes « positifs » ou « négatifs »	→ *invaluable freedom, best, most important, other kinds of sacrifice...*
• les sentiments et réactions (adjectifs, modaux, formes d'insistance...)	→ *perfect, happy* → *what is stressing them, I therefore conclude...* → *success not by salary...*
Les mots de liaison... • qui permettent d'expliquer de manière logique une opinion (cause, conséquence...)	→ *so, because, therefore*
• qui permettent de nuancer l'opinion (concession)	→ *but, however, despite, nevertheless*
• qui introduisent deux points de vue différents	→ *on the one hand.... on the other hand...*
Les justifications de l'opinion • les paragraphes : chaque paragraphe correspond souvent à une justification de l'opinion	→ *the way they are working (at the office) is stressing them*
• les arguments : l'auteur explique son opinion	→ *when I am at home I work at my own rhythm*
• les exemples : l'auteur illustre ce qu'il dit en citant des faits	→ *If I have errands to run, or shopping to do, or the kids to pick up from school, I can do it and still find time to get my job done.*

→ À vous

Identifiez les opinions et leurs justifications dans le texte : pages 48-49 **ou** ▶ www.didierpassword.fr

Le jour du Bac

Toutes séries

→ voir aussi : *Entraînement Bac* p. 70 et 92

• Un, deux ou trois textes **en lien avec une notion du programme** pourront vous être proposés.

• À l'issue de la première lecture, demandez-vous **quel est le but du texte** :
- raconter une histoire, vraie ou fictive (texte narratif) ?
- présenter et expliquer des faits de manière neutre (texte explicatif) ?
- exprimer une opinion et inciter le lecteur à s'engager dans un débat (texte argumentatif) ?

• Pour gagner du temps, **organisez vos repérages** : surlignez en deux couleurs :
- les arguments qui expliquent l'opinion soutenue ;
- les arguments contraires présentés.

• **Associez** le thème abordé dans le texte à l'une des quatre notions du programme.

• **Identifiez l'idée principale** de chaque paragraphe : aidez-vous des champs lexicaux.

• Si une phrase vous semble longue et complexe, **réduisez-la** pour en comprendre le sens général : nom sujet - verbe - nom complément.

• **Reformulez** avec vos propres mots les expressions ou les passages difficiles.

FINAL TASKS

Promotional campaign

task 1

Speaking

Advocate telecommuting

You are taking part in a radio campaign to boost telecommuting.

1. Get ready

- **Work in pairs.** Choose who you want to target: employers or employees.
- List the arguments and examples you are going to use.

2. Action!

- Address the people you want to persuade.
- Be lively and sound convincing. Don't read your notes.

task 2

Reading

Identify the target

- Your teacher will give you a series of texts promoting telecommuting. Read them and identify which of these groups each text is aimed at:

administrators | business managers | environmentalists

Bac

Compréhension de l'oral

Listen to a speech:
Work-life delicate balance

1. Listen to the document three times and take notes.

2. Write a report in French of what you have understood.

Expression orale

Oral presentation

1. Using what you have learnt in this chapter, prepare notes explaining how **technological progress** changes working conditions.
You can follow those guidelines:
- Information Technologies → new opportunities.
- Telecommuting → new daily routine, new lifestyle.
- Impact on personal and social relationships.

Illustrate your presentation with relevant examples.

2. Give your oral presentation.

3. Be ready to discuss the topic.

→ **Aide**

Utilisez la fiche *Recap* du workbook p. 50 ou sur www.didierpassword.fr pour préparer cette synthèse orale.

Compréhension de l'écrit

Study a set of documents

Your teacher will give you several documents. Read them carefully and answer the questions.

Expression écrite

Write two different texts

Using the elements given by your teacher, write:

1. A post to have your say

2. A newspaper article

Good reads

"I knew I had the job"

↑ A still from *The Devil Wears Prada*, 2006

Andrea Sachs has been looking for a job and gets an interview at the plush Manhattan offices of* Runway*, the world's most fashionable magazine. She meets several assistants and then the editor, Miranda Priestly.

Since I'd never seen so much as a picture of Miranda Priestly, I was surprised to see how willowy she was. The hand she held out was small-boned, feminine, soft. She had to turn her head upward to look me in the eye, although she did not stand to greet me. Her expertly dyed blond hair was pulled back in a chic knot, deliberately loose enough to look casual but still supremely neat, and while she did not smile, she did not appear particularly intimidating. She seemed rather gentle and somewhat fragile behind her ominous black desk, and although she did not invite me to sit, I felt comfortable enough to claim one of the uncomfortable black chairs that faced her. And it was then I noticed: she was watching me intently, mentally noting my attempts at grace and propriety with what seemed like amusement. Condescending and awkward, yes, but not, I decided, particularly mean-spirited. She spoke first.

"What brings you to *Runway*, Ahn-dre-ah?" she asked in her upper-crust British accent, never taking her eyes away from mine.

"Well, I interviewed with Sharon, and she told me that you're looking for an assistant," I started, my voice a little shaky. When she nodded, my confidence increased slightly. "And now, after meeting with Emily, Allison, and Cheryl, I feel like I have a clear understanding of the kind of person you're looking for, and I'm confident I'd be perfect for the job," I said, remembering Cheryl's words. She looked amused for a moment but seemed unfazed[1].

It was at this point that I began to want the job most desperately, in the way people yearn for things they consider unattainable. It might not be akin to getting into law school or having an essay published in a campus journal, but it was, in my starved-for-success mind, a real challenge – a challenge because I was an imposter, and not a very good one at that. I had known the minute I stepped on the *Runway* floor that I didn't belong. My clothes and hair were wrong for sure, but more glaringly out of place was my attitude. I didn't know anything about fashion and I didn't *care*. At all. And therefore, I had to have it. Besides, a million girls would die for this job.

I continued to answer her questions about myself with a forthrightness and confidence that surprised me. There wasn't time to be intimidated. After all, she seemed pleasant enough and I, amazingly, knew nothing to the contrary. We stumbled a bit when she inquired about any foreign languages I spoke. When I told her I knew Hebrew, she paused, pushed her palms flat on her desk and said icily, "Hebrew? I was hoping for French, or at least something more useful." I almost apologized, but stopped myself.

"Unfortunately, I don't speak a word of French, but I'm confident it won't be a problem." She clasped her hands back together.

"It says here that you studied at Brown[2]?"

"Yes, I, uh, I was an English major, concentrating on creative writing. Writing has always been a passion." *So cheesy*, I reprimanded myself. *Did I really have to use the word 'passion'?*

"So, does your affinity for writing mean that you're not particularly interested in fashion?" She took a sip of sparkling liquid from a glass and set it down quietly. One quick glance at the glass showed that she was the kind of woman who could drink without leaving one of those disgusting lipstick marks. She would always have perfectly lined and filled-in lips regardless of the hour.

"Oh no, of course not. I adore fashion": I lied rather smoothly. "I'm looking forward to learning even more about it, since I think it would be wonderful to write about fashion one day." Where the hell had I come up with that one? This was becoming an out-of-body experience.

Things progressed with the same relative ease until she asked her final question: Which magazines did I read regularly? I leaned forward eagerly and began to speak: "Well, I only subscribe to *The New Yorker* and *Newsweek*, but I regularly read *The Buzz*. Sometimes *Time*, but it's dry, and *US News* is way too conservative. Of course, as a guilty pleasure, I'll skim *Chic*, and since I just returned from traveling, I read all of the travel magazines and..."

"And do you read *Runway*, Ahn-dre-ah?" she interrupted, leaning over the desk and peering at me even more intently than before.

It had come so quickly, so unexpectedly, that for the first time that day I was caught off-guard. I didn't lie, and I didn't elaborate or even attempt to explain.

"No."

After perhaps ten seconds of stony silence, she beckoned for Emily to escort me out. I knew I had the job.

Lauren Weisberger,
The Devil Wears Prada
(2003)

1. unfazed: not confused
2. Brown University is a private Ivy League university

Lauren Weisberger (born 1977)

American novelist. Author of the 2003 bestseller The Devil Wears Prada*, a novel inspired by her first job experience at the fashion magazine* Vogue*. Based on the novel, a movie of the same name was released in June 2006, starring Meryl Streep and Anne Hathaway.*

UNIT 7 Museum restitution

Moai **(stone statue), from Easter Island, Polynesia, around AD 1000.**
British Museum, London.

Whose cultural treasure is it?

Look at the photo, its caption and the question above.
Discuss what the expression "cultural treasure" means.
Suggest an answer to the question.

FINAL TASKS

P. 146

TV debates

Speaking
Debate and have your say!

Listening
Choose partners for your debating team

CULTURE	COMMUNICATION	TOOLS
• Exploring the debate over museum restitution. • Learning about the meaning of cultural artefacts: - in their countries of origin, - where they are displayed. • Social study: Kwame Opoku, *"When will Britain return looted golden Ghanaian artefacts?"* • Literary work: Janet Frame, *You Are Now Entering the Human Heart*	Discussing the issue of restitution, giving arguments and examples. Identifying the main points and opinions in a documentary or a news report. Understanding opinions and arguments in articles.	**★ Words** • Restitution • Museums • Pillage • Agreement/Disagreement • Heritage • Virtual repatriation • Identity **★ Pronunciation** • Intonation in rhetorical questions • Linking up words **★ Grammar** • Rhetorical questions • *Talk sb into doing sth*

Bac

Stratégies
→ *Défendre un point de vue, justifier, convaincre* p. 144

Évaluation
→ *4 situations d'évaluation* p. 147

The issue of restitution

1 "Return our artefacts!"

http://www.sciencebuzz.org

Even before the word "archaeology" was invented, people have been removing artefacts from their original context — or location. Objects have been taken to be sold for profit, saved as souvenirs, and put in museums. Often, historically important artefacts that have been placed in large, national museums have become points of national pride. Think of the Egyptian Rosetta Stone in the British Museum, or the Greek "Nike of Samothrace" at the Louvre in Paris (the French call it the "Winged Victory of Samothrace").

↑ The Nike of Samothrace

In the past few decades, some governments have politely asked for objects that they feel have been pillaged from their countries to be returned. During the 2004 Summer Olympics in Athens, Greece attempted to pressure Great Britain for the return of the displaced Parthenon or "Elgin marbles" by announcing the building of a brand new museum for them, the Acropolis Museum. Italy recently returned an obelisk that was taken from Ethiopia just before World War II.

Recently however, the demand for the return of these has taken a more formal, and perhaps less polite, turn. Egypt recently announced that

↑ The Elgin Marbles

it has decided to sue two museums, one in England and one in Belgium for the return of two pharaonic reliefs — or tomb carvings. Egypt says that if the museums don't return the artefacts in question, archaeologists who work in those museums will not be allowed to continue digging in the "Land of the Pharaohs". [...]

Some archaeologists are nervous that the return of the Elgin marbles or the Rosetta Stone will open the "flood-gates" for the return of hundreds if not thousands of artefacts. Museums like the British Museum have argued that they not only promote scientific research on these objects, but having them in places like London, Paris, and New York allows millions of visitors to come and visit them every year. Others argue that it is important for countries to have the objects which reflect their cultural heritage and national history in their own museums.

Detail from the Rosetta stone →

1. **Before reading**, look at the pictures on this page and say what you know or would like to know about these objects.
2. **Read the blog above** and discuss what you have understood.
3. **Read again and identify**:
   - what happened to the objects mentioned;
   - where they come from and where they are now;
   - what some governments have asked and how;
   - the reactions to their demands.
4. **Share** your findings.

2 Maori head repatriated to New Zealand

video 11

A New Zealand TV documentary, 2011

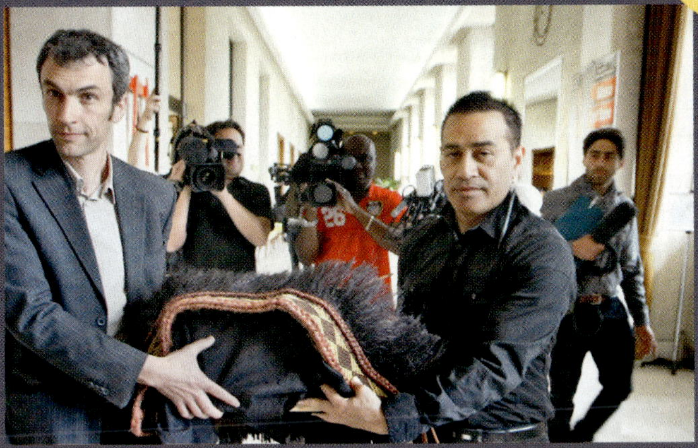

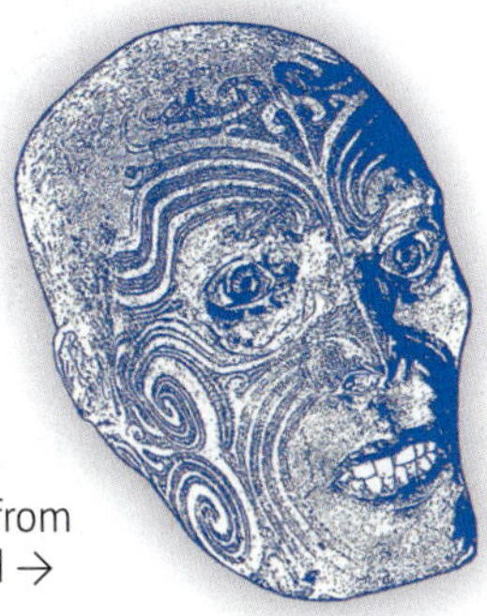

Drawing of a tattoed Maori head from New Zealand →

1. **Before watching**, say what you know about Maoris and New Zealand.
2. **Watch the video** and say what you have understood.
3. **In groups**. Watch again and pick out information about:
   - the event that took place in France in May, 2011 and why;
   - the past story of the Maori head;
   - what will happen to the head from now on.
4. **Share** your findings.

Recap → Comment on this quotation: "Cultural sensitivities have changed". page 54

LANGUAGE TOOLS

★ **WORDS**

Restitution
- re**turn**, hand **o**ver, give back, hand back, res**to**re
- po**ssess**, own
- repatri**a**tion, re**co**very

Museums
- cu**ra**tor, regis**trar**
- exhi**bi**tion, **gal**lery,
- mu**seum** piece, **ar**tefact, loan from a museum
- ex**hi**bit, dis**play**
- **vi**sit

Pillage
- steal, raid, loot *(piller)*, **plun**der, ap**pro**priate
- de**spoil**, **de**secrate: show disrespect for something sacred
- **van**dalism, **loo**ting, spoli**a**tion

TRAINING TASK

A two-minute talk

1. Choose one of the objects on page 134 (the Elgin Marbles, the Rosetta Stone or the Nike of Samothrace).
Search the Internet to find out more about it: what its use was, when it was removed, how, why, etc.

2. Give the class a brief talk about the object.

↑ The Nike of Samothrace being removed

Conflicting points of view

1 The "property of humankind"?

When will Britain return looted golden Ghanaian artefacts?

Many of the stolen/looted Asante items are in the Wallace Collection.

The British do not appear to be in the mood to discuss the return of some of these looted objects to Ghana. [...]

The justification presented in the House of Lords debate was that the looted items were part of an indemnity agreed to by the Asantehene Kofi Karkari[1]. So the Asantes are to pay for a war they did not start against a European power that came from thousands of miles from Europe to attack the Asante. [...]

"The British Museum said yesterday that its trustees[2] had no power to dispose of such material as the regalia. That was forbidden under the British Museum Act, 1963. The museum said there would probably have to be a special Act of Parliament to allow the return of the objects". [...]

The Parliament says you have to talk directly to the museum and the museum says an act of parliament prevents it from returning any object. [...]

The invitation to Africans to view the display of looted African cultural artefacts [in Western countries] is also an invitation to put a distance between themselves and the culture that produced those objects or at least to recognize such a distance in time and space. Normally, others should not be showing me my cultural artefacts. I should be showing them my cultural objects. The French do not show the British, British cultural artefacts. Normally, I should not travel thousands of miles to other countries and continents to see the icons of my culture. Others should come to my country to see my culture. But with respect to African culture, the situation has been reversed by the West to such an extent that what would generally be considered as perverse is becoming normal. This is also part of the general scheme to appropriate all useful and valuable African material culture and other materials whether this be gold or diamond and to present them as part of the property of humankind. Thus most African cultural objects are now being presented as part of the cultural heritage of mankind and thus entitling all to possess them. The West contests the right of Africans to seek the return of the looted treasures. Unfortunately, even some highly educated Africans and peoples of African descent are beginning to accept and propagate the Western idea that African artefacts are better kept in the West. The alienation of the African from his land, property and culture that was begun in the colonial days seems to be making tremendous progress since Independence. [...]

↑ Gold mask seized by the British from Ghana, in 1874 and now in London.

These treasures are of great research and educational value. They embody in them silent testimony of the expanse of influences that went into the making of our civilization. Also most of the regalia depict symbols in which one may find the summation of our ancestors' teachings on political life, and of their moral, social and political philosophies. Thus, while to their present owners and admirers abroad, these may be at best exotic, artistic and romantic value, to us, they hold the key to the wisdom and even the history of our ancestors." ■

Dr Kwame Opoku, 5/01/2011
www.modernghana.com

The Asante Empire was a state in West Africa which became part of Ghana.

▶ **1874**: the British colonize parts of the country and appropriate artefacts including the "Asante regalia" (the traditional clothes and decorations worn by royals).

▶ **1957**: Ghana gains its independence.

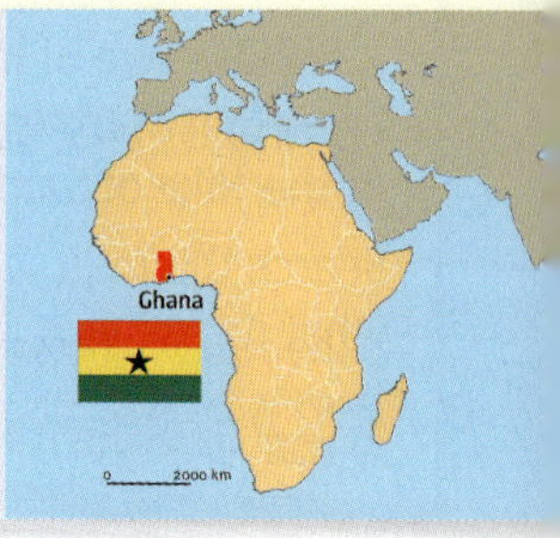

1. King of the Asante Empire at war with the British in 1874
2. administrators

1. **Before reading**, explain the link between the title or the article p. 136 and the information provided on Ghana.
2. **Read the article** and say what you have understood.
3. **Read again and highlight:**
   - the reasons why the items have not been returned;
   - what they represent for the British and for Dr Opoku;
   - Dr Opoku's arguments in favour of restitution;
   - other African people's opinions. page 51
4. **Share** your findings and explain Dr Opoku's point of view.

2 Radio debate

track 45

Should works of art be rapatriated?

1. **Before listening**, say what arguments you expect to hear.
2. **Listen** to the radio programme.
   a. **List the arguments**.
   b. **Share** your findings.
3. **Classify** the arguments and **discuss** them.

Recap → List the arguments for and against restitution.
Explain which arguments are the most important in your opinion. page 54

LANGUAGE TOOLS

★ WORDS

Agreement
- ac**cord**, under**stan**ding, as**sent**
- sup**port**, de**fend**, ad**mit**, com**ply**

Disagreement
- dis**sen**sion, dis**pute**, strife, con**tro**versy
- **dif**fer, dis**sent**, de**ny**, re**fute**, con**test**

Heritage
- **trea**sure, **le**gacy, in**he**ritance, **pa**trimony, es**tate**, **an**cestry

★ PRONUNCIATION → p. 142

Intonation in rhetorical questions

★ GRAMMAR → p. 143

Rhetorical questions

→ How can you say so? This argument is just unacceptable!

TRAINING TASK

UNESCO

Convention for the fight against the illicit trafficking of cultural property

↑ UNESCO logotype

The debate goes on

Listen to various points of view about the issue of museum restitution. Sort out the arguments **for** or **against** the repatriation of cultural treasures.

track 46

Homecoming, real or virtual?

SOCIETY

Should museums change their approach to restitution?

Today, **the debate on museum restitution** is evolving as more museums start to return artefacts as normal practice. Key to this has been the introduction of a system where representatives from both parties, museum and source community, discuss disputed objects as equals, rather than expecting source communities, many of whom have few resources, to justify their claims. In some cases, also, modern technology might offer a compromise solution that avoids physical restitution – but is that enough for source communities?

"One way of keeping culture heritage alive is to present it in a digital format"

University of Ulster academic Dr Bill Hart is to play a key role in a multi-disciplinary research initiative that will make Sierra Leone's rich cultural heritage accessible to a worldwide audience.

The project, *Reanimating Cultural Heritage,* has secured £456,000 funding from the Arts and Humanities Research Council (AHRC) to digitise the Sierra Leonean collections of three UK museums for use by students and researchers in the west African countries and elsewhere.

Presenting the UK-based artefacts in a digitised form will mean that people in Sierra Leone will be able to access them through a form of "virtual repatriation". By utilising advances in interactive digital technologies, the project could prompt a significant revaluation of how information is presented in museums.

[...] Dr Hart said: "Sierra Leone, like many other African countries, has a rich cultural heritage and one way of keeping this alive for future generations is to present it in a digital format."

"Our partner institutions in the project [...] have historically important collections of artefacts from Sierra Leone, most of which are held in storage and not on view to the public.

"Presenting photographic and other documentation relating to them in digital form will help bring those collections to life and make them accessible to a wider audience. Looking further ahead, we can envisage developing the database to include documentation from other museum collections in the UK and elsewhere."[...] Dr Hart says that in present circumstances it is not feasible to consider physical repatriation of artefacts to Sierra Leone. [...] "So we have to look at other ways to keep a sense of heritage alive and one way of doing this is through virtual repatriation."

NEWS ARCHIVES,
University of Ulster, Trina Porter, 23rd February 2009

1. **a. Read the introduction** and pick out elements indicating how "the debate on museum restitution is evolving".
b. Skim-read the document and explain why "modern technology might offer a compromise solution".

2. In groups, study one of the two articles.
Identify and explain:
- Dr Hart's opinion *(group 1 – p. 138)*
- Dr Opoku's opinion *(group 2 – p. 139)*

3. Discuss the different viewpoints and give yours.

Recap → List all the arguments for or against "virtual repatriation". page 54

Tattooed preserved Maori heads are covered with cloaks at the Te Papa Museum, in Wellington, NZ, after being returned from different parts of Europe (2011).

"There is no substitute for the physical transfer of cultural objects"

Where does this all leave the often presented argument that in this age of digitalization, the location of artefacts is not important and that there is no need to transfer physically looted African artefacts? We have never considered as serious the spurious argument based on digitalization for even if the Asante objects in the Wallace Collection were to be digitalized, how many Ghanaians could afford purchasing individual computers in order to see their cultural artefacts? Besides, would anyone seriously argue that the King of the Asantes, the Asantehene, could do with a digitalized sword instead of the swords in the museum? How does one fight or dance with a digitalized sword or wear a digitalized ring? The Asante objects once more demonstrate that the argument based on digitalization has no validity at all as far as cultural objects are concerned and that there is no substitute for the physical transfer of such objects from Western museums that do not need them to Africans who use them in their living culture.

DR KWAME OPOKU,
5 January, 2011

LANGUAGE TOOLS

★ **WORDS**

Virtual repatriation

- com**pu**ter **i**mage, **di**gital form, **di**gitised/di**gi**talized form
- un**real**, false, fake, mock
- **ac**tual, real, au**then**tic, **ge**nuine

↑ Wooden mask, Nigeria

TRAINING TASK

A discussion about restitution

In pairs. Imagine a conversation between a representative of the British Museum and a representative of an African museum demanding the restitution of artefacts.

- They mention the different possible types of repatriation.
- They give their points of view.

Restoring identity and respect

1 Animated objects

In *First Light*, Carol O'Biso, of the American Federation of Arts in New York, writes about her trip to New Zealand to prepare *Te Maori*, an exhibition of ancestral Maori treasures which was shown in New-York in 1984.

HERE IS AN EXTRACT FROM HER BOOK:

Carved wooden Maori treasures, Rotorua, NZ.

"Peta [a young Maori] spoke as if to himself. We listened with equal distance, each silently enveloped in an unreachable place of our own. He explained that it had been difficult for the Maori people to discuss their art with the Americans. There is no single word for art in the Maori language. A piece of wood has no significance. It is transformed through the art process. The contact with people, the words and stories built into the piece of wood during its making and in the centuries that might follow, turn it into a taonga, something treasured. The object is actually clothed with words, animated and transformed into a cultural object whose mana, or psychic force and power, are increased by continued association with people and events during its lifetime."

CAROL O'BISO FIRST LIGHT: A MAGICAL JOURNEY, 1989

THE PUTORINO
AN EXAMPLE OF ANIMATED OBJECT

One of the enigmas of Oceanic music is the putorino, a flute-like instrument once made by the Maori people of Aotearoa (New Zealand). Fashioned from a piece of split wood, hollowed out and then bound back together to form the body of the instrument, putorino have a single hole at the top and a figure-eight-shaped hole at the center. It is uncertain exactly how the instrument was originally played but the musician possibly blew into or across the hole at the top and used a finger to cover or uncover the central hole to modify the sound. Putorino were reportedly played as flutes, trumpets (with the lips vibrating), and also used as megaphones to modify the human voice. The sound was said to represent Hineraukatauri, a female ancestor who personified flute music.

METROPOLITAN MUSEUM OF ART, NEW YORK

1. **Look at the photos**: what strikes you?
2. **Read this magazine page. Explain**:
   - why it was "difficult for the Maori people to discuss their art with the Americans";
   - how the putorino illustrates what is said by Carol O'Biso.

2 A totem pole comes home

video 12

A documentary about the restitution of a totem pole

← Members of the Haisla Nation look at the G'psgolox totem pole on its return to Vancouver, British Columbia, in April 26, 2006.

1. **Before watching**, look at the photo. What do you expect to learn?
2. **Watch the video** and give your first reaction.
3. Watch again and identify:
   - what happened/is going to happen to the totem pole;
   - what the adults want to teach the children;
   - the symbolism of the pole and the adults' feelings.
4. **Share** your findings.

Recap → Explain how cultural artefacts can be differently regarded. page 54

LANGUAGE TOOLS

★ WORDS

Identity

- soul, tra**di**tion, **va**lue, be**lief**, rite, **spi**rit, em**bo**diment, recog**ni**tion
- ex**press**, voice, em**bo**dy, repre**sent**, stand for, de**pict**

★ GRAMMAR → p. 143

Talk somebody into doing something

→ The Swedish authorities were talked into returning the totem pole.

★ PRONUNCIATION → p. 142

Making liaisons

TRAINING TASK

Writing workshop

An exhibition displaying Maori / American Indian / African artefacts is about to open in a western museum.

As a journalist, write an article presenting the exhibition and stressing the importance of the objects displayed (220 words).

★ WORDS

❶ Arguing

track 45

Listen again to the debate on p. 137 and list all the expressions which can be used in a debate. Classify them.

	you can say...
To agree	Absolutely!
To disagree	Not at all!
To add something	I'm sorry to interrupt but I wanted to add...
...	...

❷ Going to the museum

Match the following words and their definitions.

curator | registrar | exhibition | display | artefact (UK) also **artifact** (US) | exhibit | loan

1. a show of paintings, photographs, or other objects that people can go and see
2. put objects in a place where people can see them easily
3. someone who is in charge of a museum
4. an object such as a tool, weapon etc. that was made in the past and is historically important
5. an object shown to the public for interest or instruction
6. someone who is in charge of official records
7. when you lend something to someone

❸ Talking about cultural exchanges

Bac

20 words related to cultural exchanges are hidden in this grid.
Find them out, and use them to write 5 sentences about museum restitution.
Orally sum up the issue.

E	X	H	I	B	I	T	E	E	P	S
S	D	I	G	I	T	I	Z	E	D	M
Y	E	C	A	T	A	J	N	N	U	R
M	M	R	H	U	L	R	I	E	R	E
B	A	T	T	R	K	E	R	G	H	P
O	N	H	V	K	S	P	E	O	E	R
L	D	E	W	L	F	A	S	T	R	E
E	M	B	O	D	Y	T	T	I	I	S
A	P	P	R	O	P	R	I	A	T	E
R	A	R	E	D	R	I	T	T	A	N
T	R	I	T	I	O	A	U	I	G	T
E	G	N	U	S	P	T	T	O	E	A
F	U	E	R	C	E	I	I	N	C	T
A	E	J	N	U	R	O	O	L	L	I
C	L	U	T	S	T	N	N	Y	A	O
T	I	E	T	S	Y	G	R	P	I	N
S	T	Q	A	L	O	A	N	Z	M	A

★ PRONUNCIATION

❹ Intonation in rhetorical questions

track 47

Listen to the following sentences.
For each question, say whether the intonation is rising (↗) or falling (↘), then indicate if they are real questions or rhetorical ones. Conclude.

1. "This artefact should stay where it belongs." "Come on, artefacts belong to everyone, don't they?"
2. "I was told the British Museum is great. Have you visited it?"
3. "I would love to see a real Egyptian mummy." "Haven't you seen one yet?"
4. "To me, museums are universal. How can't you agree with me?"

❺ Making liaisons

track 48

a. Here is a short paragraph about museum restitution.
Listen to it and pay attention to the liaisons.

> Artefacts belong‿to their country‿of‿origin and repatriation is the right thing to do. They‿have a unique‿connection with the place where they were produced and‿are‿an‿essential part‿of the cultural history‿of that‿area.

b. Practise reading the paragraph aloud.

★ GRAMMAR

Rhetorical questions

Observe

"I don't see why artefacts should be sent back. Aren't they part of an international cultural heritage? Culture belongs to everyone. Don't you agree?"
"No, I don't. I think seeing an artefact in the place where it belongs gives it more value. Don't you think so?"
"Of course not! Could you afford to travel thousands of miles to see those treasures? You know they're better preserved in our museums, don't you?"
"No, I don't!"

- **Étudiez les questions surlignées en vert et celles en rose en faisant attention aux réponses.**
- **Dites ce qui les différencie. Lesquelles sont dites « rhétoriques » ? Pourquoi ?**

Practise

6 Read these three dialogues and pick out the rhetorical questions.

a. "Have they reached an agreement with Ghana?"
"Not yet. The decision seems to be... how shall I put it? ... tough to make."

b. "I did not know this masterpiece would be transferred. Did you?"
"Not at all."
"How can the government pay for the repatriation of all those artefacts?"
"I have no idea!"

c. "According to you, why don't they want to return the artefacts?"
"If one artefact is given back, shouldn't they all? And it would be a good idea."
"How can you say so? It is just unacceptable!"

7 You are talking to a friend about your last visit to the Quai Branly museum. Try to persuade her/him to visit it as well, using rhetorical questions.

Talk somebody into doing something

Observe

1. It is said some Greek people were bribed into giving the Parthenon Marbles to the English.
2. Do not try to delude them into believing you respect their ancestors when you don't!
3. They coaxed them into leaving Ghana.
4. After long discussions, the Swedish authorities were talked into returning the totem pole.

bribe: offer money to a person to influence that person's views or conduct
delude: make someone believe something that is not true
coax: kindly convince

- **Lisez les phrases 1, 2 et 3. Aidez-vous de la définition des verbes pour expliquer le sens de ces phrases.**
- **D'après vous, que veut dire la phrase 4 ?**
- **Observez et décrivez la structure des quatre phrases. Que pouvez-vous conclure sur ce qu'exprime cette structure ?**

Grammaire (19) p. 208

Practise

8 a. Use the following elements to make three sentences.

a. the British - coax - return masks to Ghana
b. the West - deceive - Africans - think their artefacts would be sent back
c. the Unesco - frighten - the British Museum - return some of the mummies

b. Write three more sentences about the issue of museum restitution, using the structures you have observed.

More exercises in your Workbook → p. 52-53

Stratégies

Défendre un point de vue, justifier, convaincre

Lors d'une discussion vous serez souvent amené à défendre votre point de vue et à le justifier afin d'obtenir l'assentiment de votre interlocuteur, voire le faire changer d'avis.

Entraînez-vous à partir de la question suivante :
Should all national museums be free to enter?

Arguments possibles

For	Against
→ *Museums are educational, so they should be open to everybody.* → *It will attract more tourists in the country.* → *Collections in museums are a source of inspiration (design, art, architecture...).*	→ *Museums are expensive to run: the state can't pay for them all.* → *People shouldn't have to pay taxes to fund museums.* → *Collections will be limited in number.*

1 Rendez vos arguments convaincants

Techniques	Exemples
Introduisez clairement votre point de vue : • exprimez votre opinion, • marquez votre accord/désaccord.	→ *"I think.../to my mind.../as far as I am concerned.../ personally/in my opinion/I'm convinced that..."* → *"I agree/You are right/That's exactly how I see it"* → *"I don't think so/I don't see things that way"*
Expliquez et justifiez vos arguments à l'aide de faits avérés (statistiques, résultats d'enquête...).	→ *"More people will visit museums if admission is free. In the UK, National museums have doubled visitor numbers in a decade of free entry".*
Présentez vos arguments logiquement... • en insistant sur les causes et les conséquences *(because, as, since, so, therefore, that's why...)*. • en faisant des hypothèses *(if, provided, in case, as long as, unless...)*.	→ *"Some people are not interested in visiting museums, therefore they shouldn't have to pay taxes to fund these museums."* → *"If free museum entry were considered a cultural right, shouldn't the state make theatre tickets free as well?"*
Mettez vos arguments en valeur : • répétions, emphase • accentuation de certains mots • intonation descendante ↘	→ *"Admission fees do deter people from going to museums."* ↘ → *"Museums are not only a source of education but they are also a source of inspiration."* ↘

→ À vous

Utilisez le tableau des arguments et les techniques ci-dessus pour rendre vos arguments convaincants : faites un brouillon d'oral puis enregistrez-vous. Réécoutez et voyez si vous avez été convaincant.

2 Impliquez votre interlocuteur

Techniques	Exemples
Mettez-le dans une situation où il sera incité à adopter votre point de vue.	→ *"Imagine museums can't increase their collections, would you wish to visit them?"*
Demandez-lui de répéter, de donner des exemples ou de préciser ses propos.	→ *"I beg your pardon, I didn't hear/understand what you said."* → *"Can you give me examples?"* → *"Do you mean that tourists will be deterred from visiting our country if our museums are expensive?"*
Remettez en cause son point de vue.	→ *"You say that admission fees don't deter visitors. However, visitors to the Victoria and Albert Museum in London declined by 15% after it started charging for admission."*
Amenez-le à être d'accord avec vous, en utilisant des questions rhétoriques.	→ *"Don't you think that/Can you deny the fact that admission fees deter some people from visiting museums?"* ↘ → *"Do you want museum collections to get poorer?"* ↘
Reprenez ses arguments à votre compte en utilisant la concession *(however, yet, still, although, even if...)* **ou la comparaison** *(like, likewise).*	→ *"Even if education should be a priority, does it mean the state has to pay for all educational opportunities?"*

→ À vous

Utilisez le tableau des arguments et les techniques ci-dessus pour impliquer votre interlocuteur.

3 Impliquez-vous dans l'échange

a. Le regard

Regardez vos interlocuteurs pour maintenir leur attention et leur faire partager votre conviction.

b. La voix

Parlez d'une voix calme et claire.

Le jour du Bac

Toutes séries

→ voir aussi *Entraînement Bac* p. 150

- À la fin de votre présentation, l'examinateur vous posera une série de questions pour vous inciter à **développer** certains de vos arguments, à **préciser** ou **donner des exemples**.
- Lors de votre préparation, **imaginez deux ou trois questions** que l'examinateur pourra vous poser : vous réagirez ainsi plus facilement aux sollicitations.
- **Si vous n'avez pas compris la question** ou si vous n'êtes pas sûr d'avoir bien compris, n'hésitez pas à demander à l'examinateur de la **répéter** ou d'**expliquer** un mot que vous ne connaissez pas. Cela fait partie de l'interaction.
- Lorsqu'on vous pose une question, **développez vos réponses**.

FINAL TASKS

TV debates

The representative of a museum in Africa

A journalist specialized in art

The representative of an English museum

task 1

Speaking

Debate and have your say!

You are taking part in a TV debate:

"Should cultural artefacts be returned to their countries of origin?"

1. Get ready

- Discover the part you are going to play.
- Jot down a few arguments.
- Anticipate the other guests' arguments.

2. Action!

- Don't read your notes.
- Take the other guests' remarks into account.
- Keep the debate going.

task 2

Listening

Choose partners for your debating team

You are a member of a group that is going to debate in favour of museum restitution.
You need debaters who completely share your point of view:

- listen to several people's opinions about the topic,
- choose those who will be part of your team.

Bac

Compréhension de l'oral

Listen to a radio programme

An imaginary museum

1. Listen to the document three times and take notes.

2. Write a report in French of what you have understood.

↑ The Metropolitan Museum in New-York

Expression orale

Oral presentation

1. Using what you have learnt about **museum restitution**, prepare notes explaining what part museums play in the **exchanges between countries**.

You can follow these guidelines:

- The places where cultural treasures originated from and where they are exhibited.
- How they changed hands.
- What they represent for people in different parts of the world.

Illustrate your presentation with relevant examples you may know.

2. Give your oral presentation.

3. Be ready to discuss the topic with your teacher.

→ Aide

Utilisez la fiche *Recap* du workbook p. 54 ou sur www.didierpassword.fr pour préparer cette synthèse orale.

Compréhension de l'écrit

Study a set of documents

Your teacher will give you several documents. Read them carefully and answer the questions.

Expression écrite

Write two different texts

Using the elements given by your teacher, write:

1. A letter

2. A dialogue

Good reads

"I'm not afraid"

↑ *Moment of truth*, by Morrison Desmond (1998)

I looked at the notice. I wondered if I had time before my train left Philadelphia for Baltimore in one hour. The heart, ceiling-high, occupied one corner of the large exhibition hall, and from wherever you stood in the hall you could hear its beating, *thum-thump-thum-thump*. It was a popular exhibit, and sometimes, when there were too many children about, the entrance had to be roped off, as the children loved to race up and down the blood vessels and match their cries to the hearth's beating [...]. The notice "You Are Now Taking the Path of a Blood Cell Through the Human Heart", hung askew. I wanted to see more of the Franklin Institute and the Natural Science Museum across the street, but a journey through the human heart would be fascinating. Did I have time?

Later. First, I would go across the street to the Hall of North America, among the bear and the bison, and catch up on American flora and fauna.

I made my way to the Hall. More children, sitting in rows on canvas chairs. An elementary class from a city school, under the control of an elderly teacher. A museum attendant holding a basket, and all eyes gazing at the basket.

He lowered his voice. "The best way to get through to the children is to start with the teacher," he said to Miss Aitcheson. "If they see you're not afraid, then they won't be."

She must be near retiring age, I thought. A city woman. Never handled a snake in her life. Her face was pale. She just managed to drag the fear from her eyes to some place in their depths, where it lurked like a dark stain. Surely the attendant and the children noticed?

"It's harmless," the attendant said. He'd been working with snakes for years.

Miss Aitcheson, I thought again. A city woman born and bred. All snakes were creatures to kill, to be protected from, alike the rattler, the copperhead, king snake, grass snake venom and victims. Were there not places in the South where you couldn't go into the streets for fear of the rattlesnakes?

Her eyes faced the lighted exit. I saw her fear. The exit light blinked, hooded. The children, none of whom had ever touched a live snake, were sitting hushed, waiting for the drama to begin; one or two looked afraid as the attendant withdrew a green snake about three feet long from the basket and with a swift movement, before the teacher could protest, draped it around her neck and stepped back, admiring and satisfied.

"There," he said to the class. "Your teacher has a snake around her neck and she's not afraid."

Miss Aitcheson stood rigid; she seemed to be holding her breath.

"Teacher's not afraid, are you?" the attendant persisted. He leaned forward, pronouncing judgement on her, while she suddenly jerked her head and lifted her hands in panic to get rid of the snake. Then, seeing the children watching her, she whispered. "No, I'm not afraid. Of course, not."' She looked around her.

"Of course not," she repeated sharply.

I could see her defeat and helplessness. The attendant seemed unaware, as if his perception had grown a reptilian covering. [...] "Would someone like to come out and stroke teacher's snake?"

Silence.

One shamefaced boy came forward. He stood petrified in front of the teacher.

"Touch it," the attendant urged. "It's a friendly snake. Teacher's wearing it around her neck and she's not afraid."

The boy darted his hand forward, rested it lightly on the snake, and immediately withdrew his hand. Then he ran back to his seat. The children shrieked with glee.

"He's afraid,"' someone said. "He's afraid of the snake."

The attendant soothed. "We have to get used to them, you know. Grown-ups are not afraid of them, but we can understand that when we're small you might be afraid, and that's why we want you to learn to love them. Isn't that right, Miss Aitcheson? Isn't that right? Now who else is going to be brave enough to touch teacher's snake?"

Two girls came out. They stood hand in hand side by side and stared at the snake then at Miss Aitcheson.

I wondered when the torture would end. The two little girls did not touch the snake, but they smiled at it and spoke to it and Miss Aitcheson smiled at them and whispered how brave they were.

"Just a minute," the attendant said. "There's really no need to be brave. It's not a question of bravery. The snake is *harmless*, absolutely *harmless*. Where's the bravery when the snake is harmless?"

Suddenly the snake moved around to face Miss Aitcheson and thrust its flat head towards her cheeks. She gave a scream, flung up her hands, and tore the snake from her throat and threw it on the floor, and, rushing across the room, she collapsed into a small canvas chair beside the Bear Cabinet and started to cry.

I didn't feel I should watch any longer. Some of the children began to laugh, some to cry. The attendant picked up the snake and nursed it. Miss Aitcheson, recovering, sat helplessly exposed by the small piece of useless torture. It was not her fault she was city-bred, her eyes tried to tell us. She looked at the children, trying in some way to force their admiration and respect; they were shut against her. She was evicted from them and from herself and even from her own fear-infested tomorrow, because she could not promise to love and preserve what she feared. She had nowhere, at the moment, but the small canvas chair by the Bear Cabinet of the Natural Science Museum.

I looked at my watch. If I hurried, I would catch the train from Thirtieth Street. There would be no time to make the journey through the human heart. I hurried out of the museum. I was freezing cold. The icebreakers would be at work at the Delaware and the Susquehanna: the mist would have risen by the time I arrived home. Yes, I would catch the train from Thirtieth Street. The journey through the human heart would have to wait some other time.

Janet Frame, *You Are Now Entering the Human Heart* (1983)

Janet Frame (1924-2004)

One of New Zealand's most distinguished writers. She was a Nominee for the Nobel Prize in Literature. Her first book, The Lagoon, *published in 1951, started her exploration into the lives of lonely and isolated people.*

Expression orale (2)

Phase d'expression en interaction

L'épreuve d'expression orale se déroule en deux temps : une phase d'expression en continu, une phase d'interaction.

Séries ES, S et technologiques
« La prise de parole en continu sert d'amorce à une conversation conduite par le professeur, qui prend appui sur l'exposé du candidat. Cette phase d'interaction n'excède pas 5 minutes. »
Série L
« La prise de parole en continu sert d'amorce à une conversation conduite par l'examinateur, qui prend appui sur l'exposé du candidat. Cette phase d'interaction n'excède pas 10 minutes. »
Instructions officielles, B.O. du 24 nov. 2011

Le jour du Bac

Utilisez la phase de préparation à l'épreuve orale

Lors des 10 min de préparation (voir ***Entraînement Bac*** p. 30), *prenez le temps d'anticiper la phase d'interaction sur votre « brouillon d'oral ».*

- Choisissez les exemples ou les explications que vous garderez « en réserve » pour illustrer ou développer certains points lors de la phase d'interaction.
- Prévoyez de mentionner dans votre conclusion un point nouveau, sur lequel vous aimeriez revenir lors de la phase d'interaction.
- Imaginez les questions que pourrait vous poser l'examinateur et préparez-vous à y répondre.

Entraînez-vous à partir de la notion « lieux et formes du pouvoir » étudiée dans le chapitre 1 *Going to university*.

- Vous prévoyez de mentionner lors de votre exposé : *"Students are more responsible if they have to pay for their studies."*

→ ***À vous :*** prévoyez deux ou trois explications ou exemples pour développer ou illustrer ce point :
Ex.: *"If they borrow money, they must pay it back so it can incite/ motivate them to succeed in their studies."*

- Vous prévoyez d'introduire dans votre conclusion le point suivant : *"Many people think that access to university should depend on 'merit' but they have to agree on the definition of 'merit'"*.

→ ***À vous :*** préparez-vous à développer ce que vous entendez par *merit*.

- Vous prévoyez de formuler l'idée suivante lors de la phase d'expression en continu : *"Education gives you the means to keep up with the changing ways of the world and contributes to making you more influential."*

→ ***À vous :*** Imaginez trois questions que l'examinateur pourrait vous poser sur ce point.

Impliquez-vous dans l'échange

- Demandez poliment de répéter ou de préciser.
- Assurez-vous de bien comprendre et d'être bien compris.

- *I didn't catch what you said, could you please repeat your question? / Would you mind repeating your question?*
- *I'm not sure I understand what you mean, could you explain, please?*
- *When you say ..., do you mean...?*
- *Does that make sense to you? / Do you see what I mean?*
- *Indeed..., more precisely...*

- Précisez et expliquez vos propos.

→ **À vous :** indiquez la fonction des expressions suivantes :

	Reformuler ou rectifier	Expliquer ou préciser
I'd like to add that...		
Actually I didn't mean... I meant		
In other words...		
As a matter of fact...		
What I mean is that...		
That is to say...		
Let me put it another way		
What I'm trying to say is that		
Perhaps I should say...		

- Réagissez aux sollicitations : lorsque l'examinateur vous pose une question, développez vos réponses (justifiez votre point de vue, donnez des exemples, expliquez certains termes).

- *"Do you think too many people go to university? "*
"Yes I think so / No I don't think so"... " in fact..."

→ **À vous :** Réagissez à la question suivante : *"Do you think access to university is a matter of money?"*

- Personnalisez votre propos : expliquez l'intérêt que vous avez personnellement porté au thème, vos sentiments, qu'ils soient positifs ou négatifs.

- *"What I found particularly interesting is that different countries have different approaches to the problem, for instance... / It made me think of my own future... as a matter of fact..."*
- *"It is a scandal that some students are denied access to university because..."*

→ **À vous :** expliquez vos réactions sur la question de la sélection à l'entrée à l'université.

Adressez-vous à l'examinateur

- Évitez de porter votre regard en permanence sur vos notes, regardez votre interlocuteur : vous comprendrez mieux ce qu'il vous dit et serez plus apte à réagir à ses sollicitations.
- Asseyez-vous confortablement, centré(e) sur votre chaise, bras et mains posés calmement afin de faciliter la communication.

UNIT 8 British characters

↑ ***Alice in Wonderland*** (Lewis Caroll, 1865) **and *Robinson Crusoe*** (Daniel Defoe, 1719)

What do British characters tell us about britishness?

What do you know about these characters?
How would you link them to your idea of "britishness"?

FINAL TASKS

P. 166

Favourite British icons

Writing
Present your favourite British character

Reading
Help website visitors discover heroic figures

CULTURE

- Learning about iconic figures in British fiction.
- Exploring British traits.
- Social studies:
  - Alice Thomson, *"What does it mean to be British?"*
  - Isabel Taylor, *"Exploring British eccentricity"*
- Literary works:
  - Joseph Conrad, *Heart of Darkness*
  - Anthony Horowitz, *The House of Silk*
  - Arthur Ransome, *Swallows and Amazons*
- Cinema:
  Oliver Parker, *Johnny English*

COMMUNICATION

Writing descriptions presenting characters or events and giving explanations.

- Reading literary texts; understanding the main facts, the characters, their actions and what they embody.
- Reading articles, understanding opinions, arguments and examples.

Presenting and explaining some aspects of britishness.

TOOLS

★ Words
- Symbol
- Heroes and characters
- Tolerance
- Sailors and adventurers
- Personal traits
- Companionship
- Admiration
- Eccentricity and humour

★ Pronunciation
- Pronouncing "-s" in plurals
- Stress on negatives

★ Grammar
- Verb + *-ing*
- *Have-en / had-en*

BAC

Stratégies
→ *Écrire un texte explicatif* p. 164

Évaluation
→ *4 situations d'évaluation* p. 167

"Of course we are unique"

1 "We, the British"

What does it mean to be British?

This week, in a West London swimming pool, I watched as two large West African women plunged into the water topless in their knickers. No one commented until one woman said: "They look like they're having fun." It was only when they went into the café afterwards and one lit a cigarette in a no-smoking zone that someone complained.

This sums up the British. [...]

So what does it mean to be British? Jacques Chirac thinks it's about bad food. Tourists cite Buckingham Palace and the double-deck bus – which has become even more iconic since the bombings[1]. The series *Little Britain* shows a nation of eccentrics with a sense of humour. According to the Australians, the British always lose at cricket. Others told me that, for them, Britain was all about curries, roasts, toast, kettles, gardens, gnomes, tea cosies, rain, the Queen and her corgies[2].

Statistically, the country is divided in each census into the English, Welsh and Scottish, into ethnic minorities, and into religions. But britishness is about more than this. It is what unites, rather than what differentiates us, that is particularly interesting. [...]

Emma Soames, the editor of *Saga Magazine*, says that the older generation has a very strong view of britishness. "Ginger beer, James Bond, pony club camp, a deep love of animals and an ambivalence towards children. We also have a great sense of pageantry[3] and dressing up which we mustn't lose." [...]

← Wallace and Gromit: classic with a twist?

Andrew Roberts, author of a biography of Lord Salisbury[4], says that britishness is easy to define. "We have a profoundly different history to the rest of the world – partly because of our geographical insularity, partly because we are the most constitutionally mature. We were the first to have an industrial revolution and we don't lose wars. We once covered one quarter of the world. Of course, we are unique." [...]

Brooke Shields, the American actress now appearing in London, thinks it's easy to define. "Fudge and pubs." But britishness is not about just a set of values or sweets – it is also about the people who have made Britain.

Baroness Susan Greenfield, the director of the Royal Institution, points to the fact that Britain produced Newton, Darwin, Watson and Crick, and has won more Nobel prizes than any country except America.

The British are also great innovators, explorers, story-tellers, soldiers and sailors – a tradition carried on by Ellen MacArthur sailing round the world, Tim Berners-Lee inventing theInternet and J. K. Rowling writing about Harry Potter.

"It's about being classic with a twist," says Geordie Greig, the editor of *Tatler Magazine*. "About combining the best of British with abroad, having Zadie Smith[5] and Shakespeare, Kelly Holmes[6] and Paula Radcliffe[7], Ikea furniture and castles."

Mriganka Chatterjee, one of the first to take the new citizenship test, says: "I could have chosen worse," showing another British trait – understatement. Even if you are proud to be British, you should never brag about it.

***The Telegraph*, July 2005**
By Alice Thomson

1. Bombings: on July 7, 2005, a series of bomb attacks on the London transport system killed about 30 people and injured some 700 others
2. Corgies: dogs
3. Pageantry: grand display/pomp
4. Lord Salisbury: British Prime Minister (1886-1892)
5. Zadie Smith: a British novelist of Jamaican origin from her mother
6. Kelly Holmes: a British middle distance athlete of Jamaican origin from her father; a gold-medalist at the Summer Olympics in 2004
7. Paula Radcliffe: a British long distance runner from North West England; a Marathon world champion in 2005

1. **Read the first paragraph** and explain *"This sums up the British"* (l. 12).
2. **Now read the text. Discuss** what you have understood.
3. **a. In groups. Focus on...**
   - everyday life and attitudes *(group 1)*,
   - history and geography *(group 2)*,
   - famous people and reasons for their fame *(group 3)*.

   b. Share your findings with the other groups.
4. **Whole class**: explain *"It's about being classic with a twist... and castles."* (l. 81-88)
5. **Conclude** about how the British see themselves. What definition of britishness is given here?

LANGUAGE TOOLS

★ WORDS

Symbol
- **fi**gure, **i**cons, role **mo**del
- arche**ty**pal /ˌɑːkɪˈtaɪpl/, **le**gendary
- em**bo**diment, quin**te**ssence

Heroes and characters
- **won**drous, awe-ins**pi**ring
- in**fa**llible, un**er**ring, **fault**less
- **vi**llain, dis**re**putable, re**mote**

Tolerance
- open-**min**ded, broad-**min**ded
- fair, un**pre**judiced

★ GRAMMAR → p. 163

Verb + *-ing*
→ Being British

2 Remarkable characters

track 57

Writer Sebastian Faulks talks about remarkable characters and heroes in British litterature

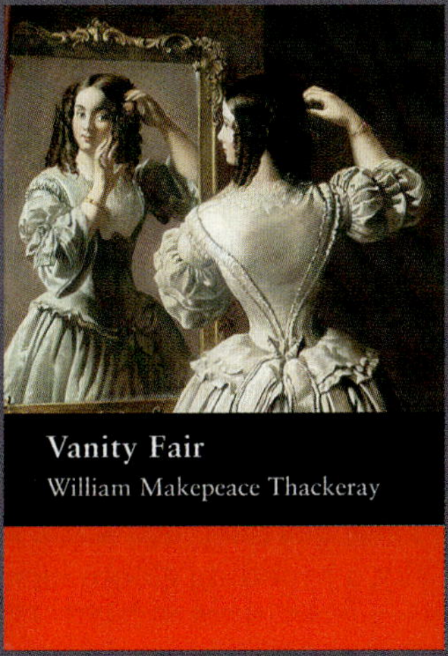

1. **Listen** and discuss what you have understood.
2. **a. In groups**: listen again and pick out information about:
   - Robinson Crusoe and Beckie Sharp *(group 1)*;
   - what Faulks says about novelists and their heroes *(group 2)*.

   b. Organize your findings and share them with the other group.
3. **Explain** what British readers find in those characters.

Recap → List some characteristics of britishness. page 61

TRAINING TASK

TV heroes

In groups: do research on one of these TV series:

Coronation street | The Avengers | Goodness Gracious me | Little Britain | Luther | Monty Python's Flying Circus

↑ Monty Python

Present the series to the class, stressing what, in your opinion, makes it typically British.

Men who follow the sea

"Seamen and wanderers"

The sailing boat* Nellie *has just entered the Thames estuary, downstream from London. The narrator and the other sailors are looking at the view of the city and of the river from the boat.

We looked at the venerable stream not in the vivid flush of a short day that comes and departs for ever, but in the august light of abiding memories. And indeed nothing is easier for a man who has, as the phrase goes, "followed the sea" with reverence and affection, than to evoke the great spirit of the past upon the lower reaches of the Thames. The tidal current runs to and fro in its unceasing service, crowded with memories of men and ships it had borne to the rest of home or to the battles of the sea. It had known and served all the men of whom the nation is proud, from Sir Francis Drake to Sir John Franklin, knights all, titled and untitled – the great knights-errant of the sea. It had borne all the ships whose names are like jewels flashing in the night of time, from the Golden Hind returning with her rotund flanks full of treasure, to be visited by the Queen's Highness and thus pass out of the gigantic tale, to the Erebus and Terror, bound on other conquests — and that never returned. It had known the ships and the men. They had sailed from Deptford, from Greenwich, from Erith — the adventurers and the settlers; kings' ships and the ships of men on 'Change; captains, admirals, the dark "interlopers" of the Eastern trade, and the commissioned "generals" of East India fleets. Hunters for gold or pursuers of fame, they all had gone out on that stream, bearing the sword, and often the torch, messengers of the might within the land, bearers of a spark from the sacred fire. What greatness had not floated on the ebb of that river into the mystery of an unknown earth! ... The dreams of men, the seed of commonwealths, the germs of empires. [...]

Lights of ships moved in the fairway – a great stir of lights going up and going down. And farther west on the upper reaches the place of the monstrous town was still marked ominously on the sky, a brooding gloom in sunshine, a lurid glare under the stars.

"And this also," said Marlow suddenly, "has been one of the dark places of the earth."

He was the only man of us who still "followed the sea." The worst that could be said of him was that he did not represent his class. He was a seaman, but he was a wanderer, too, while most seamen lead, if one may so express it, a sedentary life. Their minds are of the stay-at-home order, and their home is always with them – the ship; and so is their country – the sea. One ship is very much like another, and the sea is always the same. In the immutability of their surroundings the foreign shores, the foreign faces, the changing immensity of life, glide past, veiled not by a sense of mystery but by a slightly disdainful ignorance; for there is nothing mysterious to a seaman unless it be the sea itself, which is the mistress of his existence and as inscrutable as Destiny.

Joseph Conrad, *Heart of Darkness* (1899)

Joseph Conrad
(1857 -1924)
Of Polish origin, he is regarded as one of the greatest English novelists. His stories are renderings of dangerous life at sea and in exotic places and depict man's inner battles with good and evil.

↑ *The Egremont Sea Piece*, 1802, a painting J.M.W. Turner

1. Before reading, look at the title, the introduction and the painting. Comment on them.

2. Read the text from line 1 to line 26. Say what you have understood and sum up the situation.

3. a. Highlight references to:
- the river,
- "men who followed the sea".

pages 55-56

b. Share your findings.
c. Explain the narrator's feelings.

4. Read from l. 27 to the end of the passage. Discuss the character of Marlow.

Recap → How did great sea voyages influence heroes in British fiction?

page 61

LANGUAGE TOOLS

★ WORDS

Sailors and adventurers
- ship crew, **sea**man, ma**ri**ner, **pi**rate, bucca**neer** /ˌbʌkəˈnɪər/, **cor**sair
- dis**co**ver, chart, map
- risk, **pe**ril, **ha**zard /ˈhæzəd/, **je**opardy /ˈdʒepədɪ/

Courage
- brave, bold, **da**ring, **for**ward, un**daun**ted /ʌnˈdɔːntɪd/
- in**tre**pid, in**do**mitable

★ PRONUNCIATION → p. 162

"-*s*" in plurals
→ explorers, places, ships

TRAINING TASK

Voyages and adventures

1. In groups, search the web about one of the following:

Sir Francis Drake | Sir John Franklin | the Golden Hind vessel | the Erebus and Terror

2. Organize your notes and present your results to the other groups.

3. Whole class: find out what they have in common and discuss what makes them memorable.

The science of detection

Remarkable Sherlock Holmes

Arthur Conan Doyle (1859-1930) published the last adventure of Sherlock Holmes in 1927. In* The House of Silk*, writer Anthony Horowitz gives the detective and his friend Watson a new life.

"Influenza is unpleasant," Sherlock Holmes remarked, "but you are right in thinking that, with your wife's help, the child will recover soon."

"I very much hope so", I replied, then stopped and gazed at him in wide-eyed astonishment. My tea had been halfway to my lips but I returned it to the table with such force that the cup and the saucer almost parted company. "But for Heaven's sake, Holmes", I exclaimed. "You have taken the very thoughts from my head. I swear I have not uttered a word about the child nor his illness. You know that my wife is away – that much you might have deduced from my presence here. But I have not yet mentioned to you the reason for her absence and I am certain that there has been nothing in my behaviour that could have given you any clue". [...]

Holmes replied, "I can tell that you have just returned from Holborn Viaduct. That you left your house in a hurry, but even so missed the train. Perhaps the fact that you are currently without a servant girl is to blame".

"No, Holmes", I cried. "I will not have it!".

"I am wrong?"

"No. You are correct on every count. But how is it possible...? "

"It is a simple matter of observation and deduction, the one informing the other. Were I to explain it to you, it would all seem painfully childish".

"And yet I must insist that you do just that".

"Well, since you have been so good as to pay me this visit, I suppose I must oblige," returned Holmes with a yawn. "Let us begin with the circumstance that brings you here. If my memory serves, we are approaching the second anniversary of your marriage, are we not?"

"Indeed so, Holmes. It is the day after tomorrow".

"An unusual time then, for you to separate from your wife. As you yourself said just now, the fact that you have chosen to stay with me, and for a prolonged period of time, would suggest that there was a compelling reason for her to part company with you. And what might that be? As I recall, Miss Mary Morston – as she once was – came to England from India and had no friend or family here. She was taken on as a governess, looking after the son of one Mrs Cecil Forrester, in Camberwell, which is of course where you met her. Mrs Forrester was very good to her, particularly in her time of need, and I would imagine that the two of them have remained close".

"That is indeed the case"

"And so, if anyone were likely to call your wife away from home, it might well be her. I wonder then what reason might lie behind such a summons, and in this cold weather the sickness of a child springs to mind. It would, I am sure, be very comforting for the afflicted lad to have his old governess back".

"His name is Richard and he is nine years old", I concurred. "But how can you be so confident that it is influenza and not something altogether more serious?"

"Were it more serious, you would surely have insisted upon attending yourself". [...]

"And the rest of it?".

" The fact that you have lost your maid and that you left the house in a hurry? The smudge of black polish on the side of your left cuff clearly indicates both. You cleaned your own shoes and you did so rather carelessly. Moreover, in your haste, you forgot your gloves –"

"Mrs Hudson took my coat from me. She could also have taken my gloves ".

"In which case, when we shook hands, why yours have been so cold? No, Watson, your entire bearing speaks of disorganization and disarray".

"Everything you say is right", I admitted. "But one last mystery, Holmes. How can you be so sure that my wife missed her train?"

"As soon as you arrived, I noticed a strong scent of coffee on your clothes. Why would you be drinking coffee immediately before coming to me for tea? The inference is that you missed your train and were forced to stay with your wife for longer that you had intended. You stowed your case at the left luggage office and went with her to a coffee house. [...]

There was a short silence and then I burst into laughter.

"Well, Holmes," I said, "I can see that I had no reason to worry about your health. You are as remarkable as ever".

Anthony Horowitz, *The House of Silk* (2011)

1. Read the text. Discuss what you have understood.

2. a. In groups: read again. Focus on...
- Watson *(group 1)*,
- Holmes *(group 2)*.

pages 57-59

b. Describe their relationship.

3. Whole class: explain what Holmes has observed and what his deductions are. Would you agree with Watson that Holmes is "as remarkable as ever" (l. 63), or do you think it is "all painfully childish" (l. 23)?

4. Discuss what, in your opinion, each of the two characters embodies.

Recap → What makes Sherlock Holmes a "British character"? page 61

LANGUAGE TOOLS

★ WORDS

Clever and smart
- ingenious, astute, shrewd /ʃruːd/
- art, skill, ability, knack, expertise
- figure out, deduce, infer, analyse, presume

Cool, calm and collected
- composed, unruffled, cold-headed
- phlegmatic, detached, aloof

Companionship
- friendship, partnership, affinity

Admiration
- marvel at, praise, look up to
- astounded, mystified, baffled

★ PRONUNCIATION → p. 162

Stress on negatives

★ GRAMMAR → p. 163

Have-en* vs *had-en

TRAINING TASK

Portrait of a genius

Dr Watson recalls the episode in his diary, insisting on what a genius Sherlock Holmes is.

1. a. In groups: decide on the arguments Watson could use to demonstrate Holmes' brilliance.

b. Organize your ideas.

2. On your own, write the entry (150 words).

A B(r)it different

1 Exploring British eccentricity

↑ Fashion designer Vivienne Westwood in London.

The English are unusual in the degree to which they regard eccentricity as a positive trait. A euphemism for 'strange' in many other Western countries, 'eccentric' is often a compliment in England. We seem to regard eccentricity as endearing, or positively attractive. [...]

Whatever form it takes, eccentricity is a mild form of rebellion against authority and social convention, so it appeals to the often-noted anarchic streak[1] in the English character. It is a declaration of independence on a small (and moderate) English scale, an assertion of the free-born English person's right to dispose of their own leisure time uninterfered with.

↑ British punk rocker in London.

Our fierce attachment to our freedom in leisure pursuits is proverbial, and it explains the outcry in the media every time "government busybodies" start "sticking their noses in" to somebody's hobby; why shouldn't Mrs Jones cover her garden with pottery cats if she wants to, and who is anybody else to try and stop her? Like humour, to which it is often closely allied, English eccentricity is a way of letting off steam. By providing an outlet for the frustrations that must inevitably build up in a densely-populated and fairly cohesive society, eccentricity paradoxically helps to prop up the very order that it appears to so recklessly flout[2], both by providing the exceptions that prove the rules and by working off tensions that could otherwise pose a real threat to social (and governmental) stability. The fact that eccentricity is an important mental safety valve also helps to explain why many eccentric English people seem to radiate an otherwise inexplicable serenity. Giving in a little to the irrational probably keeps many of us fundamentally sane, and may have added something to our generally fairly steady and placid temperament. [...]

Eccentricity is [...] closely tied to English creativity and inventiveness. This can be clearly seen in all the arts, particularly in fashion and music, as well as in our tradition of nonsense literature. English fashion designers have long attempted to tap into the allure of the conscious type of eccentricity by evoking it in their collections, so that self-parody is now regarded as a hallmark of English fashion. Likewise, eccentricity has been reflected in English music. English music fans often want to be entertained and amused more than uplifted and enlightened by the music that they listen to. Thus a tinge of eccentricity has helped to produce some of the best English music of the past fifty years, especially noticeable on some of the great rock albums, such as *Sgt. Pepper* and *Dark Side of the Moon*. Perhaps the high point of eccentricity in English music (a tradition which includes Gilbert and Sullivan, Kate Bush, the Kinks, the Streets, and many others) was the wild and woolly Bonzo Dog Doo Dah Band, headed up by the most flamboyant eccentric of our time, the late Vivian Stanshall. [...]

However, we should not rest on our laurels. Sometimes it seems as if eccentrics of the grand old school are becoming fewer and fewer; truly original eccentricity, one of the motive forces which propel the development and renewal of English culture, is harder to find these days. Let us be bold and inventive — we must not allow our culture to stagnate. Who's for tabletop croquet?

© Isabel Taylor (2006)

1. **streak:** tendancy

2. **flout:** defy, ignore

1. a. **Look at the titles and photos** on p. 160 and react.
   b. **Give some examples** of British eccentricity.
2. **Read the first paragraph** and explain what is specific about British eccentricity.
3. a. **In groups**, explore British eccentricity as described by the writer:
   - in paragraph 2 *(group 1)*,
   - in paragraph 3 *(group 2)*. pages 59-60
   b. **Explain** what you have discovered to the other group.
4. **Whole class**: explain the last paragraph. Can you find examples that show British eccentricity is still alive and kicking?

LANGUAGE TOOLS

★ **WORDS**

Eccentricity
- biz**a**rre, odd, **we**ird, **goo**fy
- **sin**gular, non con**for**mist, **quir**ky

Clumsiness
- in**a**dequacy, **short**coming, ina**bil**ity
- in**ept**, **awk**ward, **help**less
- make **blun**ders, act **fool**ishly, make a fool of one**self**

Self-confidence / self-criticism
- sure of one**self**, **self**-assured, **co**cky ≠ **self**-conscious, des**pon**dent

Humour
- joke, jest, **fun**niness
- de**ri**sion, **mo**ckery, de**bun**king
- **pa**rody, pas**tiche**, **sa**tire

2 Johnny English

video 13

A trailer for *Johnny English*, a 2003 British film

1. **Watch the trailer** and discuss:
   a. what kind of film it is, and what other films it resembles,
   b. what the plot is,
   c. how the main character is portrayed, and who he may be inspired by.
2. What British traits does it emphasize?

Recap → How would you define British eccentricity? Give examples. page 61

TRAINING TASK

A flyer

Imagine a new fund-raising event for a British charity, and create the flyer.

1. Decide on a cause and on an event (like *Wrong Trousers Day*), inspiring yourself from some British traits you've seen in the chapter.
→ *...Day intends to... by... The funds will be used to...*

2. List arguments you will use to convince people to join in.

3. Write and design your flyer.

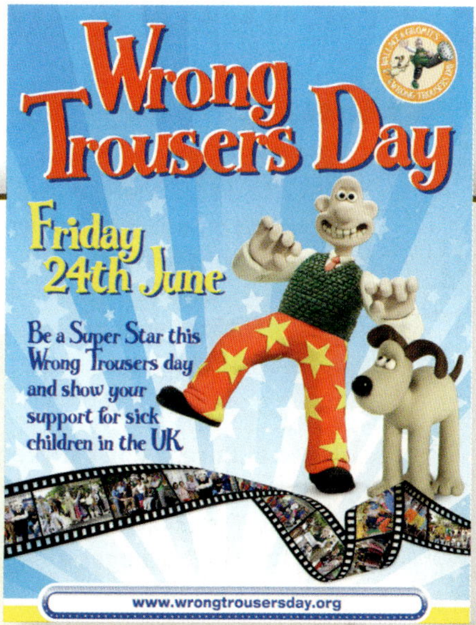

Wrong Trousers Day raises thousands of pounds each year by encouraging the people of Britain to pay a pound to wear "the wrong trousers" to work, school, or even the supermarket! The funds raised are used for sick children in over 50 hospitals and hospices across the UK. This year is no exception, with the aim to beat last year's record of attracting over 400,000 participants to join in!

★ WORDS

❶ Describing heroic characters

Here are adjectives that could be used to describe heroic characters. For each list, find at least one more adjective with a similar meaning and two antonyms.

1. astute, judicious...
2. strong-willed, resolute...
3. mild, unassuming...
4. stubborn, obstinate...
5. rebellious, defiant...

❷ The odd one out

a. Here are verbs that can be used to explain and to comment. In each list, spot the odd one.

1. stress - emphasize - conceal - highlight - point up
2. refer to - mention - hint at - deny - point out
3. reveal - impart - mask - bring to light - expose
4. embody - represent - exclude - illustrate - symbolize

b. Look at the film poster on the left. Using some of the verbs above, write a short paragraph to talk about this British icon.

❸ Talking about British characters

Bac

a. Find as many words as possible in order to create a 'British characters' word map.

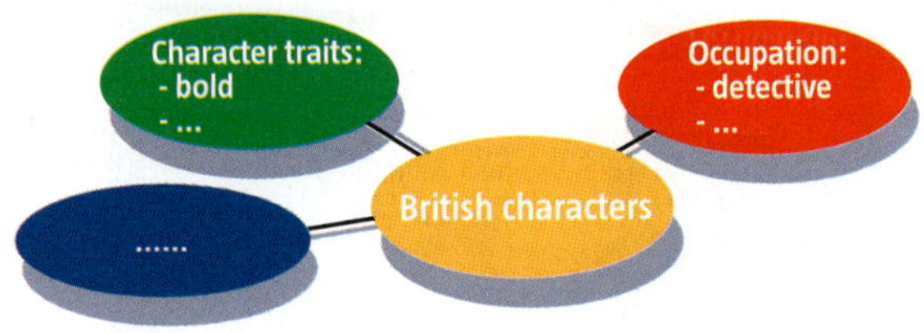

b. Use those words to speak about one or two characters you've studied in this chapter.

★ PRONUNCIATION

❹ Stress on negatives

track 52

"But for Heaven's sake, Holmes, I swear I have not uttered a word about the child nor his illness. You know that my wife is not at home. But I have not yet mentioned to you the reason for her absence.

Les formes négatives sont toujours accentuées car elles apportent des informations essentielles au message.

Listen to a conversation between Sherlock Holmes and Doctor Watson. Pay attention to the stress on negatives. Then practise saying this short dialogue.

track 53

❺ "-s" in plurals

track 54

a. Listen to the following nouns and indicate whether the final "-s" is pronounced /s/, /z/ or /iz/. Practise reading them aloud.

- citizens - tourists - eccentrics - gardens - values - traditions - explorers - sailors - castles - ships - dreams - heroes - kids - lives - places - streets - symbols - adventurers - buses - wars

b. Practise reading the following lines, paying attention to the pronunciation of "-s" in plurals.

Hunters for gold or pursuers of fame, they all had gone out on that stream, bearing the sword, and often the torch, messengers of the might within the land, bearers of a spark from the sacred fire. What greatness had not floated on the ebb of that river into the mystery of an unknown earth! ... The dreams of men, the seed of commonwealths, the germs of empires.

c. Now listen and check.

track 55

★ GRAMMAR

Verb + *-ing*

Observe

1. Being British is more than just eating fish and chips and curries.
2. After years of being embarrassed about our past, we are now proud to be who we are.
3. It is their individuality that is particularly interesting.
4. The beginning of this new James Bond film is as surprising as its ending.
5. Some British dishes may not sound tempting or appetizing but I can assure you most of them are very tasty.

Observez les formes en *-ing* ci-dessus. Quels types de mots permettent-elles de former ?

g → Grammaire ③ p. 192

Practise

6 **Complete these sentences using Verb + *-ing* forms.**
1. Being a James Bond means...
2. Being a hero implies...
3. Reading novels, ..., ..., ... is not my cup of tea.
4. Solving crimes requires...

7 **Write an e-mail to your new English-speaking penpal explaining what, in your opinion, being French is or is not. Give as many details as possible, using Verb + *-ing* forms.**

Have-en / had-en

Observe

1. I have always been impressed by Holmes's perspicacity and he keeps baffling me. Yesterday, as soon as he saw me, he discovered why I had not come earlier.
2. Holmes told me he had not discovered any new pieces of evidence, but I know he has already found some interesting ones.
3. I was surprised to hear that Holmes had not yet identified the murderer, but I am sure he has nearly solved the case.

Observez les formes verbales surlignées en rose et en bleu. Qu'expriment-elles ? Qu'est-ce qui les différencie ?

g → Grammaire ⑪ p. 200

Practise

8 **Put the verbs between brackets in the appropriate verbal form: *have-en* or *had-en*.**

Both of us *(hear)* about the art dealer when he contacted us and we couldn't believe he *(be robbed)*. He knew that Holmes already *(solve)* many cases, and he wanted him to investigate the case. Holmes asked the art dealer if he *(notice)* anything strange the day before, but apparently he *(have not)*. So far, Holmes *(manage)* to solve all the cases presented to him. I *(know)* him for years now, and I totally trust him and his expertise.

9 **Say what you have learnt about British characters:**
→ I've learnt that...
→ I hadn't heard of... before.
→ I had already read about...

More exercises in your Workbook → p. 60

Stratégies

Écrire un texte explicatif

Lorsque vous rédigez un texte explicatif, votre objectif est de faire comprendre le plus clairement possible un fait, un phénomène, un sujet, une opinion ou des sentiments.

Entraînez-vous à partir du sujet suivant :
In your opinion, how and why do some people become heroes?

1 Préparez et organisez votre explication

Étapes	Conseils	Exemples
Définissez le sujet et ses différents aspects.	• Différenciez le sens des mots. • Repérez les termes clés et vérifiez leur définition si besoin. • Reformulez le sujet.	→ *how = in many ways, why = because* → *hero, in your opinion* *hero = a man/woman of distinguished courage or ability, admired for his brave deeds and noble qualities* → on me demande de donner et de justifier mon avis sur...
Rassemblez vos connaissances sur le sujet.	• Appuyez-vous sur des exemples. • Balayez différents domaines. • Faites des recherches : encyclopédies, internet... • Faites des comparaisons.	→ *Rosa Parks, soldiers ....* → *politics, sports, science, art, everyday life... past - present* → *heroes' attitudes / other people's attitudes*
Faites un plan.	• Commencez par l'aspect le plus évident pour aller vers le moins évident.	→ **À vous** **Faites un plan pour répondre à la question posée ci-dessus.**

2 Rédigez un texte cohérent

Étapes	Conseils	Exemples
Introduisez le sujet.	• Captez l'attention du lecteur à l'aide d'une question, d'une citation...	→ *Why do some people do all they can to save a stranger while others are unable to act?*
Faites des paragraphes.	• Développez une idée par paragraphe.	→ *concern for other people*
Développez les exemples.	• Décrivez, racontez une scène.	→ *When he saw that the house was on fire, he just ran to the entrance door in order to try and save his neighbour.*
Marquez les étapes de l'explication.	• Utilisez des connections.	→ *first, second, third, last but not least, finally*

Étapes	Conseils	Exemples
Insistez sur la logique de l'explication.	• Indiquez clairement les liens de cause et de consequence	→ *because, since, all the more as...* → *so, then, as a result, that's why...*
Concluez.	• Résumez en une phrase ce que vous avez dit dans le texte.	→ *Simply put, I would say that the key to heroism is a concern for people in need*

→ À vous

Développez l'idée suivante en un paragraphe de 5 ou 6 lignes :
Who do you consider a hero? Explain why.

3 Retravaillez votre texte

Étapes	Conseils	Exemples
Évitez les répétitions.	• Utilisez des mots de substitution *(who, that, the other...).*	→ *The firefighter rescued his neighbour. His neighbour was injured.* → *The firefighter rescued his neighbour, who was injured.*
Précisez vos idées.	• Évitez les mots « passe partout » *(good, bad, very, nice...).*	→ *amazing, disappointing, funny, smart, extremely...*
Veillez à la cohérence des temps.	• Le présent pour parler de faits généraux. • Le passé lorsque vous racontez des événements.	→ *Courageous people are ready to give their lives.* → *When the fire broke out, his wife started yelling.*
Vérifiez la ponctuation.	• La ponctuation permet de donner du sens à la phrase.	→ *He is very courageous, he didn't mind risking his life to save his neighbour.*

→ À vous

Retravaillez le passage ci-contre.

The courage people show during times of disaster, it makes them different from others. They have courage and are very good. In Mumbai after the floods last year many people become heroes, they save other people. Perhaps they don't know they risk their lives, they rescue people and they don't think of themselves but they think of the other people; their lives are more important for them. They are nice people.

Le jour du Bac

Toutes séries

→ voir aussi *Entraînement Bac* p. 72

Lors de l'épreuve d'expression écrite du baccalauréat, vous serez amené(e) à rédiger un ou plusieurs textes construits.

- Appuyez-vous sur **ce que vous connaissez** et sur les éléments du texte qui vous sera fourni en **épreuve de compréhension de l'écrit** pour nourrir vos idées.
- Prenez le temps de faire un **brouillon**.
- **Présentez clairement** votre texte : soignez l'introduction et la conclusion, sautez des lignes pour marquer les différents paragraphes.
- Vérifiez l'**orthographe** et la **ponctuation**.
- N'oubliez pas d'écrire **lisiblement**.
- **Relisez-vous** attentivement.

FINAL TASKS

Favourite British icons

task 1

Writing

Present your favourite British character

Your class intend to publish a book entitled *A Gallery of British Icons and Remarkable Characters.*

1. Get ready

- Choose a character (fictional or real) you find typically British.
- Look up for information about him/her and take notes:

personal life | occupation | hobbies | qualities/faults

2. Action!

- Sort out the information gathered, keeping only the most striking characteristics.
- Write a short text (200 words) presenting your character and explaining why you think he/she embodies the true British icon.

task 2

Reading

Help website visitors discover heroic figures

As a contributor to an interactive website dedicated to heroic figures:

- read some posts expressing people's likes in movies or books,
- choose the heroic figure that would suit each person's tastes best.

Bac

Compréhension de l'oral

Listen to an interview:
My favourite fictional character

1. Listen to the document three times and take notes.

2. Write a report in French of what you have understood.

Expression orale

Oral presentation

1. Using what you have learnt about **British fictional heroes**, prepare notes about **British fictional characters** and to what extent they can be seen as **iconic figures**. You can follow these guidelines:

- How the British see themselves.
- What aspects of the British national character are echoed in remarkable fictional heroes?
- What real people or events inspired their creation?

Illustrate your presentation with relevant examples.

2. Give your oral presentation.

3. Be ready to discuss the topic with your teacher.

→ Aide

Utilisez la fiche *Recap* du workbook p. 61 ou sur www.didierpassword.fr pour préparer cette synthèse orale.

Compréhension de l'écrit

Study a set of documents

Your teacher will give you several documents. Read them carefully and answer the questions.

Expression écrite

Write two different texts

Using the elements given by your teacher, write:

1. An entry in a logbook

2. Your opinion about British characters

Good reads

"Hullo, Robinson Crusoe"

↑ A still from the film *Swallows and Amazons*, 1974

Four children, John, Susan, Titty and Roger, are holidaying with their mother on the shores of an unnamed lake in England. They have received permission to set sail on the dinghy* Swallow *to camp on a deserted island on the lake and have been there for some time.

"Hullo Man Friday," said Titty joyfully.

"Hullo, Robinson Crusoe," said Mother. That was the best of Mother. She was different from other natives. You could always count on her to know things like that.

Robinson Crusoe and Man Friday then kissed each other as if they were pretending to be Titty and Mother.

"You didn't expect to see me so soon after yesterday," said Mother, "but I came to say something to John. I supposed he's with the rest of the crew in that secret harbor of yours that poor natives are not allowed to see."

"No. He isn't on the island just at present," said Titty. "No one is except me... and now you too."

"So you really are Robinson Crusoe," said Mother "and I am Man Friday in earnest. If I'd known that I'd have made a good big footprint on the beach. But where are the others?"

"They're all right," said Titty. "They're coming back again. They've gone in *Swallow* on a cutting-out expedition." More than that she could not well say, because, after all,

Man Friday might be Mother, but she was also a native, even if she was the best native in the world.

"I expect they've gone to meet the Blackett children", said Mother.

"Man Friday ought not to know anything about them," said Titty.

"Very well, I won't," said Mother. "But what are you doing all by yourself?"

"Properly I'm in charge of the camp," said Titty. "But while they're not here it does not make any difference if I'm Robinson Crusoe instead."

"I am sure it doesn't," said Mother. "Have they left you anything to eat?"

"I've got my rations in the tent," said Titty.

"Well, it's high time you ate them," said Mother. "Will you let Man Friday put some more wood on the fire and make some tea? I can't stay very long but perhaps they'll be back before I go."

"I don't think they will," said Titty. "They've sailed across the Pacific Ocean. Timbuctoo is nothing to where they've gone."

"Well, I'll make some tea anyhow," said Mother. "Let's see what they've left you in the way of rations." [...]

When they had eaten their meal, which was a very good one, Robinson Crusoe said, "Now Man Friday, would you mind telling me some of your life before you came to this island?"

Man Friday began at once by telling how she had nearly been eaten by savages, and had only escaped by jumping out of the stew-pot at the last minute.

"Weren't you scalded?" said Robinson Crusoe.

"Badly," said Man Friday, "but I buttered the places that hurt most."

And then Man Friday forgot about being Man Friday and became Mother again, and told about her own childhood on a sheep station in Australia, and about emus that laid eggs as big as baby's heads, and opossums than ran about with their young ones in a pocket in their fronts, and about kangaroos that could kill a man with a kick, and about snakes that hid in the dust.

Here Robinson Crusoe, who had forgotten that she was Robinson Crusoe, and had turned into Titty again, talked about the snake which she had seen herself in the cigar-box that was kept in the charcoal-burners' wigwam. Then she told Mother about the dipper*, and how it had bobbed at her, and flown under water. Then Mother talked about the great drought on the sheep stations, when there was no rain and no water in the wells, and the flocks had to be driven miles and miles to get a drink, and thousands and thousands of them died. Then she talked of the pony she had when she was a little girl, and then of the little brown bears that her father caught in the bush, and that used to lick her fingers for her when she dipped them in honey.

Time went on very fast, much faster than when Robinson had been alone.

Arthur Ransome, *Swallows and Amazons* (1931)

* dipper: a species of birds that can dive and swim under water

Arthur Ransome (1884-1967)

English writer and journalist born in Leeds. He lived in St Petersburg and Moscow where he reported about the Russian Revolution for The Observer *and* The Manchester Guardian. *Today Arthur Ransome is best known for writing the* Swallows and Amazons *series. All remain in print and have been widely translated.*

UNIT 9 News from the world

↑ *The Times* - from print to online edition

How is the newsroom changing?

React to the photo, the title of the chapter and the question above. **Say** what you know or would like to know about news media.

FINAL TASKS

P. 184

Online messages

Writing
Have your say on an online forum

Reading
Pick out the best tweet

CULTURE	COMMUNICATION	TOOLS
• Learning about news media and their evolution. • Discovering new forms of journalism. • Social studies: - Eric Alterman, *"Out of print – The death and life of the American newspaper"* - Charlie Beckett, *"Is new media killing journalism?"* • Literary works: - Catherine O'Flynn, *The News Where You Are* - John Grisham, *The Last Juror*	Expressing an opinion, taking into account other points of view. Understanding key information and arguments in a press article and a narrative. Reporting facts and stating opinions.	★ **Words** • The press • Gullibility • Reliability • Editing • Exposure • Censorship/Freedom • Contributing • Audience • Worth ★ **Pronunciation** • Stress to contrast past and present • Verbs and adjectives ending in *"-ate"* ★ **Grammar** • *Used to / would* • *The more..., the more...*

Bac

Stratégies
→ *Écrire un texte argumentatif* p. 182

Évaluation
→ *4 situations d'évaluation* p. 185

Changing times

1 "How do you get your news?"

A survey by Boston University's students

1. **Before watching the video**, use the elements above to say what sort of document you expect to see and what it may be about.
2. **Watch the video** and say what you have understood.
3. **a.** Watch the video again and pick out:
   - the news outlets these people use,
   - how often they use them.

   b. Complete a pie chart showing these people's habits.

   page 62 or www.didierpassword.fr
4. **Link** your findings to the graph below. What conclusions can you reach?

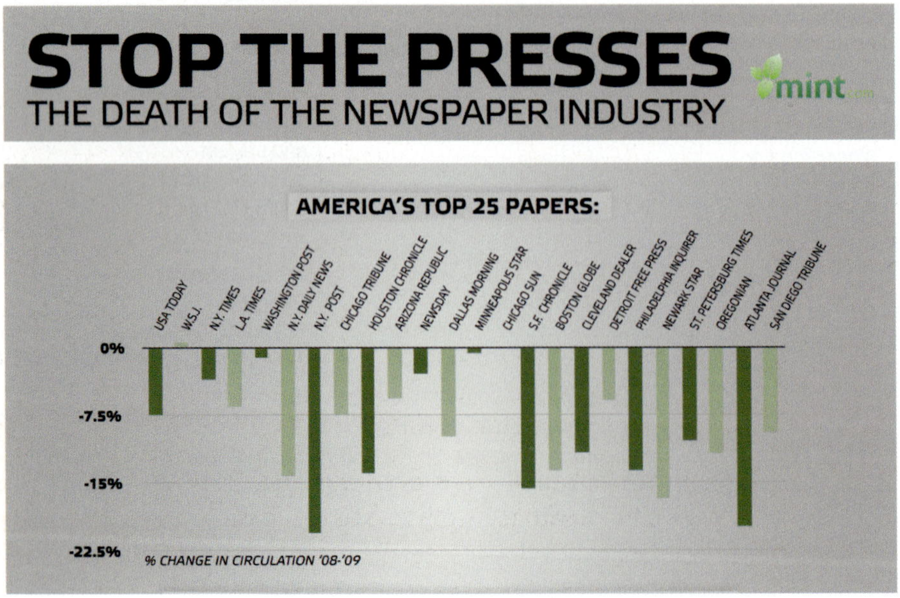

← **% change in newspaper circulation between 2008 and 2009**

e.g. *The Wall Street Journal* (W.S.J.) is the only newspaper to have increased its circulation between 2008 and 2009.

2 "A new era"

There are three ways to look at how society is informed.

The first is that people are gullible and will read, listen to, or watch just about anything.

The second is that most people require an informed intermediary to tell them what is good, important or meaningful.

The third is that people are pretty smart; given the means, they can sort things out for themselves, find their own version of the truth.

The means have arrived. The truth is out there. Throughout history, access to news and information has been a privilege accorded to powerful institutions with the authority or wealth to dominate distribution. For the past two centuries, an independent press has served as advocate for society and its right to know — an essential role during an era of democratic enlightenment.

It feels like a new era has been thrust upon us — an era of enlightened anxiety. We now know more than ever before, but our knowledge creates anxiety over harsh truths and puzzling paradoxes.

The Media Center at the American Press Institute, July 2003

1. **Read the title and the source of the article**: what information do you expect to get?
2. **Read the article** and say what you have understood.
3. **a.** Read again. **Pick out information** about:
   - the different types of press readers,
   - how they have had access to information throughout history.

   page 62

   b. Share your findings.
4. **Focus on the last paragraph** and explain how the journalist represents the "new era".

Recap → Explain how information has changed in recent years. page 71

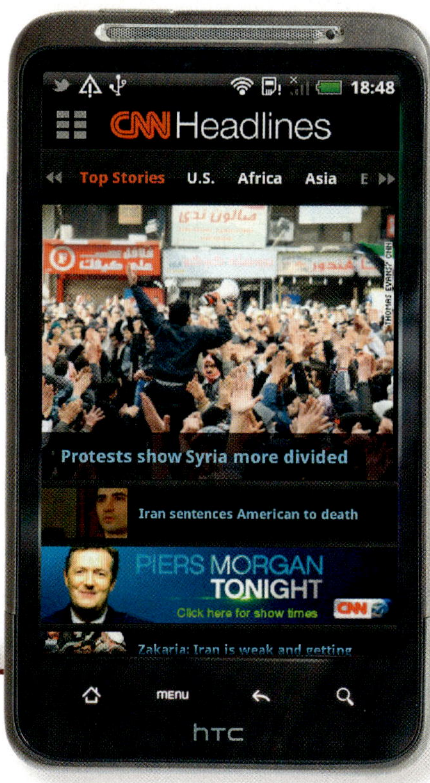

LANGUAGE TOOLS

★ WORDS

The press

- **dai**ly, **week**ly, **month**ly, peri**o**dical
- **me**dia, **news out**let, **news**room, **press a**gency
- high/low circu**la**tion, **rea**dership
- **co**lumnist, **e**ditor
- edi**to**rial, **co**lumns, dis**patch**, **press** release

Gullibility

- na**i**vety, cre**du**lity, blind
- **gu**llible, na**ive**, **cre**dulous, un**wa**ry, **can**did

★ PRONUNCIATION → p. 180

Stress to contrast past and present

→ Ten years ago people didn't read news on their computers, now a lot do.

Training Task

Conducting a survey

1. **In groups**: interview 5 friends, 5 relatives and 5 people in the street.
   - How do they get their news?
   - Have they changed their habits?
2. Present your findings as percentages (%), and compare them with the statistics seen in class.

The explosion of news websites

1 A shared enterprise

Founded by Ariana Huffington and Jonah Peretti, The Huffington Post *was launched in May 2005. A Canadian edition and a UK version followed in 2011. The French version was started in 2012.*

Out of Print - The death and life of the American newspaper

by Eric Alterman - March 31, 2008
The New Yorker

The Huffington Post started out by aggregating political news and gossip; it also organized a group blog, with writers drawn largely from Huffington's alarmingly vast array of friends and connections. [...]

On the Huffington Post, Peretti explains, news is not something handed down from above but "a shared enterprise between its producer and its consumer." Echoing Murdoch*, he says that the Internet offers editors "immediate information" about which stories interest readers, provoke comments, are shared with friends, and generate the greatest number of Web searches. An Internet-based news site, Peretti contends, is therefore "alive in a way that is impossible for paper and ink."

Though Huffington has a news staff (it is tiny, but the hope is to expand in the future), the vast majority of the stories that it features originate elsewhere, whether in print, on television, or on someone's video camera or cell phone. The editors link to whatever they believe to be the best story on a given topic. Then they repurpose it with a catchy, often liberal-leaning headline and provide a comment section beneath it, where readers can chime in. Surrounding the news articles are the highly opinionated posts of an apparently endless army of both celebrity [...] and non-celebrity bloggers – more than eighteen hundred so far. The bloggers are not paid. The over-all effect may appear chaotic and confusing, but, Lerer argues, "this new way of thinking about, and presenting, the news, is transforming news as much as CNN did thirty years ago." Arianna Huffington and her partners believe that their model points to where the news business is heading. [...]

Additional oddities abound. Whereas a newspaper tends to stand by its story on the basis of an editorial process in which professional reporters and editors attempt to vet their sources and check their accuracy before publishing, the blogosphere relies on its readership – its community – for quality control. At the Huffington Post, Jonah Peretti explains, the editors "stand behind our front page" and do their best to insure that only trusted bloggers and reliable news sources are posted there. Most posts inside the site, however, go up before an editor sees them. Only if a post is deemed by a reader to be false, defamatory, or offensive does an editor get involved. ■

* **Murdoch:** founder, Chairman and CEO of News Corporation, the world's second-largest media conglomerate.

2 "Unprocessed and raw"

www.scoop.co.nz

Unique, independent and necessary in NZ media...

Scoop.co.nz is New Zealand's leading news resource for news-makers and the people that influence the news (as opposed to a news site for "news consumers")

Scoop INDEPENDENT NEWS

Freedom, expression, ideas, information, empowerment, transformation

The scoop.co.nz publication is a new media, born of the Internet and populated by material of the Internet. It delivers news in a totally new way – unprocessed and raw "from the horse's mouth". Scoop.co.nz is transforming the news environment – providing an open forum for a variety of perspectives to co-exist just as the sources intended.

In the paper you read digested news – usually late. On the radio and TV you receive sound-bite news – compressed to fit demographic formats that must select and discriminate. Censor.

The majority of Internet based news services are based on feeds of news from the old – real-world – media, transcribed and regurgitated online. scoop.co.nz is not – it's raw news as it gets released.

On Scoop you can read the news at the same time that the media are reading it. It is all here... the good oil... the whole story... the whole speech... what the Prime Minister really said, not what the reporter heard them say. Better yet you get to hear it when the Prime Minister said it. Not tomorrow.

Scoop believes in the power of information to transform lives. It believes in the power of the Internet to resolve conflict. And it believes in the power of compelling ideas to propel themselves into political consciousness if they are able to get exposure and be debated. Scoop is, necessarily, a forum that is neither censored through its own prejudices nor controlled by a multinational media conglomerate.

1. Look at the documents on p. 174-175 and briefly state what news media they are about. Say what you know about this type of media.

2. a. In groups: choose to focus either on the *Huffington Post (group 1)* or *Scoop (group 2)*. Read the text and pick out information about:
- new sources of information,
- how the information is processed and edited,
- the purpose of the media. page 63

b. Organize your findings.

3. a. Report your findings to the other groups.
b. Compare the two news media.

4. Discuss what issues are raised by the explosion of news websites.

Recap → Compare news websites and traditional newspapers. page 71

LANGUAGE TOOLS

★ **WORDS**

Reliability
- **re**levant, **a**ccurate, rel**i**able, **trust**worthy
- ir**re**levant, in**a**ccurate, unde**pen**dable, unrel**i**able, un**sound**, un**true**

Editing
- pro**cess**, com**pose**, cut, **am**plify, re**lease** news
- **ve**rify, check, vet, **cen**sor

Exposure
- reve**la**tion, un**co**vering, dis**clo**sure, un**mas**king
- in**ves**tigate, con**vey**
- im**part** infor**ma**tion

TRAINING TASK

Posting comments

You decide to post a comment (either on *The Huffington Post* or *Scoop*) about what you think the purpose of a news website should be. Write it in about 120 words.

A participatory revolution

Is new media killing journalism?

The public are now becoming partners with journalists in the production of news.

Media freedom is about power and it is time for that power to shift. Journalists have always been the subject of our concerns about press freedom, but now the public must become part of the equation. Working together, journalists and citizens can secure our fragile media freedoms in the face of global threats.

The amount of media freedom has increased since the end of the Cold War and the liberalisation of media markets around the world. Improving levels of literacy, increasing wealth and progressive political changes mean we have more information, debate and reporting of our world than ever before. New technology means that it is harder for authoritarian regimes to control the flow of media. News is exponentially faster, fuller and more accessible – from Burma to Birmingham.

At the same time professional journalists are still subject to familiar hazards such as violence, censorship and commercial pressure. Some would argue that these have taken new and sinister forms in places such as China, Russia or even the west. Superficially, freedom is expanding, but in practice, professional journalism is still constantly under threat. So how do we save it?

In my new book, *SuperMedia*, I argue that in the end only politics can protect press freedom but that there is a lot that the news media can do. The first step is to embrace networked journalism.

This is the idea that traditional journalism opens itself up to the public. It shares the production process from start to finish. It uses new technologies to include the citizen in every aspect of news-gathering, production and publication. It means using a lot of jargon like crowd-sourcing, social networking, *wikis* and *Twittering*. Many of these techniques build on existing journalism methods and are already out there. But it will also require a participatory revolution in the way we make the news.

Participatory journalism

The act of a citizen, or group of citizens, playing an active role in the process of collecting, reporting, analyzing and disseminating news and information. The intent of this participation is to provide the independent, reliable, accurate, wide-ranging and relevant information that a democracy requires.

OhmyNews was created in 1999 by OH, a South Korean journalist, who was concerned by the imbalance of power in the media environment in South Korea. It is now the most influential online news site in South Korea, attracting an estimated 2 million readers a day. It is produced by more than 26,000 registered citizen reporters. Its first international edition was launched in 2004.

Blogging is the least of it. Much more important, for example, is the use of camera phones by citizens, capturing news as it happens and sending it to news organisations around the world. This produced the images of demonstrations by monks in Tibet or police beatings in Zimbabwe that would otherwise have been out of the range of the professional photographers' lens. That is media freedom. [...]

In future we must think about media freedom as the human right to free expression, not just as the protection of a trade. And that means that journalists must accept that they can no longer be the privileged gatekeepers to information or the sole arbiters of editorial judgement. [...]

But the power shift to the public in news production means that the journalist is now not alone in the struggle for press freedom. If the public are part of the process and they value what is created then they will also want a more free and open news media. It's a new compact of trust.

This may sound a tad idealistic. It is the opposite. Networked journalism is both a business model and a practical strategy to secure the future of journalism and its freedom. ■

Charlie Beckett,
The Guardian,
May 2008

1. **Read the definition of "participatory journalism" and the information about *OhmyNews*.**
   What are the main characteristics of this online newspaper?
2. **Read the title and the standfirst of the article.**
   Discuss what you expect to read.
3. **a. Read the article** and say what you have understood.
   b. Highlight elements illustrating this idea: *"the public must become part of the equation"* (l. 6). pages 64-65
4. **Explain** Charlie Beckett's opinion about "The power shift to the public in news production" (l. 80).

Recap → Explain the possible benefits of participatory journalism. page 71

LANGUAGE TOOLS

★ WORDS

Censorship/freedom
- **pre**ssure, **stru**ggle, demon**stra**tion
- en**dan**ger, **threa**ten, **jeo**pardize, be under threat, se**cure free**dom

Contributing
- corres**pon**dents, **ci**tizen re**por**ters, **blo**ggers, **part**ners
- sub**mit sto**ries/news, con**tri**bute to, pro**vide** infor**ma**tion, de**bate**
- **news**-gathering = co**llec**ting/re**por**ting news
- **crowd**-sourcing = unpaid online collaboration

★ GRAMMAR → p. 181

Used to/would

→ She used to work in this newsroom. I remember she would write her articles every morning.

↑ Pakistani university students use their mobile phones to record video of a protest, Jan. 7, 2011.

TRAINING TASK

A Tweet

After reading Charlie Beckett's article, write a Tweet to react to it (140 characters).

The professional journalist's role

"Who are we making the programmes for?"

Frank and Julia, two TV journalists, are talking about their job.

"That man is such an idiot. He has such a low opinion of the viewers. He thinks they're imbeciles." She paused, but Frank could tell she was only just getting started. "'He's not the only one, of course. I wonder sometimes who we are making the programmes for. People who are desperate to hear us repackage press releases from the fire service? People who demand no greater interactivity than an email address on the screen? People who can't focus on anything longer than one minute and a half? All we do is bombard people with these random, decontextualized jumbles of facts and faces. Don't you ever wonder who actually watches this programme?"

"Well, people do watch us – there are viewing figures."

"Watch us? Really watch us? Do you reckon? Okay, maybe older people who've always watched us. But the bulk of those figures – we're just on in the background. A familiar noise while they're eating their tea."

Frank shook his head. "But regional news is important. The small-scale, the local – that matters to people, it matters to me. Why shouldn't we be able to see stories that happen here? Why shouldn't we have a sense of our own identity?"

Julia laughed. "Are you joking? [...] If they want to know about the rest of the country, they'll watch the main stories on the national news. If they want local news, they want news about their locality. The only identity this programme reflects is whichever fool has been put in charge of the control for this day."

"Sometimes we get it right."

"Rarely – more by chance than design. Most of the time we're dicking about in no-man's land with stories that are neither specific nor broad enough to interest anyone. Sometimes I feel as if we have a deliberate policy of avoiding the news, of reporting anything that actually matters."

Frank reflected on this. "It's just a time of transition – we've been through them in the past. The internet has changed everything and we're still trying to work it out, but I think we will. In the meantime I don't think we're doing anything evil or wrong."

↑ A still from *Morning Glory*, directed by Roger Michell, 2010

Julia smiled. "No. Just utterly pointless. I like working with you, Frank – you know that, and don't take any offence – but this is just the place you come every day for a few hours. It's just a job for you. You've got family and stuff outside of work and you never let this be important to you. But my work means everything to me. I want it to define me. If I think I'm doing a shit job, I feel worthless – it eats away at me."

Frank smiled a little.

"What's funny?"

"It's nothing."

"What?"

"I was thinking how you actually sound like the kind of journalists you see in films – you know, fire in the belly – you sound like the real thing."

Julia nodded sadly. "I've got to get out of here, Frank."

"I'm not sure you'll find things very different wherever you go."

Catherine O'Flynn,
***The News Where You Are* (2010)**

1. Read the title: guess who "we" may be and suggest answers to the question.

2. Read the text. Say what you have understood.

3. In groups, read the text again. Highlight information about viewers, news content, and the journalist's job:
- in Julia's opinion *(group 1)*,
- in Frank's opinion *(group 2)*.

pages 66-67

4. a. Explain: *"In the meantime..."* (l. 49-51) *Julia smiled. "No. Just utterly pointless".*
b. Discuss the meaning of Frank's final statement.

5. Look at the two cartoons: to what extent do they illustrate the text?

Recap → What are the different views on a professional journalist's role? page 71

LANGUAGE TOOLS

★ WORDS

Audience
- **vie**wers, (online) **vie**wing figures, **me**dia ratings

Worth
- **va**luable ≠ **va**lueless
- **worth**while ≠ **worth**less
- **mea**ningful ≠ **mea**ningless, **point**less, insig**ni**ficant
- be **news**worthy

★ GRAMMAR → p. 181
The more..., the more...

★ PRONUNCIATION → p. 180
Words ending in *-ate*

TRAINING TASK

Applying for a new job

Julia decides to apply for a new job at a news channel that broadcast news 24hrs a day.

1. List at least five arguments and reasons she gives...
- for quitting her present job,
- for choosing the new job.

2. Draft her application letter.

★ WORDS

❶ Matching

Match the words below and their definitions.

1. news item 2. circulation 3. a weekly 4. headline 5. standfirst 6. news-stand	a. outside place where newspapers are sold b. number of papers sold c. short title d. explanatory text under the main heading of a news article e. newspaper printed once a week f. event recorded in the press

❷ Newspaper sections

Explain what the following newspaper sections deal with.

- agony column, review, horoscope, sports, national news, lifestyle, international news, leaders, entertainment, feature, business, obituary, editorial

→ *editorial = a piece of writing that gives the editor's opinion*

❸ Talking about the press (Bac)

a. Link verbs to complements in order to find as many expressions as possible.

verbs	complements	
denounce	an event;	wrong-doings
publish	a report;	a counter power
report	news;	political scandals
file	conflicts;	massive coverage
leak	stories;	provocative comments
represent	a force;	embarrassing facts
cover	views;	demonstrations
provide	information;	press releases
launch		specific geographic areas
expose		
investigate		

→ *represent a counter-power*

b. Talk about the power of the press, using some of the expressions you have found in *a*.

★ PRONUNCIATION

❹ Stress to contrast past and present (track 56)

In the past, only a few people would read newspapers. Today, nearly everyone can get the news from the Internet.

Lorsque le locuteur souhaite marquer la différence entre un « avant » et un « après », il accentue plus fortement les éléments qui ont évolué.

a. Listen to the following sentences and say which words are more stressed. Then practise reading them. (track 57)

1. Before the advent of technology, access to information was a privilege but now, most citizens in the world have unlimited access to international news.
2. Centuries ago, it was not easy to know what was going on in the rest of the world. Nowadays, information is just a click away.
3. Now this news website is one of the most influential. But when it was created in 2000, it was hardly visited.

b. Practise in your workbook. pages 68-69

❺ Verbs and adjectives ending in *"-ate"* (track 58)

a. Listen to the following words:

1. *Verbs:* communicate - dominate - educate - originate - illustrate - create
2. *Adj.:* immediate - accurate - illiterate - desperate - adequate - passionate

b. What do you notice about the pronunciation of *"-ate"*?

c. Practise reading the following words aloud:

verbs	adjectives
investigate	separate
advocate	delicate
separate	legitimate
legitimate	deliberate
deliberate	intricate
circulate	ultimate
participate	surrogate
cooperate	intimate

d. Listen and check. (track 59)

★ GRAMMAR

Used to / would

Observe

1. My parents didn't use to read newspapers on line but now they do. I remember how they would keep telling me they did not trust the Internet.

2. She used to work for a local newspaper when she was in her thirties and would always make sure her reports never hurt anyone she knew.

3. When I was younger I used to read a lot of comics. I would stay in my room for hours and read them over and over again. It would drive my parents crazy.

4. When he was a schoolboy, my father used to deliver newspapers early in the morning. He enjoyed it so much he would even do it in the holidays.

- **Qu'expriment les formes verbales surlignées ?**
- **En quoi diffèrent-elles au niveau du sens ?**

g → Grammaire ⑬ p. 202

Practise

6 What was it like before the rise of the internet?

Ex. Christmas cards / a fortune on stamps
→ People used to post Christmas cards. They would spend a fortune on stamps.

1. Long distance phone calls / wait ages and get no connection
2. Political events in far away places / no immediate knowledge
3. Read only one favourite newspaper / limited point of view
4. Prepare a trip abroad with printed guides / no access to various people's experiences

7 Imagine you're talking to your grand-children in 50 years' time. Tell them what it was like when you were younger.

"See kids? This is a LETTER. A LETTER. Back when I was a kid, people would send these all the time. There was no such thing as e-mail."

The more..., the more...

Observe

1. The more copies you sell, the more profits you make.
2. The fewer readers, the less profit.
3. Which magazine do you want? The glossier the better?
4. Join our team. The more, the merrier!

- **Qu'expriment les éléments soulignés ?**
- **Observez et décrivez leur construction.**

g → Grammaire ⑦ p. 197

Practise

8 The following 'vicious circle' describes the problems journalists are facing today. Write sentences explaining the problems.

many media → much competition → low prices → low salaries → few journalists → little investigation → low quality in reports → many comments from the readers → little credibility
→ *The more media, the more competition; the more competition...*

9 A new member has joined your school magazine team. Tell him what is expected in the magazine.
→ *The more events we cover, the happier the readers.*

More exercises in your Workbook → p. 69-70

Écrire un texte argumentatif

On écrit un texte argumentatif pour défendre un point de vue, en s'appuyant sur des arguments susceptibles d'emporter l'adhésion du lecteur.

Entraînez-vous à partir du sujet suivant :

"Better technology, better informed". Do you agree?

1 Rassemblez vos idées

Étapes	Conseils	Exemples	→ À vous
1. Identifiez la problématique (la question que l'on se pose à partir d'un thème).	• Repérez les **mots clés** et assurez-vous de comprendre **leur sens** (cherchez des synonymes une explication, des exemples). • Mettez-les en relation et reformulez le sujet.	→ *technology* → *informed: getting news* → *better... better: a comparison (better than before, better than without technology).* → *Which news media to use? (press, websites, TV...)*	**Identifiez le thème et la question que l'on se pose.**
2. Rassemblez vos idées	• **Mobilisez vos connaissances** et notez toutes les idées et les exemples qui vous viennent à l'esprit. • **Trouvez des idées** en faisant des associations. • **Relativisez** l'idée exprimée dans le sujet. • **Cherchez à la contredire**. • **Complétez** par quelques recherches (internet, presse...)	→ *access to worldwide media thanks to the Internet/online news media* → *immediate news/no delay* → *maybe not really reliable/ not processed* → *in some parts of the world, the press is not free, so information is biased.*	**Ajoutez vos propres idées sur la question.**

2 Élaborez votre plan

La clarté de votre propos dépendra de l'organisation de votre texte. Bâtissez un plan thématique dans lequel vous aborderez successivement différents aspects du problème. Par exemple :

Aspect 1 : *Amount of information*	
Opinion	→ *We are better informed*
Explication	→ *We can have access to news websites worldwide*
Exemple	→ *No problem with language, thanks to international editions of news websites such as* The Huffington Post
Prise en considération d'un avis différent sur ce même aspect	→ *Some people believe online journalism always highlights the same stories*

→ À vous

Préparez un plan thématique pour classer les idées notées lors de l'étape 1.

3 Rédigez votre texte

Éléments		Exemples	→ À vous
L'introduction	• Introduisez le thème et la problématique (citation, question…). • Donnez l'opinion que vous allez défendre. *ou* • Donnez l'opinion opposée à celle que vous allez défendre pour la mettre d'emblée en question. *ou* • Donnez des opinions nuancées et indiquez de quelle opinion vous vous sentez le/la plus proche.	→ *The globalisation of news can be connected to the advances in technology, but does that mean we are better informed?* → *I personally don't think so…* → *Some people claim this is definitely so.* → *The question has triggered much debate, even if it is widely believed that the information age has brought change and improvement.*	**Rédigez votre introduction.**
Les paragraphes	• Variez l'**expression de l'opinion** (verbes, adverbes, adjectifs, modaux)	→ *There is no denying that much online journalism is repetitive.*	**Rédigez un paragraphe en vous appuyant sur le plan que vous avez élaboré en 2.**
	• Insistez sur les **articulations logiques** pour marquer les étapes du raisonnement (cause, conséquence : *as, because, that's why, therefore*) et relier des idées différentes (concession : *however, nevertheless, and yet…*).	→ *I would argue that while we spend more time getting our news through the Internet, I'm not sure if this means we are more or less informed.*	
	• Utilisez la **comparaison**, l'expression de l'**hypothèse** pour présenter vos arguments et vos exemples.	→ *If we couldn't use all these new technological devices, like our laptops or smartphones, we wouldn't be able to…*	
La conclusion	• Résumez les **enjeux principaux**. • Ouvrez de **nouvelles perspectives**	→ *To conclude, I would say that the way we get our information is undoubtedly changing.* → *The new media may have the potential to make us more informed, but they haven't yet.*	**Proposez votre conclusion.**

Le jour du Bac

Toutes séries

→ voir aussi *Entraînement Bac* p. 72

• Donnez-vous le temps de bien **identifier la problématique** afin d'éviter les hors sujets (c'est-à-dire de parler d'autre chose).

• Prenez également le temps d'**organiser votre texte au brouillon** : la clarté de votre organisation contribuera à convaincre votre lecteur.

• **Soyez sûr(e)** de ce que vous affirmez pour être convaincant et **illustrez** le propos par des exemples.

• Ne cherchez pas à traiter le sujet de manière exhaustive : **choisissez deux ou trois points** qui vous semblent importants pour traiter la problématique et concentrez-vous sur l'écriture, en respectant le nombre de mots.

• **Respectez la mise en forme** :
- pour un texte : marquez les paragraphes en allant à la ligne ;
- pour un dialogue : passez à la ligne quand vous changez de personnage et contrôlez les marques de ponctuation.

FINAL TASKS

Online messages

task 1

Writing

Have your say on an online forum

http://topics.journalism/ — journalism forum

WHO SHOULD BE CALLED A JOURNALIST?

In an age when anyone can use new media to share information with the world, who should be called a journalist? What do you think?

Post reply

April 11
By chazbennett

Topic: Who should be called a journalist?

Having worked as a journalist for some time now, I'm often agitated by what is referred to as 'journalism' and how any story by any contributor or a person with a view gets pushed and given more prominence on the cover than the work of true journalists.

April 16
By xohxoh29

Re: Who should be called a journalist?

A journalist is a person who is capable of presenting information accurately, truthfully and in a balanced way. A good journalist always observes the ethics of his profession, without exception.

May 04
By Claire

Re.Re: Who should be called a journalist?

I think the conventional definition of a journalist has changed with the popularity of social media and the development of information technology.

1. Get ready

- Read the comments posted on this forum.
- **In groups**: make sure you understand them and discuss your contribution to the forum.

2. Action!

- Organize your answer taking into account what has been written.
- **On your own**: write your comment (200 words).

task 2

Reading

Pick out the right tweet

Your teacher will give you an article and several tweets: read them all, then decide which tweet best corresponds to the article.

Bac

Compréhension de l'oral

Listen to a radio programme:
American journalism in peril

1. Listen to the document three times and take notes.
2. Write a report in French of what you have understood.

Expression orale

Oral presentation

1. Using what you have learnt about the changing newsroom, prepare notes about how the evolution of news media changes the power of the press.
You can follow these guidelines:
    - The impact of technology on news media and how the newsroom has changed in recent years.
    - The evolution of the role of journalists and their audience: who will be able to report/cover news in the future? how? who for?
    - To what extent the contribution of the public to the "fourth estate" can be a power check.
    - The purpose of the media.

    Illustrate your presentation with relevant examples you may know.
2. Give your oral presentation.
3. Be ready to discuss the topic with your teacher.

→ Aide

Utilisez la fiche *Recap* du workbook p. 71 ou sur www.didierpassword.fr pour préparer cette synthèse orale.

Compréhension de l'écrit

Study a set of documents

Your teacher will give you several documents. Read them carefully and answer the questions.

Expression écrite

Write two different texts

Using the elements given by your teacher, write:

1. A contribution to an online forum
2. A letter to the editor

Good reads

Lofty dreams

↑ Robert Capa, world-acclaimed photojournalist, in 1937

J.W. Traynor dreams of becoming an investigative reporter for a famous national newspaper, but his poor academic record forces him to reconsider his choice of a career.

I grew up in Memphis and studied journalism at Syracuse for five years before my grandmother got tired of paying for what was becoming an extended education. My grades were unremarkably low, and I was a year away from a degree. Maybe a year and a half. She, BeeBee, had plenty of money, hated to spend it, and after five years she figured my opportunity had been sufficiently funded. When she cut me off I was very disappointed, but I did not complain, to her anyway. I was her only grandchild and her estate would be a delight.

I studied journalism with a hangover. In the early days at Syracuse, I aspired to be an investigative reporter with the *New York Times* or the *Washington Post*. I wanted to save the world by uncovering corruption and environmental abuse and government waste and the injustice suffered by the weak and oppressed. Pulitzers were waiting for me. After a year or so of such lofty dreams, I saw a movie about a foreign correspondent who dashed around the world looking for wars, seducing beautiful women, and somehow finding the time to write award-winning stories. He spoke eight languages, wore a beard, combat boots, starched khakis that never wrinkled. So I decided I would become such a journalist. I grew a beard, bought some boots and khakis, tried to learn German, tried to score with prettier girls. During my junior years, when my grades began their steady decline to the bottom of the class, I became captivated by the idea of working for a small-town newspaper. I cannot explain this attraction, except that it was at about the time that I met and befriended Nick Diener. He was from rural Indiana, and for decades his family had owned a rather prosperous county newspaper. He drove a fancy little Alfa Romeo and always had plenty of cash. We became close friends.

Nick was a brilliant student who could have handled medicine, law or engineering. His only goal, however, was to return to Indiana and run the family business. This baffled me until we got drunk one night and he told me how much his father cleared each year off their small weekly – circulation six thousand. It was a gold mine, he said. Just local news, wedding announcements, church socials, honor rolls, sports coverage, pictures of basketball teams, a few recipes, a few obituaries, and pages of advertising. Maybe a little politics, but stay away from controversy. And count your money. His father was a millionaire. It was laid-back, low-pressure journalism with money growing on trees, according to Nick.

This appealed to me. After my fourth year, which should've been my last but wasn't close, I spent the summer interning at a small weekly in the Ozark Mountains of Arkansas. The pay was peanuts but BeeBee was impressed because I was employed. Each week I mailed her the paper, at least half of which was written by me. The owner/editor/publisher was a wonderful old gentleman who was delighted to have a reporter who wanted to write. He was quite wealthy.

After five years at Syracuse my grades were irreparable, and the well ran dry. I returned to Memphis, visited BeeBee, thanked her for her efforts, and told her loved her. She told me to find a job.

At this time Wilson Caudle's sister lived in Memphis, and through the course of things this lady met BeeBee at one of those hot tea drinkers' parties. After a few phone calls back and forth, I was packed and headed to Clanton, Mississippi, where Spot was eagerly waiting. After an hour of orientation, he turned me loose on Ford County.

In the next edition he ran a sweet little story with a photo of me announcing my "internship" at the *Times*. It made the front page. News was slow in those days. [...]

After years of financial trouble,* The Times *goes bankrupt. With money loaned by BeeBee, J.W. buys the newspaper and becomes the owner and editor.

The new *Times* debuted on March 18, 1970 [...]. It was almost an inch thick and loaded with more photos than has ever been published in a county weekly. Cub Scouts troops, Brownies, junior high basketball teams, garden clubs, book clubs, tea clubs, Bible study groups, adult softball teams, civic clubs. Dozens of photos. I tried to include every living soul in the country. And the dead ones were exhalted like never before. The obits were embarrassingly long. [...]

The news was light and breezy. Absolutely no editorials. People love to read about crime, so on the bottom left-hand corner of the front page I launched the Crime Notes Section. Thankfully, two pickups had been stolen the week before, and I covered these heists as if Fort Knox had been looted.

[...] I was proud of my staff. We had worked around the clock for ten days, and our first edition was a great success. We printed five thousand copies and sold them all. I sent a box of them to BeeBee, and she was most impressed.

For the next months, the new *Times* slowly took shape as I struggled to determine what I wanted it to become. Change is painful in rural Mississippi, so I decided to do it gradually. The old paper was bankrupt, but it had changed little in fifty years. I wrote more news, sold more ads, included more and more pictures of groups of endless varieties. And I worked hard on the obituaries.

John Grisham, *The Last Juror* (2004)

John Grisham (born 1955)

John Grisham is considered the master of the legal thriller. He began his career as a lawyer in Mississippi, but became a full-time writer following the success of his second novel, The Firm.

SOMMAIRE

L'énoncé : quelques définitions préalables

L'ÉNONCÉ : QUELQUES DÉFINITIONS PRÉALABLES

Parler une langue, c'est **exprimer des idées**, les partager, les confronter. Ces idées sont véhiculées à travers des énoncés, messages écrits ou oraux, simples (ex : *« Pardon » / « Laure parle anglais. »*) ou complexes (ex : *« Bien que Laure ne soit jamais allée en Angleterre, elle parle anglais couramment. »*), que l'on produit en contexte, dans **une situation donnée**. Cette situation s'appelle **la situation d'énonciation**. Elle met en scène un **énonciateur** (celui qui produit l'énoncé) et un **co-énonciateur** (le destinataire de l'énoncé).

Ce précis grammatical vous aidera :

- à repérer et analyser les formes que peuvent prendre les groupes nominaux, les groupes verbaux et les phrases en anglais.
- à mieux saisir leurs sens et ainsi à mieux les utiliser lors des différentes situations de communication dans lesquelles vous vous trouverez.

Quelques définitions utiles

Adjectif :	Mot qui détermine et qualifie un nom/groupe nominal.
Adverbe :	Mot qui modifie le sens d'un verbe, d'un adjectif, d'un autre adverbe ou d'une phrase.
Agent :	Celui qui fait l'action.
Auxiliaire :	mot qui permet de construire diverses formes verbales. On l'utilise notamment pour former des énoncés négatifs et interrogatifs. Trois auxiliaires en anglais : *DO, BE, HAVE* auxquels s'ajoutent les auxiliaires modaux.
Base verbale :	→ Voir : *Infinitif*
Coordination :	Juxtaposition de deux noms/groupes nominaux/groupes adjectivaux/ propositions liés entre eux par une conjonction de coordination (ex : *and, but, so, consequently, however*).
Infinitif :	Forme nue du verbe, appelée aussi « base verbale » (ex : *walk, work, eat, sing*).
Préposition :	Mot qui permet d'introduire un complément (ex : *at, by, from, in, on*).
Proposition :	Ensemble de mots composé en général d'un sujet et d'un groupe verbal, parfois simplement d'un groupe nominal.
Subordination :	Lien entre une proposition subordonnée rattachée à une proposition principale par une conjonction de subordination (ex : *although, whereas, while*).
Verbe transitif :	Verbe suivi d'un complément direct ou indirect (par opposition à « verbe intransitif »).

I — Le groupe nominal

En anglais, le nom est **déterminé** par des éléments qui viennent se placer directement à sa gauche. Les compléments que l'on trouve à sa droite relèvent de l'**expansion** du groupe nominal.

Détermination du nom			Nom	Expansion du nom
• article • adjectif démonstratif • quantifieur • génitif /adjectif possessif	adjectif (s) qualificatif(s)	nom	nom	proposition(s) relative(s)

Their amazing video report, which was about incredible people, came out on TV yesterday.

1 Noms dénombrables et indénombrables

a. Noms dénombrables

Ces noms renvoient à des éléments distincts que l'on peut séparer, quantifier à l'aide d'adjectifs numéraux *(one, two, three...)* ou de quantifieurs *(many, a lot of)*.

pen → ten pens   *flower → a bunch of flowers*   *book → many books*

b. Noms indénombrables

Ces noms renvoient à quelque chose de global, envisagé comme un tout. Ils n'ont qu'une forme singulier et le verbe qui suit est lui aussi singulier. Parmi eux, on trouve des termes qui renvoient à des activités *(swimming, reading)*, des catégories *(wood, sand, tea)*, des notions abstraites *(knowledge, luck, peace, freedom, courage)*. Il est possible de les quantifier :

money → plenty of money   *coffee → a cup of coffee*   *bread → a loaf of bread*

⚠ **Certains noms dénombrables en français sont indénombrables en anglais :**

Français	Anglais
bagage / bagages	*luggage*
meuble / meubles	*furniture*
information / informations	*information*
conseil / conseils	*advice*

Si l'on souhaite faire référence à un ou plusieurs de ces éléments, il faut utiliser *'a piece of' (a piece of luggage/furniture, two pieces of information/advice)*.

2 Pluriel des noms

- Comme en français, la plupart des noms prennent un -s final.

room → rooms   *tree → trees*   *book → books*   *pea → peas*

⚠ **Prononciation**

Selon les lettres qui précèdent le -*s* final, la prononciation sera /s/ *(roofs, rats)*, /z/ *(trees, games)* ou /ɪz/ *(houses, bushes)*.

- Toutefois, certains noms ont des terminaisons particulières.

Terminaisons	Marques du pluriel	Exemples	
-y	→ *-ies*	*cherry → cherries* *story → stories*	*party → parties*
-o, -s, -z, -x, -sh, -ch	→ *-es*	*potato → potatoes* *bus → buses* *fox → foxes*	*waltz → waltzes* *bush →bushes*
-f(e)	→ *-ves*	*wife → wives* *life → lives* *wolf → wolves*	*dwarf → dwarves* *knife → knives* *leaf → leaves*
Pluriels irréguliers		*(wo)man → (wo)men* *medium →media* *foot/tooth →feet/teeth*	*child → children* *crisis → crises*

⚠ **La présence d'un *-s* en fin de mot n'indique pas nécessairement une forme pluriel.**
Economics (l'économie), *news* (l'information), *politics* (la politique), *a series* (une série), *a means* (un moyen), *a species* (une espèce)

3 Dérivation et composition

a. Dérivation

Les noms, adjectifs et adverbes dérivés sont formés à partir d'un « mot racine » auquel on ajoute un ou plusieurs préfixes (avant la racine) et/ou suffixe(s) (après la racine). Ce principe est très actif en anglais et permet de transformer un nom en adjectif ou en adverbe, un verbe en nom, etc. :

happy → unhappy, happiness, happily
friend → friendly, friendship
play → player, playful

Préfixes		Exemples
sens privatif ou contraire	***a-, anti-, dis-, il-, im-, in-, ir-, mal-, mis-, non-, un-***	*amoral, dislike, illegal, impossible, irregular, misunderstand, unreasonable*
référence temporelle	***after-, neo-, post-, pre-***	*afterthought, postgraduate, premature*
Suffixes		**Exemples**
absence ou approximation	***-less, -ish***	*hopeless, greyish*
activité ou action	***-al, -ation, -ing, -ment***	*arrival, negociation, reading, experiment*
agent	***- ant, -er, -ess, -or***	*attendant, driver, actress, actor*
catégorie ou nationalité	***-ese, -ian, -ish, -ism, -ist***	*Chinese, Italian, Irish, capitalism, extremist*
état	***-dom, -hood, -ness, -ship***	*freedom, brotherhood, hopelessness, friendship*
matière ou manière de faire	***-y, -ly***	*silky, softly*

b. Composition

• Les noms et adjectifs composés sont formés de deux éléments. Le deuxième élément est le mot principal ; le premier élément joue le rôle d'adjectif : il vient préciser le sens du deuxième élément et c'est souvent lui qui est accentué (→ *Précis de prononciation p. 219*).

a tea room *a chat room* *a living-room* *a dining room*

dark blue *self-sufficient* *ill-equipped*

• Lorsqu'ils sont formés de deux noms, les noms composés peuvent prendre les formes NN *(a raincoat)*, NØN *(a gold watch)* ou N-N *(a post-office)*.

• Ils peuvent aussi être formés d'un nom et d'une base verbale: N + BV-er *(a bus driver)*, N + BV-ing *(rock climbing)* ou BV-ing + N *(a cleaning woman)*.

LES DÉTERMINANTS DU NOM

4 Articles et adjectifs démonstratifs

Le système des articles en anglais diffère largement du français : comme on ne distingue pas le masculin et le féminin, il n'y a pas d'articles de sens masculin ou féminin. Le choix de l'article ou de l'adjectif démonstratif se fait en fonction :
- du sens que l'on souhaite véhiculer (général ou particulier) ;
- de la catégorie (dénombrable ou non) du nom.

a. Article indéfini *a/an*

Il permet de mentionner UN élément pour la première fois.

Give me a banana, please. *There was a student in the library.* *Come back in a year.*

⚠ **Si le nom commence par une consonne ou par le son [j] *(university/year/European)*, on utilisera l'article *a*.**
S'il commence par une voyelle ou un «h» non aspiré – qu'on ne prononce pas *(hour/honour/heir)*, on utilisera l'article *an* **(→ *Précis de prononciation p. 221*)****.**
I would like an orange first. *We have been waiting for an hour.*

⚠ **Emplois particuliers**

• L'article *a* peut aussi faire référence à un élément représentatif d'une classe.
A dog can become dangerous if you don't feed him.
→ Un chien peut devenir dangereux si on ne le nourrit pas.
Everybody needs a computer today.
→ Tout le monde a besoin d'un ordinateur de nos jours.

Ici, on parle d'un chien ou d'un ordinateur en général.

• Contrairement au français, les **noms de métiers** sont toujours précédés de l'article *a*.
He is a baker. *She works as a secretary.*

• Pour exprimer un rapport au temps, au poids, à la distance, on utilise aussi l'article *a*.
90 miles an hour *3 pounds a kilo* *once a month*

b. Article défini *the*

Il permet de déterminer UN OU PLUSIEURS éléments particuliers dont on a déjà parlé ou qui sont connus du co-énonciateur. Cet élément peut être caractérisé par :

- Les compléments qui le précèdent ou le suivent :
  The girl I met yesterday *is their niece.* *At the end* of the film, *she started to cry.*
- La situation ou le contexte dans lesquels on se trouve :
  Will you buy me the book? (sous-entendu « le livre dont je t'ai parlé »)
  Give me the salt, please. (sous-entendu « le sel qui est sur la table »)
- Leur unicité, leur spécificité, leur renvoi à la connaissance générale du monde :
  the British anthem, the French government, the Atlantic ocean
  the earth, the sun, the sky, the moon, the internet...

⚠ **Prononciation**

- Si le nom commence par une consonne, *the* se prononce /ðə/ *(the dog, the cat)*.
- Si le nom commence par une voyelle ou un « h » non aspiré, *the* se prononce /ðɪ/ *(the hour, the apple)*

c. Article zéro Ø

Il permet de faire référence à UN ENSEMBLE d'éléments (pluriel de ***a/an***) ou à une classe/sous-classe, lorsqu'il est associé à des noms dénombrables pluriels.

Ø Whales are amazing animals. *Ø Babies often cry.* *I am afraid of Ø black cats.*

⚠ **Lorsqu'il est associé à des noms indénombrables, il a une valeur généralisante.**

Ø Money doesn't buy happiness. *Ø Freedom is a basic human right.*

⚠ **Lorsqu'un nom propre est précédé d'un titre ou d'une fonction, il n'y a jamais d'article. Il en va de même pour les noms de pays et les langues.**

Ø Queen Elizabeth, *Ø President Obama.* *Ø France is north of Ø Spain.*
Ø Chinese is a lovely language. *I love speaking Ø English.*

NB : Certains noms de pays sont toujours précédés de ***the*** :

The United Kingdom *The United States* *The Netherlands*

d. Adjectifs démonstratifs

Les adjectifs démonstratifs ***this*** (pluriel ***these***) et ***that*** (pluriel ***those***) correspondent aux déterminants français « ce/cet(te)/ces » mais n'ont pas les mêmes caractéristiques.

This/ These	+ qque chose dont l'énonciateur n'a pas encore parlé, ou qui n'est connu que de lui.	• *This is my new boyfriend. His name is Patrick.* (personne nouvellement présentée) • *Can you lend me this book, please?* (*'this book'* : information nouvelle)
That/ Those	+ qque chose dont l'énonciateur a déjà parlé ou qui est déjà connu du co-énonciateur.	• *Have you heard what happened? Oh yes, I've heard about that story!* (histoire connue du co-énonciateur)

⚠ ***This*** **et** ***that*** **peuvent aussi être pronoms ou adverbes.**
Give me this!
(*'this'* remplace un nom → « Donne moi ceci immédiatement ! »)
He has just found 100 dollars but he does not look that happy.
(*'that'* restreint le sens de *'happy'* → Il vient de trouver 100 dollars mais il n'a pas l'air si heureux que ça)

5 Quantifieurs

Les quantifieurs permettent de spécifier la quantité donnée d'un nom ou d'un groupe nominal. Cette quantité peut être précise, chiffrée, ou plus indicative. Les quantifieurs varient selon la nature (dénombrable ou non) du nom qu'ils déterminent.

	Quantifieurs	Exemples : noms dénombrables	Exemples : noms indénombrables
Quantité nulle	*no* (négation absolue)	*There were no flowers in his garden.* (aucune)	*She has no money to buy a new car.* (pas du tout)
	not any	*There were not any flowers in his garden.*	*She hasn't got any money to buy a new car.*
	none *no one*	*None of them can help me.* (aucun d'eux)	*No one can help me.* (personne)
Petite quantité	*little*	/	*She has little money on her account.* (peu/pas beaucoup : sens négatif)
	a little (+ sing.)	/	*She has a little money on her account.* (un peu)
	few	*They have few friends.* (peu/pas beaucoup : sens négatif)	*She has little money on her account.* (peu/pas beaucoup : sens négatif)
	a few (+ plur.)	*They have a few friends.* (quelques : sens positif)	/
Grande quantité	*(not) much* *(too) much* (+ sing.)	/	*She has (not) much/too much money on her bank account* (peu de/beaucoup de/trop de)
	(not) many *(too) many* (+ plur.)	*There are (not) many/too many flowers in his garden.* (pas de/beaucoup de/trop de)	/
	a lot of / lots of / loads of / plenty of	*There are a lot of lowers in his garden* (beaucoup de)	*She has a lot of money on her bank account* (beaucoup de)
Quantité non précisée	*Some* - dans un énoncé affirmatif - dans un énoncé interrogatif (on s'attend à une réponse positive)	*Some books are very boring.* (certains) *Did you buy some books at the market?* (des/quelques)	*Give me some money, please.* (de/un peu de) *Would you have some money, please?* (de/un peu de)
	Any - dans un énoncé affirmatif - dans un énoncé interrogatif (on ne sait pas quelle sera la réponse, on demande « à tout hasard »)	*I can read any book, I don't mind.* (n'importe quel) *Did you buy any books at the market?* (des)	/ *Does she have any money?* (de)

	Quantifieurs	Exemples
De l'unité à la totalité	***One***	*Only one guest came to his party.* (un et un seul)
	Both	*Both families were proud of them.* (les deux)
	Each (+ sing.)	*Each child has a right to education.* (chaque)
	Every (+ sing.)	*Every child has a right to education.* (tous/chacun d'eux)
	Nombres précis	*Only three thousand children go to school in his country.* *Hundreds/thousands of children ...*
	Most (+ plur.)	*Most children like sweets.* (la plupart)
	The whole (+sing.)	*The whole village was flooded.* (tout entier)
	All	*All the village(s) was(were) flooded.* (tout, tous)
	Either ... or ***Neither ... nor***	*Either you or your sister can stay* .(soit... soit...) *Neither you nor your sister can stay.* (ni... ni...)

6 Génitif *(...'s)* et adjectifs possessifs

a. Utilisations du génitif

Le génitif indique un lien entre deux personnes, deux objets ou une personne et un objet. Ce lien est marqué par la présence de *« 's »*. Le premier élément détermine le second. Le lien qui unit les deux éléments peut être :

- un lien de propriété : *Mike's bike is broken.* → Le vélo de Mike est cassé.
- un lien de parenté : *I have met Mike's sister.* → J'ai rencontré la sœur de Mike.
- un lien relationnel : *Mike's friends are great!* → Les amis de Mike sont formidables !

NB : On remarquera qu'en français cette relation est souvent marquée par la préposition « de ».

On peut également trouver *« 's »* pour indiquer :

- un repère dans l'espace : *London's musicals are exceptional. America's buildings are huge.*
- un lieu : *I went to the baker's. I went to my uncle's.*
- un repère temporel : *Today's cars are very expensive. Last year's protests were violent.*
- une durée : *After a day's work, I'm always exhausted. I've just had two weeks' holidays.*

⚠ **Lorsque le mot qui précède « *'s* » est au pluriel, on indique uniquement le lien par l'apostrophe *(my cousins' house)*. Par contre, lorsque son pluriel est irrégulier, on maintient « *'s* » *(the children's games)*. Si ce mot est un nom singulier qui se termine par un « *-s* », on pourra ou non maintenir le « *'s* » *(James' book ou James's book)*.**

b. Adjectifs possessifs

Les adjectifs possessifs marquent un lien (de possession, mais pas toujours) entre deux éléments.

I	*you*	*he*	*she*	*it*	*we*	*you*	*they*
my	*your*	*his*	*her*	*its*	*our*	*your*	*their*

⚠ **Ils s'accordent en genre et en nombre avec l'élément auquel ils se rapportent, et non pas avec le nom qui suit comme en français.**

Mike likes his aunt very much. Carla often plays with her brother.

7 Adjectifs qualificatifs et comparaison

a. Règles fondamentales

• En anglais, les adjectifs qualificatifs sont toujours invariables (ne s'accordent ni en genre, ni en nombre) et sont toujours placés devant le nom, en position épithète, quel que soit leur nombre (à l'exception des adjectifs comme *alive, asleep, alone, afraid, awake* qui sont toujours en position attribut).

Mary is an intelligent pretty young girl but she often feels alone and is afraid of the dark.

• Lorsque plusieurs adjectifs qualifient un même nom, on les place selon un ordre allant du + subjectif au + objectif :

adj. + subjectif ---------- adj. + objectif – nom

opinion / taille / âge / couleur / origine / matière – nom

A nice tall young Asian girl *A beautiful comfortable new silky jersey*

• On emploie parfois un adjectif comme nom pour renvoyer à une catégorie de personnes. Dans ce cas, l'adjectif reste invariable, est précédé du déterminant ***the***, et a un sens pluriel.

the young *the rich* *the poor*

b. Comparatifs et superlatifs réguliers

Comparatif	Superlatif
Il permet de comparer **2 éléments entre eux.** Il existe **3 types** de comparatifs : • le comparatif de supériorité (plus... que) • le comparatif d'(in)égalité [(pas) aussi ... que] • le comparatif d'infériorité (moins... que)	Il permet de comparer **1 élément à tous les autres.** Il existe **2 types** de superlatifs : • le superlatif de supériorité (le plus...) • le superlatif d'infériorité (le moins...).

	Comparatif	Superlatif
infériorité	***less*** + adj. + ***than*** (moins + adj. + que...) *Mary is less selfish than her brother*	***the least*** + adj. (le/la/les moins + adj. ...) *Mary is the least selfish girl I've ever met.*
égalité inégalité	***(not) as*** + adj. + ***as*** [(pas) aussi + adj. + que] *Clara is (not) as tall as her twin sister*	
supériorité	• **Adjectifs longs*** ***more*** + adj. + ***than*** (plus + adj. + que) *The blue car is more expensive than the yellow one.*	• **Adjectifs longs*** ***the most*** + adj. (le/la/les plus + adj. ...) *Emma is the most romantic girl in the class.*
	• **Adjectifs courts**** adj. + ***-er*** + ***than*** *The blue car is cheaper than the red one.*	• **Adjectifs courts**** adj. + ***-est*** *This is the cheapest car I've ever bought.*

***Adjectifs longs** (2 syllabes – sauf ceux terminés en *-er*, *-y*, *-ow*, et *-le* ou plus) :

stupid, interesting, wonderful, extraordinary

****Adjectifs courts** (1 syllabe ou de 2 syllabes) terminés par *-er*, *-y*, *-ow*, et *-le* :

big, fat, young, short *clever, pretty, narrow, subtle*

c. Comparatifs et superlatifs irréguliers

	Comparatif	Superlatif
Good	*better*	*the best*
Bad	*worse*	*the worst*
Far	*farther/further*	*the farthest/furthest*

d. Expression de l'accroissement

	Adjectifs courts	Adjectifs longs
De plus en plus...	*Sweets are cheaper and cheaper.*	*Vegetables are more and more expensive.*
De moins en moins...	*Computers are less and less expensive.*	

Grâce aux comparatifs, on peut également formuler l'idée d'un accroissement parallèle.

Plus..., plus/moins...	*The richer he becomes, the more selfish he is.* *The richer he is, the less happy he feels.*
Moins..., plus/ moins...	*The less generous you are, the more alone you will feel.* *The less generous you are, the less popular you will be.*

LES COMPLÉMENTS DU NOM

8 Noms et propositions relatives

- Deux types de propositions relatives permettent de compléter le sens d'un nom :

- les **propositions relatives déterminatives** (ou restrictives)

The students who had finished left quickly. (a)

- les **propositions relatives non déterminatives**

The students, who had finished, left quickly.. (b)

La nature de la proposition relative change le sens de l'énoncé. En (a), seuls les étudiants qui avaient terminé sont partis. En (b), il s'agit de tous les étudiants : la relative placée entre virgules n'est qu'un simple ajout d'information.

- On utilise le pronom relatif ***who*** (ou ***that***) si le mot qui précède est sujet de la phrase et renvoie à une personne ; on utilise ***which*** (ou ***that***) si le mot qui précède est sujet ou objet de la phrase et renvoie à de l'inanimé, et ***where*** si le mot qui précède renvoie à un lieu.

⚠ **Parfois (lorsqu'il reprend un nom en position objet) le pronom relatif n'apparaît pas et peut être sous-entendu.**

The museum (which/that) I visited was quite old.
The girl (that) I met last week is fantastic!

- Il existe deux autres pronoms relatifs : ***whose*** (qui exprime l'appartenance) et ***whom*** qui est l'équivalent de ***who*** et s'emploie lorsque le mot qui précède est en position objet.

My uncle, whose car broke down yesterday, did not go on holidays.
→ Mon oncle, dont la voiture est tombée en panne hier, n'est pas parti en vacances.

My aunt, whom you met yesterday, lives in London.
→ Ma tante, que tu as rencontrée hier, habite à Londres.

They consulted the lawyer (whom) they had met in London.
→ Ils consultèrent l'avocat qu'ils avaient rencontré à Londres.

⚠ **Attention à la traduction de « dont » : en français, il ne renvoie pas systématiquement à l'appartenance.**

L'homme dont je t'ai parlé est ingénieur.
The man (whom) I told you about is an engineer.

⚠ ***Who's*** (= *who is* : « qui est » **ou** *who has* : « qui a ») ≠ ***whose*** (« dont »).

LES SUBSTITUTS DU NOM

9 Pronoms *(personnels, réfléchis, possessifs, réciproques)*

Par définition, les pronoms remplacent les noms auxquels ils font référence (« pro-nom » : « pour le nom »). Il existe 5 catégories de pronoms qui peuvent occuper différentes fonctions dans la phrase :

1. pronoms personnels (sujets)	2. pronoms personnels (compléments)	3. pronoms possessifs	4. pronoms réfléchis	5. pronoms réciproques
I	*me*	*mine*	*myself*	
you	*you*	*yours*	*yourself*	
he	*him*	*his*	*himself*	
she	*her*	*hers*	*herself*	*each other*
it	*it*	*its*	*itself*	*one another*
we	*us*	*ours*	*ourselves*	
you	*you*	*yours*	*yourselves*	
they	*them*	*theirs*	*themselves*	

1 et 2 : Les pronoms personnels sujets et compléments remplacent des noms en position sujet ou complément.

*Mary loves Peter → She loves him (**She*** = sujet, ***him*** = complément*)*
Georges broke a vase → He broke it.

En anglais, on n'emploie pas deux fois le pronom sujet. On marque simplement l'insistance à l'oral.

Moi, j'aime vraiment la course à pied → *I really like running.*

Attention à la traduction d'un groupe nominal composé d'un double sujet car le français et l'anglais n'ont pas recours aux mêmes pronoms.

Mon cousin et moi habitons Montpellier → *My cousin and I live in Montpellier.*

3 : Les pronoms possessifs permettent de renvoyer à l'objet possédé en évitant les répétitions.

Don't touch this dress, it's my dress. → Don't touch this dress, it's mine.

4 : Les pronoms réfléchis s'emploient lorsque le sujet et l'objet renvoient à la même personne.

He looked at himself in the mirror (***himself*** = lui-même)
≠ *He looked at him in the mirror* (***him*** = une autre personne)

- On peut également les utiliser pour insister sur une personne/un objet.
  Why don't you do it yourself?
- Ils permettent parfois de traduire certains verbes pronominaux.
  Elle s'est blessée → *She hurt herself.*

5 : Les pronoms réciproques expriment l'idée d'un échange, d'une relation entre deux ***(each other)*** ou plusieurs personnes ***(one another)***. Ils indiquent que les sujets concernés agissent l'un envers l'autre. On les emploie souvent dans le cas de verbes pronominaux français.

His uncle and aunt respect each other.
→ Son oncle et sa tante ont du respect l'un pour l'autre/se respectent.
They all know one another.
→ Ils se connaissent tous.

II — Le groupe verbal

Contrairement au français, l'anglais ne compte que **2 temps** : le passé et le présent.
À ces deux temps s'ajoutent **2 aspects** : ***have -en*** (auxiliaire ***Have*** + participe passé) et ***be -ing*** (auxiliaire ***Be*** + base verbale ***-ing***) qui permettent d'apporter de nombreuses nuances de sens.
Le système verbal anglais n'est donc pas du tout comparable au système français : à un temps grammatical français peuvent correspondre plusieurs formes verbales anglaises et inversement.

Informer	Présent simple/Prétérit
Effectuer un bilan	*have -en:* Present perfect/Past perfect
Justifier Réagir	*be -ing:* Présent *be -ing*/Passé *be -ing* Modalité : auxiliaires modaux
Repérer des faits	Marqueurs temporels : *ago, for, since*

INFORMER

Lorsque l'énonciateur présente des faits à simple titre d'information (pour annoncer ou informer), il utilise le présent simple ou le prétérit.

10 Présent simple et préterit

a. Présent simple

- **Formation** : Base verbale (BV) à toutes les personnes ; *-s* final à la 3e personne du singulier.

- **À la forme négative**, on utilise l'auxiliaire ***Do*** au présent auquel on ajoute ***not*** (forme contractée : ***n't***). À la forme interrogative, on place l'auxiliaire ***Do*** devant le sujet. *(voir 16 p. 205)*
  I/you/we/they work. *He/she/it works.*
  I don't work. *Do you work?* *He doesn't work.* *Does he work?*

- **On utilise le présent simple pour** :

1. énoncer des faits
   Water boils at 100°C. *The sun rises on the east.* *She likes strawberries.*
2. raconter une histoire et rendre un récit plus vivant (présent de narration)
   So he goes to work, and when he comes back, he discovers the truth.
3. renvoyer à un événement à venir
   His family arrives at 10 a.m. tomorrow.
   Who speaks after Mark? Peter does but then Mary enters the stage.

b. Le prétérit

- **Formation** : BV + *-d* ou *-ed* pour les verbes réguliers.

⚠ Verbes irréguliers *(voir liste p. 212-213)*.

- **On utilise l'auxiliaire *Do*** (***Did*** au passé) pour former des énoncés négatifs ou interrogatifs.
  I/you/he/she/it/we/you/they worked. *I didn't work.* *Did she work?*

- **On utilise le prétérit**, temps du récit, pour faire référence à un événement passé, souvent daté, et révolu. Le prétérit exprime une coupure avec le présent, et dans certains cas avec la réalité (voir 20 prétérit modal). On peut le traduire en français par un passé composé, un passé simple ou un imparfait.
  The wolf asked the little girl where she was going to.
  → Le loup demanda à la fillette où elle allait.
  When I was younger, I played the violin. → Quand j'étais plus jeune, je jouais du violon.

⚠ *Used to* **est uniquement employé pour marquer une rupture totale avec le présent.**
I used to go swimming when I was young → (« Aujourd'hui je ne nage plus »).

EFFECTUER UN BILAN

Lorsque l'énonciateur porte un certain regard sur un événement, notamment lorsqu'il souhaite indiquer les conséquences d'un événement passé sur la situation d'énonciation, il utilise le *present perfect* ou le *past perfect*.

⓫ *Present perfect* et *past perfect*: *have* + participe passé

a. *Present perfect*

• Formation: auxiliaire ***have*** **au présent + participe passé** (BV + *-d* ou *-ed*, ou 3e colonne des verbes irréguliers *(voir liste p. 212-213)*.

• Comme ***have*** est auxiliaire, c'est lui qui est conjugué, qui s'accorde avec le sujet auquel il se rapporte, qui porte la marque de la négation ***(not/n't)*** dans les énoncés négatifs et qui est placé devant le sujet dans les énoncés interrogatifs.

I/you/we/they have worked   *He/she/it has worked*   *I haven't worked*   *Has he worked?*

• On utilise le *present perfect* pour : porter un regard vers le passé et le lier au présent, pour faire le bilan d'une situation passée, ou parler d'un événement qui a démarré dans le passé et se poursuit au moment où l'on parle. On peut le traduire en français par du passé composé ou du présent.

He has lost his keys. → Il a perdu ses clés. (résultat : il ne peut plus rentrer chez lui)
I have worked here for 3 years. → Je travaille ici depuis 3 ans. (fait toujours d'actualité)
I have just called her; she seems to be feeling better.
I have never eaten such delicious fruits!

b. *Past perfect*

• Formation : auxiliaire ***have*** **au passé + participe passé**.

I/you/he/she/it/we/you/they had worked   *We hadn't worked*   *Had they worked?*

• Le *past perfect* correspond en général au *present perfect* dans un contexte passé. On l'utilise dans des discours rapportés ou pour effectuer des retours en arrière explicatifs. Il équivaut au plus-que-parfait français.

He told me that they had not come because they were sick.
→ Il m'a dit qu'ils n'étaient pas venus car ils étaient malades.

EXPLIQUER, RÉAGIR

Lorsque l'énonciateur souhaite expliquer, justifier, réagir à une situation il utilise l'aspect ***be -ing***, ou bien les auxiliaires de modalité.

⓬ L'aspect *be -ing*

a. Au présent

• Formation : auxiliaire ***be*** au présent + BV ***-ing***

• Comme ***be*** est auxiliaire, c'est lui qui est conjugué, qui s'accorde avec le sujet auquel il se rapporte, qui porte la marque de la négation ***(not/n't)*** dans les énoncés négatifs et qui est placé devant le sujet dans les énoncés interrogatifs.

I am working. *you/we/they are working.* *he/she/it is working.*
We are not/aren't working. *Are they working?*

- On utilise le présent ***be -ing*** pour:

1. justifier des propos ou une situation

I'm doing my homework, don't disturb me, please!
→ j'explique pourquoi je ne veux pas être dérangé.
I'm going to London next weekend. → j'explique pourquoi je ne serai pas là.

2. réagir à des propos ou à une situation

I'm sorry but I'm not cooking again. → J'en ai assez, j'ai déjà cuisiné hier et avant-hier.
He is always complaining about something. → C'est lassant, il se plaint toujours.

b. Au passé

- Formation : Auxiliaire ***be*** **au passé + BV** ***-ing*****.**

I/he/she/it was working. *you/we/they were working.* *Were they working?*

- On utilise le passé ***be -ing*** lorsqu'on veut expliquer/commenter des faits qui se sont déroulés dans le passé. On peut le traduire en français par un imparfait.

I was reading a novel when my friends called to invite me out.
→ Je lisais un roman lorsque mes amis m'ont appelée pour m'inviter à sortir.

Le passé ***be -ing*** permet de dire ce que je faisais à l'arrivée de mes amis (pour expliquer/justifier ma présence chez moi, ou pour expliquer pourquoi j'étais libre et ai pu accepter l'invitation...).

c. Au *present perfect* et *past perfect*

- L'énonciateur peut choisir de combiner l'aspect ***have -en*** à l'aspect ***be -ing*** au présent ou au passé. Dans ce cas, c'est ***have*** qui est conjugué, qui porte la marque de la négation et qui est inversé dans les énoncés interrogatifs.

They have been working *I haven't been working* *Has she been working?*
We had been working *They hadn't been working* *Had he been working?*

- Le *present perfect* + ***be -ing***, combine la valeur du *present perfect* simple (l'énonciateur fait le constat d'un fait passé) et celle de ***be-ing*** (il explique / justifie / réagit à ce fait passé).

You cough a lot; that's because you've been smoking too much!
→ Tu tousses beaucoup, c'est parce que tu as trop fumé !

- Le *past perfect* + ***be -ing*** correspond à du *present perfect* + ***be -ing*** dans un contexte passé.

I realised you had been smoking too much when I heard you cough.
→ Je me suis rendu compte que tu avais trop fumé quand je t'ai entendu tousser.

13 Auxiliaires modaux

a. Définition et caractéristiques des auxiliaires modaux

- Ils permettent à l'énonciateur de donner son point de vue sur le lien qui existe entre le sujet et le verbe auquel il est associé. Puisque le modal est choisi par l'énonciateur, qui « s'insère » entre le sujet et le verbe, il ne dépend pas du sujet grammatical. C'est la raison pour laquelle il n'est pas conjugué et ne prend jamais de *-s* à la 3e personne.

- Comme tous les auxiliaires (***do***, ***be*** et ***have***) :
  - Ils sont suivis de *not* dans les énoncés négatifs ;
  - Ils sont placés devant le sujet dans les énoncés interrogatifs ;
  - Ils sont toujours suivis d'une base verbale.

b. Les deux sens des auxiliaires modaux

Auxiliaire modal	Sens 1 Lien sujet - verbe	Sens 2 Chances de réalisation d'un événement
may *might*	**Permission** *May I open the window?* **Interdiction** *You may not talk to me like that!*	***May:*** **Hypothèse** *She may come or not, I don't know.* ***Might:*** **Hypothèse plus faible** *She might come but only if you invite her.*
must *(+ needn't)*	**Obligation/nécessité** *You must work hard or you will fail your exam.* **Interdiction** *You mustn't shout in a church.* ⚠ **Absence d'obligation/nécessité** *You needn't wait so long.*	**Quasi certitude** *She has just got married: she must be so happy!*
can *could*	**Capacité** • au présent : *He can sing, dance and play the guitar at the same time: he is a great artist!* • au passé : *When he was young, he could sing, dance and play the guitar at the same time: he was a great artist!* • au conditionnel : *She could work more, don't you think?* **Incapacité** • au présent : *He cannot run long distances because his knees hurt.* • au passé : *When he was young, he could not run long distances.* **Permission** *You can go out with your friends but only if you come back before 5 p.m.* **Interdiction** *You cannot go out, that's all!*	**Probabilité** • au présent : *We can meet wild animals here, so get prepared!* **Probabilité plus incertaine** • au passé : *We could meet wild animals here but I doubt it.* **Impossibilité certaine** *There cannot be any wild animals here, trust me. There's too much noise.*
will *would*	**Volonté** *Listen to us, will you?* **Refus** *I won't listen to you; your opinion is unacceptable.* **Volonté atténuée** *I would listen to you, but honestly, I have to go.* Je t'écouterais bien mais... **Caractéristique/habitude du sujet (actuelle ou passée)** *He will watch TV endlessly if I don't tell him to stop.* *He would watch TV endlessly when he was a kid.*	**Sens futur** *One day I will go to America!* **Conditionnel (fait irréel)** • présent : *I would travel with him if he wanted to.* Je voyagerais avec lui si... • passé : *I would have travelled with him if he had wanted to.* J'aurais voyagé avec lui si...

Auxiliaire modal	Sens 1 Lien sujet - verbe	Sens 2 Chances de réalisation d'un événement
shall *should*	**Suggestion (forme interrogative)** *Shall we go to a restaurant tonight?* Et si nous allions au restaurant ? **Conseil** *You should listen to him more.* Tu devrais l'écouter davantage. **Reproche/regret** *You should have listened to him more.* Tu aurais dû l'écouter davantage.	**Probabilité forte** *He should be back by ten tonight.* Il devrait être de retour vers dix heures ce soir.

c. Sens 1 des auxiliaires modaux et équivalents

Il existe des verbes/formes verbales qui expriment des idées équivalentes à celles véhiculées par les auxiliaires modaux lorsqu'ils sont employés avec le sens 1. Lorsque l'énonciateur utilise ces verbes, il n'exprime alors plus son point de vue, mais énonce un état de fait. Parfois il peut simplement utiliser ces verbes lorqu'il y a déjà un modal dans l'énoncé.

Sens 1	Formes modales	équivalents	Exemples
Capacité/ Incapacité	*can*	*be able to*	• au présent : *He is able to sing, dance and play an instrument at the same time: he is a great artist! He may be able to join tonight.* • au passé : *When he was young, he was able to sing, dance and play an instrument at the same time: he was a great artist!*
	cannot	*not be able to* *be unable to*	• au présent : *He is not able to/is unable to run long distances because his knees hurt.* • au passé : *When he was young, he was not able to/he was unable to run long distances.*
Permission/ Interdiction	*can* *may*	*be allowed to*	• *You are allowed to go out with your friends but only if you come back before 5 p.m.* • *Am I allowed to open the window?*
	cannot *may not* *must not* *shall not*	*not be allowed to* *be forbidden to*	• *You are not allowed to go out, that's all!* • *You are not allowed to talk to me like that!* • *It is forbidden to shout in a church.*
Obligation/ Absence d'obligation	*must*	*have to*	• *You have to work hard or you will fail your exam.*
	(+ need'nt)	*don't have to*	• *You don't have to wait so long.*
Volonté/ Refus	*will*	*want to*	• *You will have to work faster tomorrow.*
	will not	*don't want to/* *not be willing to*	*I am not willing to/don't want to listen to you, your opinion is unacceptable.*

REPÉRER DES FAITS

14 *Ago, for, since*

a. *Ago*

Ago est un adverbe de temps qui renvoie au **passé**.
Il est donc associé à du prétérit + complément de temps.

I left Moscow three years ago → J'ai quitté Moscou il y a trois ans.

b. *For*

For est une préposition qui indique une **durée**.
Elle est souvent (mais pas toujours) associée à du *present perfect*.

We have walked for three hours. It's time to have a rest.
→ Cela fait trois heures que nous marchons, il est temps de faire une pause.
I walked for three hours before getting to the train station.
→ J'ai marché pendant trois heures avant d'arriver à la gare.

c. *Since*

Since est une préposition qui indique le **début**, le point de départ d'un événement. Elle est souvent associée à du *present perfect* et correspond à la préposition française « depuis ».

I have seen him only twice since last March.
→ Je ne l'ai vu que deux fois depuis mars dernier.

PARLER DE L'AVENIR

15 *Will*, présent simple, présent *be -ing, be going to* + V

Comme il n'y a pas véritablement de temps « futur » en anglais, l'énonciateur a différents moyens de renvoyer à l'avenir.

Expressions	Valeurs	Exemples
Will	Prédit, prévoit ce qui va se passer indépendamment de la situation présente.	*It will rain tomorrow.*
Présent simple	Informe quelqu'un d'un événement prévu, planifié.	*His train arrives at 3 p.m. tomorrow, so be on time!*
Présent ***be -ing***	Présente l'événement futur comme une explication de la situation présente.	*I'm seeing Mike at 2 p.m. so I can't come with you.*
Be going to + V	Présente l'événement futur comme certain, lié de près à la situation présente.	*It's going to rain, look at those clouds!*

III — La phrase

DE L'ÉNONCÉ SIMPLE...

16 Déclarer, interroger, demander confirmation, répondre

a. Déclarer (affirmations et négations)

Parmi les énoncés déclaratifs, on trouve:

- les **affirmations** qui suivent l'ordre **S (+ Aux.) + V + Complément(s)**.

  Tom has bought a new car. *Mary studied in Los Angeles last year.*

- les **négations** qui suivent l'ordre **S + Aux. + Not + V + Complément(s)**.

Lorsque le verbe est au présent ou au prétérit (sans auxiliaire), on utilise l'auxiliaire ***do*** (***did*** au passé) suivi de la négation ***not***. Si le verbe est déjà accompagné d'un ou plusieurs auxiliaires (dans l'ordre : auxiliaire modal, ***have***, ***be***), la négation porte directement sur le premier auxiliaire.

Tom has not bought a new car. *Mary will not be studying in Los Angeles next year.*
They have not been doing much lately.

⚠ **Auxiliaire *do* de reprise**
Parfois, on utilise l'auxiliaire ***do*** pour reprendre des propos antérieurs en évitant de répéter le verbe, pour marquer l'insistance, ou pour corriger et réaffirmer un fait qui aurait été nié ou mis en doute.
He said he would come and he did. (sous-entendu : *and he did come*)
Are you sure you like me? Of course, I do like you! (valeur d'insistance)
Why didn't you go to London? I did go to London! (correction + réaffirmation)

b. Interroger (*yes/no questions*, *Wh- questions*, questions brèves)

- Parmi les énoncés interrogatifs, on trouve :

1. **les questions fermées** (ou *yes-no questions*) qui attendent une réponse de type *'yes', 'no', 'maybe'*.
2. **les questions ouvertes** (ou *Wh- questions*) qui attendent une réponse développée avec des informations précises. Toutes deux suivent l'ordre:

(pronom interrogatif) + Aux. + S + V + Complément(s)?

(1) *Did Paul visit the cathedral yesterday?* *Has Tom bought a new car?*
(2) *When did Paul visit the cathedral?* *What has Tom bought?*

Les pronoms interrogatifs commencent tous par ***'wh-'*** : ***who, what, which, when, where, why, whose, how*** (qui commençait également autrefois par «wh-») et ses composés, ***how much/how many/ how old/how tall/ long/how far/how big/ how often***.

⚠ **Lorsque le pronom interrogatif porte sur l'identité du sujet *(who)* OU sur le sujet d'action *(what)*, l'ordre sera :** *Who* + Aux. + V.
Who is coming? *Who will work with us?* *What happened?*

- **Les questions brèves** permettent de rebondir sur les propos de quelqu'un en évitant de répéter ce qui vient d'être dit. Pour cela, on reprend simplement l'auxiliaire.

  I have never met him. Have you? (sous-entendu : *Have you met him?*)

Elles permettent aussi de marquer la surprise face aux propos qui viennent d'être exprimés.

- I have worked in a factory for 10 years.
- Have you? (En français, on pourra traduire par « Ah bon ? »)

c. Demander confirmation *(Tag questions)*

Les *Tags*, spécificité anglaise que l'on traduit souvent en français par «n'est-ce pas ?» permettent de demander confirmation de ce qui a été déclaré. Ils transforment une affirmation ou une négation en question.

She is a great actress, isn't she? *She isn't a great actress, is she?*
He can't be his father, can he? *He will sing at the show, won't he?*

(intonation : → voir précis de prononciation p. 216)

d. Répondre

Les réponses brèves permettent de répondre à une question en évitant les répétitions.

- Have you finished your homework?
- Yes, I have. / No, I haven't.

« moi aussi »	***So*** + Aux. + S	• *'I love chocolate.' '<u>So do I.</u>'* (moi aussi) • *'They went to New York.' '<u>So did we.</u>'* (nous aussi)
« moi non plus »	***Neither*** + Aux. + S	• *'We haven't gone to Paris.' '<u>Neither have they.</u>'* (eux non plus) • *'He cannot come.' '<u>Neither can she.</u>'* (elle non plus)
« moi si » « moi non »	Reprise auxiliaire, forme opposée	• *'I love chocolate.' 'I don't.'* (moi non) • *'We haven't gone to the concert.' 'They have.'* (eux si)

17 S'exclamer, donner des ordres

a. S'exclamer (*What (a)/such (a)* + (Adj.) N, *How/so* + Adj.)

Si l'exclamation porte sur un groupe nominal, on utilise ***What/such (a)*** + Groupe Nominal ; si elle porte sur un groupe adjectival ou adverbial, on utilise ***How/so*** + groupe adjectival/adverbial.

	Groupe nominal		Groupe adjectival
what (a) + adj. + nom (+ S + V)!	*What a pretty girl (she is)!* Quelle jolie fille! *What strong men (they are)!* *What an actress!* *What actors!*	***how*** + adj./adv. (+ S + V)!	*How pretty (she is)!* Comme elle est jolie! Qu'est-ce qu'elle est jolie! *How strong (they are)!* *How deeply I love her!*
S + V + ***such (a)*** (+ adj.) + nom	*She is such a pretty girl!* C'est une si jolie fille! *They are such strong men!* *She is such an actress!* *They are such actors!*	S + V + ***so*** (+ adj./adv.)	*She is so pretty!* Elle est si jolie! *They are so strong!* *This novel is so beautifully written!*

b. Donner des ordres (impératif)

Formation de l'**impératif** : <u>base verbale</u> ou **impératif négatif** : ***Don't*** + base verbale.

Pars maintenant ! *Leave now!* Ne pars pas maintenant ! *Don't leave now!*

NB : Si l'on souhaite faire une **suggestion**, on utilise l'expression ***Let's*** + base verbale.

Allons au cinéma ! *Let's go to cinema!* Ne les oublions pas ! *Let's not forget them!*

...VERS L'ÉNONCÉ COMPLEXE

18 Rapporter des propos : du discours direct au discours indirect

Comme en français, on utilise le discours indirect pour rapporter des propos.
Le passage du discours direct au discours indirect implique des changements au niveau de la ponctuation (disparition des guillemets), des pronoms (sujet → complément, ***this*** → ***that***), des adjectifs et pronoms possessifs, des temps (présent → passé) et des adverbes de lieu et de temps (***here*** → ***there*** ; ***now*** → ***then*** ; ***today*** → ***that day*** ; ***yesterday*** → ***the day before*** ; ***tomorrow*** → ***the day after***).
Les propos rapportés sont souvent introduits par la conjonction de subordination *that* et par des verbes tels que ***say, tell, answer, reply, retort, explain...***

Paul: 'I found it here yesterday'
→ Paul said that he had found it there the day before.

Tina: 'I will come with you tomorrow'
→ Tina said that she would come with us the day after.

⚠ **D'autres changements peuvent apparaître selon le type de phrases.**

- **Interrogatives indirectes**

Suppression du point d'interrogation et de l'inversion Aux. + S

Paul: 'Are you eating with us?' → Paul asked me if I was eating with them.

'How many books has she read?' → Paul wondered how many books she had read.

- **Impératifs indirects**

Ajout de *'to'* ou *'not to'* devant le verbe.

Tina: 'Stay here!' → Tina told me to stay there.
'Don't stay here!' → Tina told me not to stay there.

19 Mettre en relief des éléments d'un énoncé

a. Tournures emphatiques *(what ... is // It is... that...)*

- Lorsqu'on présente des faits de manière neutre, sans mise en relief, l'ordre des mots suit le schéma traditionnel S + V + Complément(s) propre aux énoncés déclaratifs.

Prince William studied biology at Eton.

- Si on souhaite mettre en avant une information particulière, on peut réorganiser l'énoncé.

1. *It is/was at Eton that Prince William studied.*
2. *It is/was biology that Prince William studied.*
3. *It is/was Prince William who studied biology at Eton.*

Dans l'exemple 1, l'information *'at Eton'* est mise en relief, dans l'exemple 2, c'est *'biology'* qui est mise en avant et dans l'exemple 3, *'Prince William'*.
Ce type d'énoncés s'appelle une « **clivée** » et suit toujours le même schéma :
It + be **+ information mise en relief +** ***who/that*** **+ proposition**.

- On peut aussi présenter l'information de cette manière :

What Prince William studied is/was biology.

Dans ce cas, l'information mise en avant est celle placée en bout de phrase, ici *'biology'* et le schéma sera : ***What*** **+ proposition +** ***be*** **+ information mise en relief**.

b. Formes passives

An army of 500 troops saved the civilians. (forme active)
1. *The civilians were saved by an army of 500 troops.* (forme passive)
2. *This library has been built recently.*
3. *Girls are said to learn faster than boys.*

Lorsqu'on emploie une forme passive, l'objet de l'action est mis en relief et devient en conséquence sujet de la phrase. On y a recours :

- soit pour mettre l'accent sur la victime ou le bénéficiaire de l'action (1),
- soit parce que l'agent est inconnu, évident, sans importance ou parce qu'on ne souhaite pas le mentionner (2),
- soit pour présenter une généralité, une rumeur, une croyance (3).

Comme on l'observe dans les exemples ci-dessus, l'énoncé prend la forme :

Sujet + *be* + participe passé du verbe (+ préposition *'by'* + agent).

Be porte la marque du temps et/ou de l'aspect et peut être accompagné d'un modal.

⚠ • **La forme passive est beaucoup plus fréquente en anglais qu'en français. Très souvent, lorsqu'une phrase commence par « on » en français, on la traduira par une forme passive en anglais.**

On a cloné de nombreux animaux l'an dernier → *Many animals were cloned last year.*

On m'a dit que tu ne viendrais pas → *I was told that you would not come.*

• **Lorsqu'un verbe a deux compléments** *(give, ask, offer, show)*, **deux formes passives sont possibles.**

They offered me a job. → *I was offered a job.*
→ *A job was offered to me.*

c. Inversion du sujet

La mise en relief de termes négatifs tels que ***not only, never, hardly*** placés en début de phrase transforme la structure de celle-ci.

Not only did I have to wake up early, but I also had to work hard.

20 Imaginer des faits, exprimer un souhait ou un regret

a. Pour renvoyer à des faits non réels (hypothétiques, imaginés ou souhaités)

On peut avoir recours à des propositions subordonnées en *if*. La condition exprimée par la proposition hypothétique introduite par *if* a pour conséquence le résultat exprimé dans la proposition principale: *'If* X, *then* Y'. La réalisation de Y dépend donc de la réalisation de X.

- **Hypothèse réalisable : *'If* + présent ... *will'***

If he learns the rules (X), *he will play well* (Y).
If he doesn't learn the rules, he will not play well.

- **Hypothèse plus incertaine : *'If* + prétérit modal ... *would'***

If he learnt the rules, he would play well.

On parle dans ce cas « d'irréel » du présent. La forme prétérit *'learnt'* ne renvoie pas à une action passée mais à une situation fictive, souhaitée ou imaginée. Cette coupure avec la réalité est exprimée par le prétérit modal.

- **Hypothèse non réalisée : *'If* + past perfect modal ... *would have -en'***

If he had learned the rules, he would have played well.

On parle dans ce cas « d'irréel du passé » car les actions ***learn*** et ***play well*** n'ont jamais eu lieu. Comme dans la tournure précédente, la forme *past perfect* ***had learned*** ne renvoie pas ici à une action antérieure au moment passé, mais à une action qui n'a jamais eu lieu.

NB : On remarquera que ces tournures sont comparables au français.

1. S'il apprend les règles, il jouera bien.
2. S'il apprenait les règles (ce qu'il ne fait pas), il jouerait bien.
3. S'il avait appris les règles (ce qu'il n'a pas fait), il aurait bien joué.

b. Pour exprimer un souhait

On peut utiliser le verbe ***wish*** + prétérit modal.

I wish I had more money. *I wish I could win at the lottery next weekend.*

Là encore, *had* ou *could* ne renvoient pas à des situations passées mais à des situations souhaitées, irréelles, en décalage avec la réalité.

c. Pour exprimer un regret

On peut utiliser le verbe ***wish*** + *past perfect modal*.

I wish I had not written that letter.

Ici, ***wish*** renvoie à une action passée que l'on aurait souhaitée autre.

21 Étoffer des énoncés : propositions coordonnées et subordonnées

Lorsqu'on souhaite exprimer une pensée de façon plus riche et plus précise, on peut étoffer les énoncés grâce à des propositions coordonnées ou subordonnées.

a. Propositions coordonnées

Propositions indépendantes, liées entre elles par une conjonction de coordination.

Conjonctions de coordination	Exemples de propositions coordonnées
Cause : ***because, since, for, as***	*He came with us because/since he felt lonely*
Conséquence : ***so, therefore, consequently, as a consequence, thus, that's why***	• *Im feeling sick, so/thus/therefore I'm going to stay home.* •*He won the lottery, that's why he has bought a new car!*
Choix/alternative : ***or, otherwise, or else***	*You should listen to him, otherwise you will regret it.*
Opposition : ***but, yet, however, nevertheless***	*He's quite rich. Yet, he doesn't spend much money.*
Concession : ***despite, in spite of*** (malgré)	*Despite/in spite of his strength, he can't make it.*

b. Propositions subordonnées:

Propositions liées entre elles par une conjonction de subordination.
Leur syntaxe est liée : la proposition subordonnée dépend de la proposition principale.
On trouve les propositions subordonnées circonstancielles, complétives et relatives.

- **Les propositions subordonnées circonstancielles**

Propositions subordonnées circonstancielles	Exemples
Temps : ***when*** (lorsque), ***before*** (avant que), ***after*** (après que), ***until*** (jusqu'à ce que), ***as soon as*** (dès que)	• *When he was a child, he used to play badminton.* • *He played tennis until he was 12.* • *As soon as she realised her mistake, she started to cry.*
Simultanéité : ***while*** (pendant que)	• *He cooked the meal while they were washing the dishes.*
Concession/paradoxe : ***(Al)though, even though*** (alors/bien que), ***even if*** (même si)	• *Although/even though she loves him, she doesn't want to marry him.* • *I won't go, even if he asks me to.*

Propositions subordonnées circonstancielles	Exemples
Condition : *if, provided* (à condition que), *unless* (à moins que)	• *If you work better, you will be rewarded.* • *Unless you work better, you will not be rewarded.*
Contraste : *whereas/while* (tandis que)	• *She wanted to go to Nepal whereas/while he wanted to go to Kenya.*
But : *so that, in order to, so as to*	• *She studied biology in order to/so as to become a doctor.* • *She studied biology so that she could become a doctor.*

⚠ *If* comme *when* posent comme réelle une action qui n'a pas eu lieu. Contrairement au français, lorsqu'une proposition subordonnée est introduite par *when* et renvoie à une action à venir, le verbe est conjugué au présent.

Lorsque je trouverai la réponse, je te le dirai.
When I find the answer, I will tell you.

Lorsque j'aurai trouvé la réponse, je te le dirai.
When I have found the answer, I will tell you.

• **Les propositions subordonnées complétives** sont généralement introduites par la conjonction *that* mais cette conjonction est souvent sous-entendue. Elles permettent de compléter le sens d'un verbe (1) ou d'un adjectif (2).

1. *He told me (that) he wanted to go to Barcelona for the summer holidays.*
2. *I was afraid (that) he might refuse to help me.*

• **Les propositions subordonnées relatives** complètent un nom (voir ❽) ou permettent de reprendre toute une phrase. Dans ce cas, la phrase qui précède est antécédent et sera reprise par le pronom relatif *which* précédé d'une virgule.

He left England last year, which was quite unexpected. → Il a quitté l'Angleterre l'an dernier, ce qui était plutôt inattendu.

⚠ Il existe aussi des propositions relatives introduites par *"what"* qui permettent de condenser l'expression *"the things that"*.

He showed me what he had painted → Il m'a montré ce qu'il avait peint.

They told me what I needed to hear → Ils m'ont dit ce que j'avais besoin d'entendre.

㉒ Exprimer l'action qu'exerce qqu'un sur qqu'un d'autre

Lorsqu'on souhaite exprimer l'action ou l'influence qu'exerce quelqu'un sur quelqu'un d'autre, on peut utiliser les propositions infinitives ou les structures causatives.

a. Propositions infinitives

S + V1 + Complément + *to* + V2

V1: ***allow, advise, ask, expect, force, get, order, prefer, tell, want.***

She wanted her parents to help her. *They asked their neighbour to stop being noisy.*
I will get her to go and see a doctor. *What do you want me to do for you?*

b. Structures causatives

S + V1 + Complément + V2

V1: ***make, have***

She made them clean their rooms. → Elle les a obligés à nettoyer leur chambre.
She had the gardener cut off the trees. → Elle a fait couper les arbres par le jardinier.

VERBES À PARTICULES

Rappel

- **Préposition** : mot qui permet d'introduire un complément (de lieu, de temps, de manière).
  He went to Dublin. The train left at 7 a.m. They come from Italy.
- **Verbe prépositionnel** : verbe qui fonctionne avec certaines prépositions uniquement.
  He is listening to music. She waited for him. We will have to deal with this issue.
- **Particule** : adverbe de forme identique aux prépositions mais contrairement à elles, il fait partie intégrante du verbe et en modifie le sens. Il peut se placer avant ou après le complément (si c'est un pronom, il se place après).
  Get out now! He took off his coat./He took his coat off. They sent him back to prison.

PRINCIPALES PREPOSITIONS ET PARTICULES

about	à propos de, au sujet de, environ	*from*	de (provenance)
after	après	*in*	dans
against	contre	*of*	de (lien)
above	au dessus de	*off*	(arrêt)
across	à travers	*on*	sur (+ marche)
along	le long de	*out*	à l'extérieur de (+ épuisement)
at	à (lieu précis)	*over*	par-dessus
away	loin de	*through*	à travers (+ réussite)
back	derrière (retour)	*to*	à, vers, en direction de
by	par (moyen), près de	*under*	sous
down	mouvement vers le bas (échec)	*up*	en haut (+ apparition)
for	pour (destinataire)	*with*	avec

PRINCIPAUX VERBES A PARTICULES

break	*break down:* tomber en panne, rompre *break in(to):* entrer par effraction *break up:* rompre	keep	*keep out:* rester en dehors *keep up:* se maintenir
bring	*bring about:* provoquer *bring over:* amener, apporter *bring up:* élever (des enfants)	look	*look after:* prendre soin de *look back:* regarder derrière soi *look down (on):* regarder en bas, mépriser *look for:* chercher
come	*come in:* entrer *come along:* venir *come out:* sortir	put	*put aside:* mettre de côté *put off:* retarder *put on:* enfiler (un vêtement) *put up (with):* supporter
get	*get along (with):* s'entendre *get away:* partir, s'éloigner *get back:* revenir *get in:* arriver *get off:* sortir (d'un véhicule) *get out:* sortir *get up:* se lever	take	*take after:* ressembler à *take along:* emmener *take away:* emporter *take off:* enlever, ôter
give	*give away:* révéler, distribuer *give back:* rendre *give in:* se résoudre à, céder *give up:* abandonner, renoncer à	turn	*turn down:* refuser, baisser (le son) *turn into:* transformer *turn out:* s'avérer *turn up:* se présenter

base verbale	prétérit	participe passé	Traduction
awake	awoke	awoken	*se réveiller*
be	was / were	been	*être*
beat	beat	beaten	*battre*
become	became	become	*devenir*
awake begin	began	begun	*commencer*
bet	bet	bet	*parier*
blow	blew	blown	*souffler*
break	broke	broken	*casser, briser, rompre*
bring	brought /brɔːt/	brought /brɔːt/	*apporter*
broadcast	broadcast	broadcast	*diffuser (radio, etc.)*
build	built	built	*construire, bâtir*
burn	burnt	burnt	*brûler*
buy	bought /bɔːt/	bought /bɔːt/	*acheter*
catch	caught /kɔːt/	caught /kɔːt/	*attraper, saisir*
choose	chose	chosen	*choisir*
come	came	come	*venir*
cost	cost	cost	*coûter, valoir*
cut	cut	cut	*couper*
deal	dealt	dealt	*distribuer, donner*
do	did /dɪd/	done /dʌn/	*faire*
draw	drew /druː/	drawn /drɔːn/	*1. dessiner ; 2. tirer*
dream	dreamt	dreamt	*rêver*
drink	drank	drunk	*boire*
drive /draɪv/	drove	driven /drɪvən/	*conduire*
eat	ate	eaten	*manger*
fall	fell	fallen	*tomber*
feed	fed	fed	*nourrir*
feel	felt	felt	*1. (res)sentir, se sentir ; 2. toucher*
fight	fought /fɔːt/	fought /fɔːt/	*se battre, combattre*
find	found	found	*trouver*
fly	flew	flown	*voler*
forbid	forbade	forbidden	*interdire*
forecast	forecast	forecast	*prévoir, prédire*
foresee	foresaw	foreseen	*prévoir*
forget	forgot	forgotten	*oublier*
forgive	forgave	forgiven	*pardonner*
freeze	froze	frozen	*geler*
get	got	got	*1. obtenir ; 2. devenir*
give	gave	given	*donner*
go	went /went/	gone /gɒn/	*aller*
grow	grew	grown	*grandir, croître, faire pousser*
have	had	had	*avoir, posséder*
hear	heard	heard	*entendre*
hide /haɪd/	hid /hɪd/	hidden /hɪdən/	*(se) cacher*
hit	hit	hit	*frapper*
hold	held	held	*tenir*
hurt	hurt	hurt	*blesser, vexer, faire mal*
keep	kept	kept	*garder*
know	knew	known	*savoir, connaître*
lead	led	led	*mener, diriger*
learn	learnt	learnt	*étudier, apprendre*
leave	left	left	*1. partir ; 2. quitter*
lend	lent	lent	*prêter*
let	let	let	*1. laisser, permettre ; 2. louer*
lie	lay	lain	*être allongé, être couché*
light /laɪt/	lit /lɪt/	lit /lɪt/	*éclairer, allumer*
lose	lost	lost	*perdre*
make	made	made	*fabriquer, faire*

base verbale	prétérit	participe passé	Traduction
mean	meant	meant	*signifier*
meet	met	met	*rencontrer*
mistake	mistook	mistaken	*se tromper sur*
misunderstand	misunderstood	misunderstood	*mal comprendre*
overcome	overcame	overcome	*surmonter, vaincre*
pay	paid	paid	*payer*
put	put	put	*poser, mettre*
quit	quit	quit	*abandonner, quitter*
read /riːd/	read /red/	read /red/	*lire*
ride	rode	ridden	*monter cheval, moto, vélo*
ring	rang	rung	*sonner*
rise	rose	risen	*s'élever, se lever*
run	ran	run	*courir*
say	said /sed/	said /sed/	*dire*
see	saw /sɔː/	seen /siːn/	*voir*
sell	sold	sold	*vendre*
send	sent	sent	*envoyer*
set	set	set	*1. poser ; 2. (se) situer ; 3. fixer (date) ; 4. se coucher (soleil)*
shake	shook	shaken	*1. secouer ; 2. trembler*
shine	shone	shone	*briller*
shoot	shot	shot	*tirer (fusil, arc, etc.)*
show	showed	shown	*montrer*
shut	shut	shut	*fermer*
sing	sang	sung	*chanter*
sink	sank	sunk	*couler, s'enfoncer, sombrer*
sit	sat	sat	*être assis*
sleep	slept	slept	*dormir*
smell	smelt	smelt	*sentir (odeur)*
speak	spoke	spoken	*parler*
speed	sped	sped	*aller vite*
spell	spelt	spelt	*épeler*
spend	spent	spent	*dépenser*
spill	spilt	spilt	*renverser (liquide)*
split	split	split	*(se) séparer*
spoil	spoilt	spoilt	*1. gâcher ; 2. gâter (enfant)*
spread	spread	spread	*1. étaler, étendre ; 2. se répandre*
stand	stood	stood	*se tenir debout*
steal	stole	stolen	*dérober, voler*
stick	stuck	stuck	*coller*
strike	struck	struck	*frapper*
swear	swore	sworn	*jurer*
sweep	swept	swept	*balayer*
swim	swam	swum	*nager*
take	took	taken	*prendre*
teach	taught /tɔːt/	taught /tɔːt/	*enseigner*
tell	told	told	*1. dire ; 2. raconter*
think	thought /θɔːt/	thought /θɔːt/	*penser*
throw	threw	thrown	*lancer, jeter*
understand	understood	understood	*comprendre*
undertake	undertook	undertaken	*entreprendre*
undo	undid	undone	*défaire*
upset	upset	upset	*1. bouleverser ; 2. renverser*
wake	woke	woken	*réveiller*
wear	wore	worn	*porter (vêtements)*
weep	wept	wept	*pleurer*
win	won /wʌn/	won /wʌn/	*gagner*
withdraw	withdrew /wɪðˌdruː/	withdrawn /wɪðˌdrɔːn/	*(se) retirer*
write /raɪt/	wrote /rəʊt/	written /ˌrɪtən/	*écrire*

SOMMAIRE

L'INTONATION

L'ACCENTUATION

LA PRONONCIATION

REMARQUES INTRODUCTIVES

Il est parfois difficile de se faire comprendre en anglais lorsque la prononciation ou l'accentuation ne sont pas exactes. De même, on peut avoir des difficultés à comprendre un message en anglais parce que l'on ne parvient pas à reconnaître des mots, des groupes de mots, ou des intentions.

Ceci s'explique par le fait que...

• À la différence du français, l'anglais est **une langue accentuée** : certaines syllabes seront prononcées plus fortement que d'autres, et entraîneront la réduction, l'« écrasement » des syllabes voisines. Des règles permettent, à partir de la graphie d'un mot, de déduire son accentuation et sa prononciation.

track 61

- photographe /'fɔ'tɒ'graf/
  en français, 3 syllabes sont accentuées.
- *photographer* /fə'tɒgrəfə/
  en anglais, une seule syllabe est accentuée, les trois autres sont réduites.

track 62

• Le rythme qui caractérise la prononciation d'un mot caractérise aussi la prononciation d'une phrase. Les mots porteurs de sens seront plus accentués que les autres, entraînant une alternance de formes fortes et de formes faibles, à l'origine de moments d'accélération ou de ralentissement.

There was a man standing at the corner of the street.

track 63

• Les sons de l'anglais et du français ont peu de similarités, et un même mot « transparent » à l'écrit se verra souvent prononcé de manière totalement différente :

theatre / archive / muscle / trouble /outrage

L'INTONATION

L'intonation – qui correspond à des mouvements de voix qui montent ou qui descendent – permet de transmettre **des informations au-delà des mots** : elle donne des indices précieux sur les sentiments du locuteur. Son choix est ainsi chargé de sens et dépend de la situation dans laquelle le locuteur se trouve. C'est pourquoi il est important de bien la repérer pour saisir le sens des messages véhiculés.

❶ Intonation descendante

C'est l'intonation « neutre » et générale de la phrase anglaise. Elle exprime une idée de certitude. Le locuteur s'exprime sans faire de commentaires implicites sur ce qu'il dit : il détient l'information ou peut demander une précision sans remettre en cause la validation de son énoncé. On trouve généralement une intonation descendante dans les situations d'énonciation suivantes :

track 64

Situations d'énonciation	Intonation
Une affirmation, une vérité, un constat	*'My sister should work more.'* (↘) *'I hate spinach.'* (↘) *'It's going to rain tomorrow.'* (↘)
Une question ouverte commençant par *"WH"*	*'What do you study on Mondays?'* (↘) *'Why did you buy this car?'* (↘) *'When will you visit us?'* (↘)
Un ordre	*'Don't listen to him!'* (↘)
La fin d'une énumération	*'We sell telephones, computers, and TV sets.'* (↘)
Un *tag* pour renforcer une affirmation ou demander une confirmation	*'You owe me twenty pounds, don't you?'* (↘)

2 Intonation montante

Elle exprime une idée d'inachèvement, de sous-entendu, de doute. On trouve généralement une intonation montante dans les situations d'énonciation suivantes :

track 65

Situations d'énonciation	Intonation
Une incertitude	*'I thought there was a Maths test next week.'* (↗)
Une question fermée ***("yes-no question")***	*'Are you sick?'* (↗) *'Did you like the cake?'* (↗)
Des propos inachevés	*'I wanted to call him, but...'* (↗)
Une énumération	*'I bought clothes* (↗)*, books* (↗)*, a laptop* (↗)*...'*
Un *tag* pour demander une confirmation, des précisions, ou vérifier l'exactitude d'un énoncé	*'You're not leaving Boston, are you?'* (↗) *'He didn't lie to you, did he?* (↗)

3 Intonation emphatique ou contrastive

On peut choisir, dans une phrase donnée, de souligner davantage des éléments jugés importants dans le message ou d'accentuer plus fortement certains mots afin d'exprimer un **contraste**. Cette accentuation particulière de la phrase s'appelle « l'intonation emphatique ou contrastive ». Elle charge l'énoncé d'implicite.

- Le locuteur peut choisir d'accentuer plus fortement un mot pour transmettre **un sentiment, un point de vue ou une appréciation sous-entendus** :

track 66

'You should see your doctor.' (tout le monde constate que tu ne vas pas bien)
'You ***should*** *see your doctor.'* (c'est plus que conseillé, vu ton état)
'You should ***see*** *your doctor.'* (plutôt que lui téléphoner)
'You should see ***your*** *doctor.'* (pas un médecin qui ne te connaît pas)
'You should see your ***doctor****.'* (pas ton dentiste)

- Le locuteur peut aussi utiliser l'intonation pour faire **une comparaison** entre deux personnes ou choses en insistant plus fortement sur l'un et/ou l'autre de ces deux éléments :

track 67

*'**Your** apple pie is much tastier than mine.'*
*'My **cousins** have been to Los Angeles but **I** haven't.'*

4 Groupes intonatifs ou «groupes de souffle»

Si à l'écrit on trouve des virgules, des points et autres signes de ponctuation qui permettent de marquer des pauses respiratoires et de donner sens à l'énoncé, à l'oral, on divise les informations en blocs que l'on appelle en français des **groupes intonatifs** (ou groupes de souffle) et en anglais *tone units*.
Ces blocs d'informations, entrecoupés de pauses plus ou moins longues, constituent des unités de sens.

track 68

A : | *'We went to the United States | for the fourth time.'* |
B : | *'Really? | Did you enjoy it?'* |
A : | *'Yeah! | It was great! | But as soon as we arrived | we had a car accident.'* |
B : | *'Oh no! | How did it happen? | Were you hurt?'* |
A : | *'No, we weren't | but it was horrible! | We bumped into a truck | that was 30 feet long.'*

L'ACCENTUATION

5 L'accent de mot

La particularité de l'anglais est que tous les mots sont accentués, et que l'on retrouve toujours une alternance entre formes pleines **(O)** et formes réduites **(o)** à l'intérieur d'un mot de plus d'une syllabe.

a. Accent principal et accent secondaire

Aucun mot, et ceci sans exception, **ne peut commencer par deux syllabes réduites**.
Le schéma accentuel **o o O** est impossible. Ainsi, un mot de plus de deux syllabes porte un accent principal, marqué par un trait vertical placé en haut à gauche de la syllabe accentuée, et un accent secondaire, marqué par un trait vertical placé en bas à gauche de la syllabe.

track 69

refugee /ˌrefjuˈdʒiː/ **[ˌO o ˈO]**
afternoon /ˌæftəˈnuːn **[ˌO o ˈO]**
education /ˌedjuˈkeɪʃən/ **[(ˌO o)ˈO o]**
communication /kəˌmjuːnɪˈkeɪʃən/ **[o(ˌO o)ˈO o]**

b. Réduction vocalique

Afin de faire ressortir la ou les syllabes accentuées, il est nécessaire de réduire l'importance des syllabes non accentuées : ce phénomène s'appelle la **réduction vocalique**.
Prenons en exemple un mot de trois syllabes : Canada.

track 70

- en français, ces trois syllabes ont une importance égale et la lettre <a> se prononce de la même manière : Canada.
- en anglais, la première syllabe ressort très nettement tandis que les deux autres syllabes sont à peine audibles : le premier <a> se prononce avec sa forme pleine, tandis que les deux autres <a> se prononcent avec une forme réduite /ə/ : *Canada* /ˈkænədə/.

track 71

→ *À vous*

Entraînez-vous à prononcer à voix haute les mots suivants en respectant la syllabe accentuée (ici soulignée) et la réduction des syllabes non accentuées.
comfortable, vegetable, develop, Italy, ridiculous, police, entertainment, America, Japan, government, environment, Brazil, laboratory, chocolate, deliberate, catastrophe, circumstance
Vérifiez en écoutant l'enregistrement.

6 Accentuation et types de mots

Les types de mots, leur formation ou leur composition permettent parfois de prédire la façon dont ils s'accentuent. Nous allons voir ici quelques règles simples d'accentuation.

a. Mots préfixés

Les préfixes en anglais *(ab-, de-, dis-, il-, im-, in-, ir-, mis-, re-, sub-, un-,* etc.*)* sont neutres : ils n'ont pas d'impact sur l'accentuation du mot racine auquel ils s'ajoutent, que ce mot soit un nom, un adjectif, un verbe ou un adverbe. Ainsi, le mot *"legal"*, accentué sur la première syllabe, /ˈliːgəl/ maintient la même accentuation lorsqu'on lui ajoute le préfixe ***il-***: *"illegal"* /ɪlˈiːgəl/. Il en va de même pour tous les mots préfixés.

b. Mots suffixés « à terminaisons non contraignantes »

De la même manière, un certain nombre de suffixes sont neutres : ils ne modifient pas la place de l'accent principal du mot racine auquel ils s'ajoutent et sont prononcés avec une forme réduite.

track 72

*'**gov**ern* → *'**gov**ernor* /'gʌvənə/

*di'**rect*** → *di'**rect**ly* /dɪ'rektlɪ/

*de'**vel**op* → *de'**vel**opment* /dɪ'veləpmənt/

C'est le cas notamment des suffixes les plus fréquents répertoriés dans le tableau ci-dessous.

track 73

Suffixes neutres	Exemples
-able / -ible	*a'voidable, 'comfortable, ac'ceptable, irre'sistible*
-al	*en'viron'mental, techno'logical, pro'fessional, 'national, ar'rival*
-ance / -ence / -ent	*'governance, ap'pearance, 'insurance, de'pendence, 'different*
-dom	*'kingdom, 'wisdom, 'freedom*
-er / -or / -ess	*'driver, 'singer, 'actor, 'actress, 'goddess, dic'tator*
-ful	*'beautiful, 'careful, 'wonderful, 'faithful*
-hood	*'childhood, 'manhood, 'neighbourhood*
-ify / -ize	*'glorify, 'falsify, 'beautify, 'privatize, 'liberalize*
-ish	*'childish, 'foolish, 'womanish*
-ism	*'journalism, A'mericanism*
-ist	*'socialist, 'specialist, 'elitist*
-ive	*'active, at'tractive, col'lective*
-less	*'powerless, 'motionless, 'tactless, 'careless*
-ly / -y	*'easily, 'lovely, 'surely, 'cloudy, 'jealousy*
-ment	*re'tirement, de'velopment, enter'tainment, 'treatment*
-ness	*a'wareness, 'happiness, 'loneliness,*
-ship	*'friendship, 'leadership, 'readership*

c. Mots suffixés à « terminaisons contraignantes »

À l'inverse, certains suffixes modifient la place de l'accent principal du mot racine auquel ils s'ajoutent. On peut toutefois, en fonction du suffixe, généralement déterminer à l'avance où va se trouver l'accent.

track 74

Suffixes contraignants (accentuation sur l'avant-dernière syllabe)	Exemples
-ic, -ics, -ical	*'robot → ro'botics / 'irony → i'ronic*
-ity, -ety	*e'lectric → elec'tricity / 'national → natio'nality*
-ion	*'educate → edu'cation / 'celebrate → cele'bration*
-ian, -iot, -ial, -eous, -ious	*'library → li'brarian / 'courage → cou'rageous*

Suffixes contraignants (accentuation sur la dernière syllabe)	Exemples
-ese	*ˈChina → Chiˈnese / Jaˈpan → Japaˈnese*
-ee, -eer, -oo	*ˈrefuge → refuˈgee / ˈtrain → traiˈnee / ˈengine → engiˈneer*
-esse, -ette	*ˈfeature → featuˈrette / ˈsuffrage → suffraˈgette*

track 75

→ À vous

Observez les mots dérivés ci-dessous. Retrouvez leurs mots racines, puis entraînez-vous à les prononcer après avoir vérifié si le suffixe entraîne ou non un déplacement d'accent.

impossibility, irregularity, disapproval, disappearance, honestly, historically, publication, conscientious, employee, remarkable, citizenship, capitalism, Vietnamese

Vérifiez en écoutant l'enregistrement.

d. Mots composés

En général, l'accent principal d'un mot composé tombe sur la syllabe accentuée du **premier mot**.

track 76

ˈradio station, ˈhaircut, ˈtop executive, ˈflower bed, ˈcar-park, ˈswimming-pool

e. Paires alternantes

Un certain nombre de mots de deux syllabes sont à la fois noms et verbes :

- en tant que **nom**, ces mots s'accentuent **ˈO o** — *a ˈcontact*
- et en tant que **verbe** **oˈO** — *I'll conˈtact him as soon as possible.*

track 77

→ À vous

Prononcez chacun des mots ci-dessous à voix haute, une première fois en tant que nom, une deuxième fois en tant que verbe, en respectant la bonne accentuation. Vérifiez ensuite en écoutant l'enregistrement.

comment, contract, contrast, convict, escort, exploit, extract, increase, progress, protest, rebel, record

7 L'accent de phrase

En anglais, on n'accentue pas tous les mots d'une phrase, mais seulement ceux qui sont **porteurs de sens**, qui véhiculent des informations essentielles. Selon leur catégorie syntaxique, leur place dans la phrase et le type d'information qu'ils véhiculent, ils seront plus ou moins fortement accentués.

a. Formes fortes et formes faibles

- Les mots accentués, appelés **formes fortes**, correspondent souvent aux mots lexicaux (noms, verbes, adjectifs, adverbes).

- Les mots réduits, appelés **formes faibles**, correspondent souvent aux mots grammaticaux, ou mots-outils (prépositions, conjonctions, auxiliaires, déterminants, etc.).

Dans l'exemple ci-dessous (*Unit 2 the new Americans*), voici en **gras** les mots qui ressortent, et en vert, ceux qui sont réduits et qu'on entend à peine.

track 78

*As a **teenager growing** up in the **United States** in the **early 1960s, I felt** an **outsider** and **longed** for a **sense** of **belonging. My brother,** on the **other hand, felt immediately** at **home** when he **came here** and has **always taken great pride** in **being** an **Iranian-American.***

track 79

→ À vous

Entraînez-vous à accentuer correctement l'énoncé ci-dessous :

When I returned to the US in 1982, this time as a political exile, I gained new respect for the democratic institutions of this country and in time I felt more at home. But the call of my birthplace is always there.

b. Cas particuliers de formes faibles accentuées

Dans certains cas, des formes grammaticales peuvent être accentuées.

- Lorsqu'on souhaite insister pour revenir sur un propos :

  *'You said I wasn't there, but I **was** there.'*

- Lorsqu'un auxiliaire est à la forme négative :

  *'Despite his age, my brother **can't** read.'*

- Lorsqu'un auxiliaire ou une préposition se trouvent en début ou en fin de phrase :

track 80

'He was waiting for the bus.'
ici, *was* est réduit en /wəz/
et *for* est réduit en /fə/

mais :
*'I don't know what he was waiting **for**, but he was later than I **was**.'*
ici *for* et *was* retrouvent leurs formes fortes :
/fɔː/ et /wɒz/.

LA PRONONCIATION

8 Phonèmes et Alphabet Phonétique International

L'orthographe d'un mot (en anglais comme dans d'autres langues) ne permet pas toujours de savoir comment ce mot se prononce.

C'est pourquoi on utilise un système de symboles, l'Alphabet Phonétique International, constitué de **24 phonèmes consonnes** (20 en français) et **20 phonèmes voyelles** (16 en français), pour décoder le lien entre graphie et phonie. Cet alphabet (voir rabat II de la couverture de votre manuel et à la fin de ce précis) – permet de transcrire avec précision la façon dont on prononce un mot. À chaque phonème correspond un son et vice versa, si bien qu'à la lecture de la transcription phonétique d'un mot, on ne peut se tromper.

Pour plus de clarté, il importe de bien distinguer les **lettres orthographiques** (ce qu'on lit et écrit) des phonèmes (ce qu'on entend et prononce). On va donc respecter le code **<lettre>** et **/son/** et on pourra dire, par exemple, que <ch> se prononce /ʃ/ en français (chaise) mais /tʃ/ en anglais *(cheese)*.

track 81

track 82

→ À vous

Utilisez le rabat II pour retrouver les mots dont vous voyez ci-dessous la transcription phonétique :

/bəʊt/ - /kraɪ/ - /kʌlə/ - /kəˌmjuːnɪˈkeɪʃən/ - /kəmpjuːtə/ - /rʊm/ - /aɪdɪə/ - /steɪ/ - /flaʊə/ - /skrɪːn/

track 83

Entraînez-vous ensuite à transcrire vous-mêmes les mots ci-dessous :

read, pear, fighting, filling, lose, chosen, thought, crowd, low, high

9 Prononciation des consonnes

a. <h>

• **La lettre <h>** existe bien sûr en français. On ne l'entend pas mais elle manifeste néanmoins sa présence à travers le choix du déterminant qui la précède, par exemple : le haricot, le héros, le hibou *mais* l'homme, l'habitude, l'hélicoptère, l'horizon...

track 84

• En anglais, la lettre orthographique **<h>** est toujours prononcée /h/ au début d'un mot sauf dans *hour, honour, honest* et *heir* où on ne l'entend pas. Comme en français, c'est la raison pour laquelle on a :

a hero, a house, a happy hitch-hiker mais *an hour, an honourable person, an honest offer, an heir*

b. <s>

Parce qu'en français, le /s/ en position finale est toujours muet, sauf en cas de liaison, les francophones oublient souvent de le prononcer en anglais où il doit **toujours être prononcé**.

La prononciation de la lettre **<s>** dépend du dernier son du mot sur lequel elle s'accroche.

• On trouve un **<s>** final pour indiquer le pluriel des noms, le présent des verbes à la troisième personne du singulier, le génitif *('s)*, ou parfois dans des noms propres : *James, Charles*.

• Lorsque le mot se termine par le son /s/, /z/, /ʃ/, /ʒ/, /tʃ/ ou /dʒ/, **<s>** se prononce /iz/.

• Lorsque le mot se termine par une voyelle ou une consonne sonore, voisée (consonne qui produit une vibration lorsqu'on la prononce - voir tableau p. 222), **<s>** se prononce /z/

• Dans tous les autres cas, il se prononce /s/.

c. <th>

track 85

• **<th>** : en anglais pour bien prononcer /θ/ *(three, thin, think...)* et /ð/ *(the, then, there...)*, il faut que le bout de la langue empêche les dents de se fermer.

track 86

→ À vous

Entraînez-vous à prononcer les mots ou groupes de mots suivants.

• he swims - three dogs - the peaks - their roses - these churches - houses - thirty measures - those friends

• the Joneses - Saint-James's Park - Marseilles' harbour

Plus difficile !

Admidst the mists and coldest frosts,
With stoutest wrists and loudest boasts,
He thrusts his fists against the posts,
And still insists he sees the ghosts.

track 87

Tableau récapitulatif

Consonnes sourdes/non voisées		Consonnes sonores/voisées	
/p/	*pen*	/b/	*boat*
/t/	*ten*	/d/	*dad*
/f/	*fat*	/g/	*guard*
/k/	*kit*	/l/	*long*
/s/	*sin*	/m/	*mum*
/ʃ/	*show*	/n/	*now*
/tʃ/	*chin*	/ŋ/	*ring*
/θ/	*three*	/r/	*write*
/h/	*hen*	/w/	*window*
		/z/	*zero*
		/ʒ/	*measure*
		/dʒ/	*John*
		/j/	*young*
		/ð/	*then*

10 Prononciation des voyelles

La prononciation des voyelles peut varier d'un pays à un autre (États-Unis, Canada, Inde, Nouvelle-Zélande, etc.), d'une région à une autre (nord et sud de l'Angleterre, région de Manchester, de Leeds, etc.), parfois d'une catégorie sociale à une autre. Malgré les différents accents, les sons voyelles présentent cependant certaines caractéristiques invariables.

Il est donc très utile de s'entrainer à associer le son voyelle des mots au mot repère du **tableau situé sur le rabat II** de la couverture de votre manuel.

C'est ainsi que l'on peut associer :

track 88

love		*cup*
want		*clock*
law	***is the same sound as***	*door*
parent		*chair*
most		*snow*
major		*day*

track 89

→ *À vous*

Entrainez-vous à trouver le mot repère qui correspond au son voyelle de ces mots :

dive, hope, some, race, blue, great, come, wood, meat, catch, where, moon, son, aunt, blind, mint, reach, right, fine, thin, green, brown, grind, round, grey, stay, stone

a. Voyelles courtes, voyelles longues

L'opposition entre les voyelles dites « longues » et les voyelles dite « courtes » est une caractéristique de l'anglais oral. Il est important de bien marquer la distinction entre ces « paires » car une mauvaise prononciation pourrait être à l'origine d'un changement de sens et donc d'une incompréhension.

track 90

"Don't hit it, heat it!"
"I want you to leave with me, not to live with me!"

"Look at the sheep, not the ship!"